BEYOND THE MAFIA

Organized Crime in the Americas

Edited by
Sue Mahan
with Katherine O'Neil

SAGE Publications
International Educational and Professional Publisher
Thousand Oaks London New Delhi

For information:

SAGE Publications, Inc.
2455 Teller Road
Thousand Oaks, California 91320
E-mail@sagepub.com

SAGE Publications Ltd.
6 Bonhill Street
London EC2A 4PU
United Kingdom

SAGE Publications India Pvt. Ltd.
M-32 Market
Greater Kailash I
New Delhi 110048 India

Printed in the United States of America

Library of Congress Cataloging-in-Publication Data

Beyond the mafia: Organized crime in the Americas / [edited by]
Sue Mahan with Katherine O'Neil.
   p. cm.
Includes bibliographical references and index.
ISBN 0-7619-1358-0 (cloth : acid-free paper)
ISBN 0-7619-1359-9 (pbk. : acid-free paper)
   1. Organized crime—North America. 2. Organized crime—Latin
America. I. Mahan, Sue. II. O'Neil, Katherine.
   HV6453.N7 O74 1997
   364.1'06'091812—ddc21   98-19692
98 99 00 01 02 03 04 8 7 6 5 4 3 2 1

Acquiring Editor:	C. Terry Hendrix
Production Editor:	Wendy Westgate
Editorial Assistant:	Karen Wiley
Typesetter/Designer:	Danielle Dillahunt
Indexer:	Molly Hall
Cover Designer:	Candice Harman

Contents

Preface

This text provides a view of organized crime (OC) in the Americas from many perspectives. It includes descriptions of criminal groups that are significant to contemporary, as well as future and historical, criminology. In the past, the study of OC in the United States focused on the traditional crime families in New York and Chicago. This book, in contrast, includes 10 readings, each of which gives an in-depth picture of an OC group outside the traditional Mafia. The focus is expanded north to Canada and south to Latin America to provide an inter-American view of OC. However, the readings examine OC in terms of the U.S. market for illegal goods and services, which is vast and has led the rest of the world. The book is divided into five parts. Each part begins with an introduction that explains a significant concept about OC and how the readings in the part illustrate the concept.

The first part introduces the idea of OC as a crime of enterprise. It explores patterns common to both legitimate business and criminal organizations. "The Rape of the Third World," from *Corporate Corruption,* by Marshall B. Clinard, illustrates corporate crime. A second type of criminal enterprise, the production of illegal liquor, is illustrated by "The Political Economy of Mountain Dew," from Wilbur R. Miller's book *Revenuers and Moonshiners.*

Part 2 covers the concept of ethnicity and the relevance of culture to organized criminal enterprise. Chinese triads are illustrated in "Gang Characteristics," from Ko-lin Chin's book *Chinatown Gangs.* The Japanese Yakuza is described in "North America: Foothold on the Mainland," from David E. Kaplan and Alec Dubro's book *Yakuza: The Explosive Account of Japan's Criminal Underworld.*

Part 3 describes the role of violence in OC. The extremes of violence used by the Medellin cocaine cartel are illustrated by "La Comuna Nororiental," from María Jimena Duzán's book *Death Beat*. Violence associated with Chicago street gangs is illustrated by two chapters from *There Are No Children Here*, by Alex Kotlowitz.

Part 4 addresses the issue of opportunity and the ways in which the opportunities for success in OC are structured. Daniel R. Wolf illustrates the closed opportunities for women in OC with "Women and the Outlaws" in his book *The Rebels: A Brotherhood of Outlaw Bikers*. The influence of the larger economic structure on OC opportunities opening up in Eastern Europe is illustrated by "The Organizatsiya," from *The New Ethnic Mobs*, by William Kleinknecht.

Part 5 explains the relationships between criminal justice policy and OC. Criminal justice policy is relevant to the forms of OC that develop. Also, the forms of OC that develop are related to the criminal justice policies in effect as they grow. The interaction between gangs and prison policies is illustrated by "Baby Mafia or Family," from R. Theodore Davidson's *Chicano Prisoners: The Key to San Quentin*. State-organized crime is illustrated by "Pirates and Profiteers," from Frank Browning and John Gerassi's *The American Way of Crime*.

Although the 10 readings are from different sources and are written in different styles, all were chosen for their authenticity and the contribution they make to a coherent outline for a comparative study of OC.

Acknowledgments

This work would not have been possible without the assistance of many people who never knew about their contribution. Howard Abadinsky's classic text *Organized Crime* continues to capture my interest, even after 10 years of teaching a class called "Organized Crime." He provided a way of understanding that was essential to developing the framework included in this book. In addition, hundreds of students who enrolled in my class over the years made important contributions with their attention, questions, and investigations. The continuing curiosity of students provided the impetus to continue even when the project was moved to a back burner from time to time before its completion.

There are others whose contributions were more personal. Melodie Cooper and Heather Rodriguez provided valuable assistance in organization and production. Terry Hendrix and Dale Grenfell at Sage contributed support and encouragement. But without the editing and manuscript preparation of Jackie Connelly, this book would never have come to be.

For K.T.,
who taught me to meet challenges head on . . .
and to always look behind the scenes.

Introduction:
Organized Crime
in the Americas

Organized crime is as American as McDonalds.
Lupsha (1995, p. 124)

Many other authors have pointed out, in the words of the cartoon possum Pogo, that when it comes to the study of OC, "We have met the enemy and he is us" (e.g., Kenney & Finckenauer, 1995, p. 371). It may not be a new idea, but any study of OC, even in this global era, must inevitably return to the enemy within. This book follows from the work of Chambliss (1978), who demonstrated that criminal networks come and go but that the processes by which they are produced go on, and the consequences remain the same. Those processes and consequences are the subject of this book.

According to Chambliss and the authors whose readings are included in this text, OC is *not* run and controlled by a national syndicate. The "commission" or "board of directors" with a feudal-like control over underlings is more a product of fiction than reality. "It is a mistake to look for a godfather in every crime network" (Chambliss, 1978, p. 9).

The idea of a Mafia, a Cosa Nostra, or simply an "organization" that rules OC is deceptive because it implies that OC is run by a group of private citizens. This book takes the position that OC really consists of a coalition of politicians, law enforcement people, businesspeople, labor leaders, and (in some ways, least important of all) gangsters. There is an inherent tendency of business, law enforcement, and politics to engage in systematic criminal behavior. This is so not because there are too many laws but rather because criminal behavior is good business, makes sense, and is by far the best, most efficient, and most profitable way to organize the operations of political offices, businesses, law enforcement agencies, and trade unions in a capitalist democracy.

In another work, Block and Chambliss (1981) pointed out that OC must be understood within historically specific forms of political and economic organization. Patterns of OC reflect the sociology of power. In a succinct description of OC, Block and Chambliss described organizations tuned to the ebb and flow of power (p. 210). OC is not some evil and monolithic presence standing apart from American society and planning its collapse. It is not some alien conspiracy whose aims run counter to the logic and tenets of competitive capitalism. OC is the sum of innumerable conspiracies, most often local in scope, that are part of the social and political fabric of everyday life. Crime enterprises pose a threat *not* to the basic structure of society but, on a more subtle level, to basic values and morals (Van Duyne, 1996).

There are many obstacles to efforts to study the processes and consequences of OC. Cressey (1995) found that secrecy, confidentiality, filters, and perceptual screens posed serious methodological problems for the study of OC. The image of OC in the Americas was distorted and manipulated by various interest groups, including the media and gangsters themselves. The public enemy was invented by the media during the period from 1918 to 1934 (Ruth, 1996). After that, an alien conspiracy theory pervaded much of what the public came to believe about OC. The theory was built on fear of immigrants and oppressed racial and ethnic groups. In time, many in the Americas came to take a pluralist approach to OC. Many saw it as a kind of Darwinian struggle in which old ethnic groups gave up power to new and better adapted ones (Potter, 1994).

Although perceptions have focused on public enemies, the real danger of OC is quiet control over the political process. It threatens businesspeople either to deal with the syndicate or to get out of business; sheriffs not to serve notices to the syndicate or report the syndicate's illegal actions; prosecutors to refuse to investigate or prosecute the syndicate; magistrates to dismiss charges; and mayors, governors, and presidents to obstruct OC control operations (Rhodes, 1984). There are many serious contemporary efforts to study OC, but few researchers examine corruption. Not coincidentally, although there are many serious criminal justice efforts to control OC, little is done to control corruption (Smith, 1995).

Defining OC

Most writers would agree with Lavey's (1990) description of OC as synonymous with corruption, murder, extortion, terror, manipulation, and guile and as involved in conscious, willful, and long-term illegal activities. In addition, it is generally assumed that OC is carried out with a division of labor and has as its aim the realization of large financial profits as quickly as possible.

Beyond this general level of agreement, however, there are differences in definitions of what is and what is not OC. The debate about the definition of OC preoccupies many scholars, but contradictions and controversy make it unlikely that an agreement will be reached. To avoid conflict over semantics and to provide a pragmatic explanation of OC useful for further study, this book uses the term *OC* for a criminal group with the following characteristics, supplied by Abadinsky (1994):

1. *Nonideological:* The primary motivating force for OC is profit. Sometimes the group adopts a worldview and political agenda, but these are supportive of, and secondary to, the goal of making money.
2. *Hierarchical:* The group has a pyramid organization with a few elites and many operatives. In between the high and low levels, the organization is supported by midlevel gangsters who handle supply and security.
3. *Having limited or exclusive membership:* The group must maintain secrecy, and loyalty of members must be ensured.
4. *Perpetuating itself:* The group has a recruitment process and policy; new recruits are being attracted as operatives.
5. *Willing to use illegal violence and bribery:* Outside of legal authority, violence is a meaningful resource. Corruption and deceit are the essence of OC.
6. *Having a specialized division of labor:* OC groups can be thought of as task forces with members combining different talents and experiences to reach an organizational goal.
7. *Monopolistic:* Market control is essential to OC because the primary goal is maximizing profits.

8. *Having explicit rules and regulations:* Members of OC groups have codes of honor (p. 6).

Of course, that does not mean that gangsters always follow their own rules. A code of behavior is also not to be confused with an ideology. Pursuit of profit is not considered a worldview, although money as a driving force is clearly an issue in the sociology of power.

Studying OC

As we move into a new century, it becomes increasingly important to view the global interdependence of OC. The state is no longer the unit of analysis (McDonald, 1995). However, although OC enterprises conduct trade across national boundaries, they do not constitute an international authority structure (Van Duyne, 1996). Decline in political order, deteriorating economic circumstances, a growing underground economy that habituates people to working outside the legal framework, easy access to arms, the massive flow of emigrants and refugees, and the difficulties of interstate cooperation all work to the advantage of multinational criminal organizations. The wealth and power of criminal organizations have grown, and there are increasing signs of international links between various criminal organizations. This does not mean, however, that there is an integrated, centrally directed criminal conspiracy (Goodson & Olson, 1995, p. 84). Kerry (1997) described, instead of an authority, a common international infrastructure for transnational crime. The infrastructure was created by global changes in the marketplace, computerization, arms and drug trafficking, money laundering, and smuggling at ports and borders all over the world.

Study of OC has tended to examine criminal enterprise in relation to the laws of some particular nation. Research of OC must expand beyond state interests and study criminal enterprises from an international perspective. An international crime occurs when it infringes on the interests of all humanity or when the international community considers itself to be directly damaged. The international community cannot yet rely on bodies through which it might assert its authority directly on individuals. Only states can exert their authority on citizens and take punitive measures against international crime (Grassi, 1990, p. 44). The United Nations can develop guidelines and instruments for mutual assistance in judicial matters that will enhance control of OC, for example. The United Nations can also provide technical assistance to member states in combating OC. However, it can only provide what the member states permit and can support (Paris-Steffens, 1990).

For a study of OC that addresses its complex international nature, this book has borrowed Chambliss's (1978) perspective of political economy. In the view of a political economist, one of the most important theoretical tools for understanding crime in general and OC in particular is the dialectic. Use of the dialectic as a heuristic device shows that criminality reflects and stems from contradictions in the very nature of the political and economic structure of society. Contradictions create conflicts. For example, political influence peddling to gain campaign financing is a contradiction in a democratic society that is based on equality of representation. Corruption of political campaign funding leads to conflicts. The state responds with attempts to resolve those conflicts. Laws are passed; committee investigations are staged. According to the dialectic view, the resolution of one conflict in turn reveals other contradictions, which give rise to further conflicts and more attempts to resolve them. In response to new restrictions, for example, political aspirants continue to find ways to cover and recover illegal monies. In this way, the process of history unfolds. From a dialectical viewpoint, OC activities fit into, reflect, complement, and mirror the political economy of our time. As Chambliss (1978) put it, "As long as providing things that are heavily in demand is illegal, crime networks of one sort or another are inevitable" (p. 9).

Controlling OC

There are three sources of international crime statistics: Interpol, the World Health Organization, and U.N. crime surveys. The three show significant differences. There are some real problems associated with data using different rates, sources, and samples (Neapolitan, 1996). In the United States, most OC data are collected by the Federal Bureau of Investigation (FBI). Chambliss (1978) pointed out that relying on law enforcement agencies for our information may lead to an overemphasis on those who fit the stereotype of criminal and a corresponding underemphasis on the importance of businesspeople, politicians, and law enforcers as institutionalized components of America's political and economic system. Law enforcement discretion creates and perpetuates syndicates that supply the vices in our major cities (p. 9).

Without some better measures, it is difficult to speculate about the extent and amount of OC. For that reason, it is even more difficult to evaluate what measures might be used to control it. The criminal justice response to OC has not proved very effective. The traditional legal approach—one crime, one offender—is not sufficient to combat OC (Lavey, 1990). Kerry (1997) recommended a revolution in legal concepts, multiple alliances, and a three-pronged strategy: multilateral, bilateral, and unilateral (p. 188). An alternative for control may be found in the private sector. Agencies and organizations outside the law enforcement field can be resourceful in developing effective strategies against OC (Hoffman, 1987). In the past, economic and social changes have had more impact on OC than law enforcement efforts.

Some alternative targets for meaningful OC control efforts were suggested by Pace (1991):

- A permissive society in which honesty values have been eroded
- The demands and expectations of citizens for illicit goods or services
- The support from other interest groups who also hope to profit indirectly from OC gains
- The resources available to supply illicit goods in the informal economy

Without addressing these targets, meaningful control of OC is not likely. Each of these four categories is considered an "entropic" force that causes social breakdowns. To control entropic forces, antientropic forces are needed to keep social norms in check and overcome the destructive elements. What antientropic social forces might be brought to bear against OC in the 21st century remain to be seen. For the most part, anti-OC efforts have been state supported and authorized by a single nation. The influence of other kinds of private, nongovernmental, and multinational control has not been evaluated.

PART

I

ILLICIT ENTERPRISE

The first business of criminal organizations is usually business.

Goodson and Olson
(1995, p. 18)

The concept of OC may have been overused. Perhaps it lost its usefulness because it was overburdened with divergent meanings. The term *illicit enterprise* may provide a better image of the range of actions included (Smith, 1995). This term is not as culturally circumscribed as *OC* has been. *Illicit enterprise* implies that what is needed is entrepreneurial skill and willingness to exploit for illegal gain. That is not to imply that illicit enterprise is easy. Many challenges and problems must be overcome by those developing a transnational crime infrastructure (Martin & Romano, 1992, p. 114). The organization must maintain secrecy but at the same time must depend on some visibility to market illicit goods or services. Wherever they operate, OC groups must neutralize law enforcement efforts. In the three-level system of the United States, neutralizing law enforcement often involves corruption of federal, state, and local forces. To market illicit enterprises, the organization must provide a range of other services from administration to transportation, as well as communication and public relations. To succeed, the illicit enterprise must not only dispel competition but also police its own ranks and maintain order within. In an enterprise in which secrecy and corruption are basic and violence is common, maintaining order is complex and difficult. Part of the success of an illicit enterprise is based on the loyalty of its members and the acceptance of customers. For this positive connection, the enterprise must depend on rationales, justifications, and serving self-interests. To maintain a crime network, it is important that all those involved continue to experience rewards. The downfall of an enterprise can be spelled out in the failure to provide for these challenges.

Under capitalism, people are taught that competition is a good thing and that there are two kinds of people in the world, winners and losers. To be a winner, you have to do whatever it takes to get what you want. If you do not, you are a loser (Parsels, 1996, p. 42). Chambliss (1978) explained that members of crime networks are simply acting within both the logic and values of the U.S. political economy: maximizing profits, protecting investments from competition, expanding markets, and providing the goods and services that are in demand. The profit motive may necessitate compromising strict adherence to the law, but then so does mere survival in the realities of political life (p. 188).

The modern underground economy blurs the distinction between the explicitly criminal and the merely informal. The 1990s saw a tremendous growth of underground activity of many forms (Naylor, 1996). Scarpitti and Block (1987) uncovered corruption in the U.S. Environmental Protection Agency and its impact on waste disposal. The result has been long-term detrimental consequences for significant portions of the population of the Americas (p. 115). Chang (1995) described a new form of international crime arising from the high demand and incredible shortage of human organs. Criminal enterprises are involved in illegal procurement, medical administration, and even control over patients. International arms trade also involves joint OC and corporate actors. As we progress toward the 21st century, corporate actors have monopolized more and more of the arms market, leaving the most risky part of the clandestine market for OC (Ruggiero, 1996).

In Canada, criminal organizations are likely to continue to take advantage of the lack of currency and monetary reporting regulations, which opens the doors for money laundering. It is unclear what effect attempts by the legislature to amend the Canadian system may have on OC (Stamler, 1990, p. 9). As such a contradiction is targeted by lawmakers, conflict and adjustments are likely. In the late 1990s, there was a trend toward using professional launderers hired by criminal organizations to arrange to transport large illicit cash shipments into and out of Canada. Professionals provide legal and financial expertise in international financial transactions where there is evidence of mounting computer and telecommunications crime. The ability to compromise global systems of financial transactions as well as communications is a valuable criminal commodity (Criminal Intelligence Service Canada [CISC], 1996). Compromised international monetary systems may be the most potent threat from OC at the dawning of the 21st century.

Illicit enterprise depends on political contacts that flow from the apex of the criminal hierarchy. Links exist in almost every phase of social and business interaction. Elected officials receive financial support and give political favors in return. Appointed members of government receive payoffs and conduct business between criminals and elected officials. Judges receive financial contributions and give favorable decisions in return. Attorneys receive fat payoffs and give legal advice and consultation to criminals. Police officers take cash from criminals and give selective enforcement and preferential treatment in return (Pace, 1991, p. 26).

Chambliss (1978) found that the key feature of political organizations that connects them with criminal networks is the peculiar necessity for politicians to spend vast sums of money to get elected to office. Crime networks have access to billions of dollars in untaxed, unreported, and unaccountable funds—a valuable source of money to oil the political machinery of capitalism (p. 183).

As OC groups develop, they became increasingly motivated by money and move steadily away from other driving forces. Mature criminal organizations have come to focus increasingly on acts for profit as "cause" (Goodson & Olson, 1995). At the same time, as OC crime groups mature, they move covertly into legitimate businesses and associations. This movement does not imply that gangsters have given up corrupt lifestyles. On the contrary, as Martens (1990) wrote, "The message is clear: 'Money buys dignity' " (p. 114).

DISCUSSION:
Corporate Crime

The first step in understanding corporate illegality is to drop the analogy of the corporation as a person (Clinard & Yaeger, 1980). Sutherland (1949) introduced the study of corporate crime as more than the actions of individual criminals. He noted that corporate characteristics facilitate illegal activities. In illicit enterprise, it is difficult to locate responsibility. There is increased rationality, with the objective of maximizing pecuniary gain. Sutherland found that corporations had attempted not only to "fix" particular accusations but also to develop public good will and to influence the implementation of the law.

Substitute procedures such as orders to appear at a hearing, decisions by administrative commissions, and desist orders conceal the essential similarity between businesspeople and professional criminals who are arrested and face trial. It was clear to Sutherland in 1949, as it is now, that a substantial number of the violations committed by corporations are deliberate and OC. As Sutherland noted, the criminality of corporations is persistent. The illegal behavior is extensive. The difference between corporate crime and other kinds of organized crime is that businesspeople who violate regulatory laws do not usually lose status. Businesspeople express contempt for government, just as professional thieves do.

1

The Rape of
the Third World

Marshall B. Clinard

Chapter 8 (pp. 137-159) of *Corporate Corruption:
The Abuse of Power,* by Marshall B. Clinard
(New York: Praeger, 1990)

It was an unseasonably cold night in central India. In the shanty towns of Bhopal, thousands of families were asleep. A scattering of people were waiting for early morning trains nearby. At the local Union Carbide plant, a maintenance worker spotted a problem. A storage tank holding 42 tons of liquid methyl isocyanate (MIC), a deadly chemical used to make pesticides, was showing a dangerously high pressure reading. Soon, a noxious white gas started seeping from the tank and spreading with the northwesterly winds. People awoke to burning, suffocating sensations—"like breathing fire" as one victim described it. As the cloud spread, people began to run helter-skelter to retch, vomit, and defecate uncontrollably. Many collapsed and died. Dogs, cows, and buffaloes lay on the ground, shuddering in their death throes. As the gas seeped through crevices and windows, it turned hovels into gas chambers.

The following morning, the bodies of human beings and animals littered the ground; Bhopal was a city of corpses. Hundreds of people, blinded by poisonous fumes, groped their way through the streets in search of medical attention. Across the city, hospitals and mortuaries became filled to overflowing. Muslims were buried four and five deep in a single grave, while Hindu funeral pyres burned around the clock.

The chairman of Union Carbide, Warren M. Anderson, flew almost immediately to Bhopal, where state authorities promptly arrested him and just as promptly released him under pressure from government of India authorities. Some officials said that Anderson's arrest was necessary to protect him from the wrath of the victims. Within days, swarms of lawyers from the United States descended on Bhopal to sign up victims for damage suits against Union Carbide. The Indian government also moved in to file a suit against the corporation. The attorney general of Connecticut, where Union Carbide is based, said that it could be the "largest and most lucrative damage case in the history of the world."

The Bhopal disaster was the world's worst industrial accident; even the Chernobyl nuclear reactor disaster in the Soviet Union could not compare with it in terms of deaths and injuries. According to official Indian government figures, more than 2,800 people died (by 1989 this figure had risen to 3,415) and 200,000 were injured, 40,000 of them seriously. A separate study by an American investigator put the death toll at more than 8,000, as hundreds of bodies were cremated by Hindus and buried by Muslims without notifying authorities.[1] Suddenly, the world had learned that chemicals that kill insects also kill human beings, and on a grand scale. Few of Bhopal's residents knew the exact nature of the pesticides being produced at the factory; they also knew little about the dangers of the methyl isocyanate that had caused the disaster. When the massive leak occurred during that fateful night, few of the residents knew what had happened. Carbide officials took two hours that night to warn the nearby residents, although many of them lived in the shacks that surrounded the plant.

For the Bhopal survivors, recovery has been agonizing, and illnesses insidious. By 1986, two years after the tragedy, the government had received 500,000 injury claims, equivalent to approximately 60 percent of the city's population. Many Bhopal residents still suffered from shortness of breath, depression, and eye irritation. One eye specialist reported that there had been a "gross change" in the eyesight of the city's residents since the leak, and each day thousands of victims were flocking to hospitals, clinics, and rehabilitation centers. The Indian Council of Medical Research estimated that one in five of those exposed to the gas will suffer long-term lung, brain, liver, and kidney damage. By 1986, Bhopal had four times the national average in India of still births.

Union Carbide is the third largest chemical producer in the United States, and one of its 50 largest industrial corporations. It operates 700 facilities, including affiliates, in 35 countries around the world. The transnational's sales in 1988 totalled more than $8 billion, of which approximately a third came from the company's international operations. The Bhopal plant was started in 1969 and grew to a $25-million manufacturing facility sprawling over 80 acres. Although the Bhopal plant was known as Union Carbide of India, Union Carbide headquarters in the United States had authority to exercise financial and technical controls over the plant. As the parent company, Union Carbide owned just over half (50.9 percent) of the plant.

Not long after the Bhopal disaster and under pressure from a U.S. federal judge, Union Carbide agreed to pay $5 million to show "good faith." Later Union Carbide changed its prior concern for the victims and started to play hard ball. Originally, when Chairman Anderson flew to India, he said that he was moved by humanitarian motives to do whatever the corporation could to alleviate the consequences of the dreadful disaster. The corporation would give money to build hospitals, orphanages, and vocational schools, and it did contribute $1 million for this purpose. Then, a year later, Union Carbide began blaming the media for the public overreaction and was claiming that the suffering had been exaggerated.

In 1986, Union Carbide offered a $350-million settlement of all injury and damage claims brought by Bhopal survivors and the Indian government, but the Indian government rejected the offer as highly inadequate. The haggling over payments became disgraceful. At issue were huge legal fees and attorneys' desires to have suits tried in the United States rather than in India, where liability payments are much lower. A U.S. federal judge finally decided in 1986 that the damage suits should be brought in India, and this was what happened.

Late in 1986, the Indian government filed a suit in Bhopal district court on behalf of the victims, asking $3.1 billion in damages from Union Carbide. In addition, the Indian government asked for punitive damages in an amount sufficient to deter Union Carbide and other multinational corporations from "willful, malicious and wanton disregard of the rights and safety" of Indians. The suit charged that the corporation had "the means to know and guard against hazards likely to be caused . . . and to provide ways of avoiding potential hazards." It pointed out that a Union Carbide engineer was directly responsible for the final design and construction of the plant. India also charged Union Carbide with inadequate safety measures, faulty alarm systems, lack of cooling facilities, storage of excessive quantities of toxic materials, and poor maintenance. In its defense, Union Carbide claimed that the disaster had been due not to sloppy corporate practices in the Third World but to worker sabotage. The company had a hard time selling its sabotage theory.

The Bhopal residents marked the first anniversary of the disaster with a massive demonstration and the burning of hundreds of effigies of Union Carbide's chairman. They shouted, "Down with Killer Carbide," and flew black flags over most of the homes in the slums, where they conducted wakes and marched in protest. In late 1988, four years after the disaster, the people were increasingly bitter, the legal wrangling continued and a settlement still had not been reached. Consequently, an Indian High Court Judge ordered $190 million interim payments to the victims. To add to the confusion, India filed criminal homicide charges against nine Union Carbide top officers, including its former chairman, Warren Anderson, holding them responsible for the disaster. People in Bhopal were waiting to receive the grant that the government had promised each victim. However, a 40-year-old car mechanic had a different point of view: "I don't want any money," he said. He just wanted his breath back. The tragedy was finally resolved in February 1989 when the Indian government, which had unilaterally assumed the exclusive right to litigate on behalf of tens of thousands of Bhopal victims, settled with Union Carbide out of court for $470 million. It will take many months, if not years, for compensation to reach the victims.

Often corporations do not install the same plant safety devices in Third World countries or operate under the same safety standards that they would in the United States. As an example, until 1980 the India plant of Union Carbide had imported the deadly methyl isocyanate (MIC) from the United States; in order to increase profits, it then began to produce it at the Bhopal plant. In a highly dangerous manufacturing process, they used the methyl isocyanate to produce Sevin Carbaryl, a highly effective pesticide. In 1982, prior to the disaster, a team of American experts on plant safety had made an internal report of the Bhopal plant. Their report pointed out certain safety concerns, including deficiencies in instrumentation and safety valves, lax maintenance procedures, and a high turnover of both operational and maintenance staffs.[2]

The report warned that the plant presented "serious potentials for size-able releases of toxic materials." There had also been other warnings of problems at the plant. In January 1982, a phosgene leak had seriously injured 28 workers, and in October of that year, methyl isocyanate had escaped from a broken valve. Several workers were injured in this accident, and nearby residents experienced eye and breathing problems. Two similar incidents were reported in 1983.

At the time of the disaster, the plant was storing a large quantity of MIC. Even though a refrigeration unit had been installed to keep the storage tank at a temperature low enough to prevent runaway chemical reactions, the unit had not been working properly for more than five months.[3] The storage tank temperature was lower than company regulations allowed. Since the refrigeration unit was out of commission, it was vital that instruments measuring temperature and pressure in the storage tank be in good operating order. They were not. The emergency scrubber used to neutralize the gas in the event of a leak had been out of use for six weeks. Finally, the flare tower, designed as the final line of defense to burn off excess MIC, had been closed down ten days before the leak because the line to the tower had corroded. If this were not enough to cause a catastrophe, the workers who operated the faulty equipment were inadequately trained for the job.

As the Bhopal tragedy exemplified, the health and safety of workers throughout the world is threatened when multinationals shift hazardous work processes abroad in an effort to avoid strict U.S. worker protection laws. One plant safety expert posed this question about transnationals: "Why risk $100 million of liability when you can make it [the product] any way you please somewhere else?" Commenting on the differential safety standards, a leading Indian newspaper, *The Statesman*, asked, "Were the safety measures in Bhopal identical to those in force in the United States plant and equally stringent in their application?" In Third World countries, safety standards are generally quite low and government plant inspections poor, due either to understaffing or underfunding. U.S. transnationals frequently set up manufacturing operations in the very foreign countries where there is little regard for worker safety. The sulfur dioxide limit in Indian chemical plants is six times the limit allowed in U.S. chemical plants, and four times the chemical limit permissible in U.S. battery manufacturing plants. The ammonia limit is seven times greater in India than in U.S. fertilizer plants. In an Indian owned plant producing DDT, a chemical pesticide banned in the United

States, one study found that one-third of the workers were ill from its effects.

In the 1980s, Mexico had only about 230 safety inspectors for a work force of more than 20 million; Indonesia had about 300 labor inspectors for its 110,000 companies; and India had a federal environmental protection staff of only some 150. In comparison to those small staffs, and allowing for population and industrial differences, the Environmental Protection Agency alone had a much larger inspection staff of approximately 4,400.

There was widespread fallout worldwide in the aftermath of the Bhopal catastrophe. It raised serious questions elsewhere about a possible double standard in U.S. versus overseas plant operations. People asked about the comparisons between the Indian plant's safety measures and those of plants in the United States. Were the standards equally enforced? The tragedy alerted both transnational corporations and Third World governments to the greater need for effective safety requirements. With weaker regulations and enforcement in Third World countries, the possibilities for other disasters are worrisome. Other transnationals were most alarmed by the possibility that Union Carbide would be found legally liable for the event and would be financially crippled as a result. This might produce a wholesale shrinkage of multinational manufacturing investment in Third World countries.

Although Bhopal was a high-profile disaster, other plant accidents have exacted high human tolls as well. A Liberian iron ore mine under the partial management of U.S. Steel, for example, was the site of a 1982 disaster in which a rain-swollen tailings dam burst and swamped the mining camp directly below it, killing 200 persons. In 1981, tests showed that one-third of the plant workers in Pennawalt's Nicaraguan plant were suffering from mercury poisoning.[4] This plant had been poisoning Lake Managua for many years. Under the Somoza regime, which was highly favorable to U.S. corporate interests, it had been able to dump between two and four tons of mercury into the lake every year for 12 years, killing fish and polluting the adjacent area. One report indicated that toxic mercury in the air of the plant was 12 times higher than the safety level recommended by the U.S. National Institute of Occupational Safety and Health. In an Indonesian battery manufacturing plant of Union Carbide Corporation, tests showed that more than half the work force was suffering from kidney diseases attributable to mercury poisoning and contamination, according to the company physician.[5]

Some corporations may manufacture products in their plants that are considered so dangerous to worker safety that they are virtually banned in the United States. As an example, arsenic trioxide is the "white" arsenic used in herbicides; it causes a high rate of cancer among workers. Regulatory agencies in the United States have strengthened standards governing workers' exposure to it; at present, the sole producer of such arsenic in the United States is Asarco's plant in Tacoma, Washington. Arsenic production has been largely shifted to less regulated havens in the developing world; in 1980 Asarco owned a 34-percent interest in Mexico's largest mining company, which produces over 5,500 tons of arsenic trioxide annually, 75 percent of which is exported to the United States.[6] This highly dangerous product is manufactured in Mexico without the strict worker-safety restraints imposed on U.S. production.

Third World countries now produce much asbestos and asbestos products. In the United States, the manufacture of asbestos products has declined markedly because of the great concern about public safety and the strict worker-safety programs the government has imposed on asbestos production. An important factor in relocation to Third World countries is the increasing demand there for asbestos products. Following the asbestos furor in this country, Manville Corporation established an asbestos production policy that states: "We will continue to equip our plants with the best available technology to assure the highest degree of personal safety." However, the standards of safety for U.S. production are far higher than those for its Third World plants. For example, Manville has a 10-percent interest in, and receives royalties from, a large Indian-owned asbestos plant that produces thousands of tons of asbestos water pipe and sheeting materials that are sold in India, Southeast Asia, and Africa. Manville corporate officials work closely with the plant, yet, when Bob Wyrick, an American journalist, visited there in 1980, the Indian workers had no shower facilities and had to wear their own clothes.[7] Even though the company supplied its regular workers with filter masks, it did not protect entirely against asbestos exposure, and the company issued temporary workers only a bandanna for their faces. In contrast, workers in the Manville plant in the United States receive clean uniforms each day, and they must shower before they change to their street clothes when leaving the plant. There were other significant differences: Plant temperatures may exceed 100 degrees in India, and the plant was pouring liquid asbestos waste into nearby canals used for irrigation and drinking water until they ran "red, blue, purple, green and white with asbestos and other chemicals." Around the Indian factory, workers build their huts from asbestos trash thrown out of the factory such as broken pipes and flawed sheets with asbestos fibers exposed, and children play in asbestos-littered trash. An Indian health official who visited the Manville plant described the area where asbestos sheets are cut to size: "You become white with asbestos. The air is full of it like a cloud."[8] The Manville Corporation knew all about the dangerous situation at the Indian plant since receiving a 1977 report from one of its own personnel. However, in the early 1980s, the American journalist concluded: "No determined corporate effort to eliminate the obvious dangers was made until the threat of adverse publicity loomed large."

Prescriptions for Death

Although it is illegal in the United States to sell a wide range of specific pharmaceuticals, pesticides, and medical devices, every year large quantities of such American-manufactured products are sold to Third World countries. The federal government, for example, has banned, with one exception for its use, the sale in the United States of Upjohn's controversial Depo-Provera, a synthetic hormone that tests have shown to be highly effective as a contraceptive as it stops the menstrual cycle for as long as three months when injected into a woman's arm or buttocks. It is now being used as a contraceptive by about 5 million women in 82 countries, mostly in the Third World. The overseas sale of the drug provides 1 percent of Upjohn's total sales.

Upjohn tried for many years to obtain approval of Depo-Provera in the United States as a "safe" contraceptive, but the Food and Drug Administration approval has been given for its use only as a palliative for certain cancers.[9] The last Food and Drug Administration rejection for its use as a contraceptive, in late 1984, was based on the lack of conclusive evidence of its long-term safety. A number of medical studies have linked Depo-Provera to a wide range of health disorders, including cancers of the breast and uterus. U.S. law states that drug products not approved by the FDA for sale in the United States cannot be sold abroad in any country whose government has not approved its sale there. Most Third World countries, however, do not have an approval process; it is simply registered with customs. This contraceptive is now produced by Upjohn's Belgian subsidiary and then shipped throughout the Third World. This is all perfectly legal because the Belgian government has approved the Depo-Provera's sale in Belgium.

As in the case of the Upjohn drug Depo-Provera, many American corporations widely promote and sell a number of drugs or other products in the Third World that have either been banned or that have never been approved for marketing in the United States.[10] Although laws prohibit drug companies from exporting drugs that are banned in the United States, companies have gotten around this prohibition by shipping the ingredients out of the country, assembling the compounds overseas, and then selling the product in Europe and Third World countries.

Drug companies also often fail to advise both doctors and patients in the developing world about necessary restrictions on their use and the possibly dangerous side effects that certain drugs can produce. If a drug is not properly prescribed, labeled, and used, what might have alleviated pain will cause disability, and what might have saved life may bring death. A definitive study of the misuse of drugs concluded that "in the Third World, because of the nonexistence or nonenforcement of laws and regulations and perhaps the social irresponsibility of the companies, claims of product efficacy are exaggerated to an almost ludicrous degree, and hazards, some of them life-threatening, are minimized or not even mentioned."[11]

Dangerous side effects from the use of certain drugs may include damage to the circulatory system, blindness, crippling, and even death. In this respect, there is a great difference between what U.S. drug companies tell physicians and patients in developed versus undeveloped countries. Where regulations are loose, as in most Third World countries, there is a temptation to make greater profits by remaining silent or by misleading patients and physicians, and possible lethal side effects of important and widely used drugs are often either totally ignored or minimized.

Studies made in 18 Third World countries in Africa, Asia, and Latin America in the early 1980s found wide differences in drug use indications and warning labels in those countries and in the labeled information provided in the United States and Great Britain.[12] For example, when Parke Davis distributed its powerful drug chloromycetin, used in the treatment of infections that include typhoid fever in the United States and Great Britain, it labeled specific instructions for use and precise warnings of associated dangers. In the Philippines, however, the company promoted the same drug with wider use indications and fewer warnings; Indonesian labels contained far more indications for use with no warnings at all. Companies promoted specific drugs derived from tetracycline in Third World countries, but labels seldom told users that these drugs could cause injury and death if they were given to patients with impaired kidney or liver function, pregnant women in the last half of their pregnancies, or children under the age of eight. Of 35 tetracycline drugs sold in Indonesia, 19 were distributed with no warnings; in Malaysia no warnings were mentioned in 10 out of 16 tetracycline drugs distributed. Since 1969, the use of Albamycin, an antibiotic related to tetracycline and manufactured by Upjohn, has been severely restricted to use only under certain conditions in the United States due to its dangerous side effects, yet the drug was widely sold for a large variety of illnesses in Brazil, Kenya, Costa Rica, and 27 other countries. As another example:

> Consider the adverse reactions listed by the Searle Company for their oral contraceptive, Ovulen. In the United States, Searle lists "nausea, loss of hair, nervousness, jaundice, high blood pressure, weight change, and headaches" as side effects. The farther south the product is sold, however, the safer it seems to become. In Mexico, only two side effects, nausea and weight change, are named, and in Brazil and Argentina, Searle would have physicians believe that Ovulen has no harmful side effects at all.[13]

Drug companies maintain that Third World physicians can always obtain proper drug use information from the company representatives if they ask for it. To this suggestion, a Sri Lankan physician replied, "Of course the company representative or detail man will tell you about the dangers if you ask him. At least I think he will." After a study of pharmaceutical usage in developing countries, three experts have concluded:

> In most developing countries, the detail men are often considered to be only salesmen. They have been repeatedly charged with exaggerating the claims and glossing over the dangers of their products, bulwarking their arguments by passing out copies of articles reprinted from journals that are actually owned or controlled by the drug company, and using rumors, innuendos or outright lies to run down competitive products. They have induced physicians or purchasing agents, occasionally by offering bribes, kickbacks or other inducements, to purchase drugs in

enormous quantities, with the result that some of these drugs will spoil on the storage shelves long before they can be dispensed.[14]

The pharmaceutical industry achieved a long-sought objective in 1986 when the U.S. Senate, with the support of the Reagan administration, approved a bill to allow the export of drugs not yet sufficiently tested for approval for sale in the United States to 21 other countries, primarily in the Third World. The pharmaceutical industry had claimed it was losing out to foreign competitors for whom no such approval was necessary. Actually, the bill opened up the people of the Third World for greater use as experimental guinea pigs, where they have long been used, for example, in testing the effectiveness of contraceptive drugs.

Senator Howard Metzenbaum (D-Ohio) decried this legislation, charging that the bill grew out of the "greed of the pharmaceutical industry."[15] He added that "the day will come when some pharmaceuticals . . . made in this country will be used by some other nation of the world and hundreds and perhaps thousands of children or senior citizens or people generally will pay with their lives or long-lasting injury." Congressman Henry Waxman (D-Calif.) said that the legislation would allow the United States to become an exporter of unsafe drugs. "It's an immoral foreign policy that hurts our country." In signing the bill, President Reagan said that it would "increase the competitiveness of the American pharmaceutical industry abroad." Left unsaid was the stark reality that the Third World could also be a corporate drug safety testing laboratory for Americans.

Exporting Banned Pesticides

Drugs are not the only prescription for death; corporations also export pesticides banned in the United States. In 1982 the Oxford Committee on Famine Relief (Oxfam) estimated that each year in the Third World there are 375,000 pesticide poisonings with a resulting 10,000 deaths.[16] A major reason for this is that many chemical corporations export these banned pesticides to developing countries where they then cause injuries and death. American manufacturers may export even the most dangerous pesticides as long as they are marked "For export only." In order to satisfy the growing market for their products, U.S. chemical companies ship overseas at least 150 million pounds a year of pesticides that are totally prohibited, severely restricted, or never registered for use in this country. This amounts to at least 25 percent of U.S. pesticide exports. Included in the American corporations that have been reported in such sales are American Cyanamid, Union Carbide, Monsanto, Dow, Chevron, DuPont, Velsicol, Hercules, FMC, and Hooker.[17] The advertisements of American chemical corporations that appear in Third World agricultural journals extol the virtues of these banned pesticides. Two writers who won awards for having exposed the dumping of pesticides on developing countries neatly phrased the issue: "For chemical executives, exporting hazardous pesticides is not dumping. If one country bans your product, move to where sales are still legal."[18]

As another method of exporting banned pesticides, many chemical companies simply ship the separate chemical ingredients to a Third World country where they manufacture the product in what they call their formulation plants. They then either sell these products locally or export them to other developing countries. In Malaysia, for example, Dow and Shell alone manufacture one-fourth of all liquid pesticides. In addition, the U.S. transnationals often operate their pesticide-producing plants with far lower worker safety standards than they employ in their U.S. plants. Thus Third World people suffer the double risk of producing these highly hazardous components and then using them in the fields.

The group of leading pesticides that the U.S. government has banned in this country have been termed the Dirty Dozen. Some of the Dirty Dozen include DDT, paraquat, aldrin, and dioxin. Another is parathion, a pesticide that may well be responsible for half the world's pesticide-related deaths. A number of American corporations, such as American Cyanamid and Monsanto, export this product which is so toxic that a teaspoonful spilled on the skin can be fatal. These pesticides are all effective in killing insects, but they can also cause cancer, severe bladder and lung diseases, nerve damage, and male sterility in humans. Dust-cropping planes in Third World countries are likely to spray pesticides indiscriminantly on fields, field hands, and homes. The chemicals infiltrate the soil and subsequently affect those who consume the food grown there or the meat from cattle that have grazed there.

Actually, the use of banned pesticides does little to alleviate poverty and hunger in these countries; such pesticides are not generally used for domestic food production involving small farmers. Some 70 percent of the pesticides are used to increase large-scale export crops such as cotton, coffee, tomatoes, bananas, rubber, pineapple, and a variety of other cash crops grown primarily by transnational corporations or wealthy land-owners in these developing countries.[19]

A factor of considerable significance in pesticide-related deaths and injuries is the failure of pesticide producers to include warnings in Third World countries about the possible dangers of using the compounds. Seldom do they state that the pesticides should be used only with a respirator and rubber gloves, nor are workers told that they should bathe after using them. The warnings in themselves, however, may be futile, as two experts on the use of pesticides in the Third World have pointed out.

> In countries where most people cannot read, what use are warning labels on pesticide packages? In countries that outlaw unions that could protect farm workers, what chance do peasants have against the crop duster's rain of poison? In countries with neither enough scientists to investigate pesticide dangers, nor enough trained government officials to enforce regulations, should foreign pesticide makers be given a free hand to push products so dangerous they are banned at home?[20]

The mushrooming use of pesticides in the Third World is a daily threat to millions of inhabitants there, and it is also a growing threat to consumers in the United States. Banned pesticides have created a veritable "Circle of Poison" as agricultural products poisoned with banned U.S. pesticides are imported into this country for consumption. According to a 1978 report of the Food and Drug Administration, approximately 10 percent of the food imported by the United States contains varying amounts of illegal pesticides. Other FDA studies at the time showed that over 15 percent of beans and 13 percent of peppers imported from Mexico violated Food and Drug Administration pesticide standards, and nearly half of imported green coffee beans contained traces of illegal pesticides banned in the United States.[21] Large amounts of beef imported from Central America have also been contaminated by pesticides. Thus, when an American eats a hamburger or drinks a cup of coffee in a fast-food restaurant, there is always the possibility that he or she may be poisoned because of a U.S. corporation's unethical behavior in exporting a banned pesticide overseas. The conclusion is clear: In a world of growing food dependence, the United States cannot export its banned chemicals and simply forget about them.

Death by Infant Formula

In the Third World, the use of infant formula often has caused illness and death of babies. In the late nineteenth century, Henri Nestle and the Swiss company he founded developed infant formula as a substitute for breast milk, ostensibly to save the life of an infant who could not be breast-fed. However, the number of infants who cannot be breast-fed has always been small. The vigorous efforts that multinational corporations such as Swiss Nestle and U.S. corporations such as Bristol Myers, Abbott, and American Home Products have made to encourage Third World mothers to use infant feeding formulas rather than to breast-feed their infants has had disastrous consequences. With declining birth rates in industrialized nations like the United States, the sale of infant formula has also declined. On the other hand, Third World markets offer unlimited growth opportunities as birth rates there continue to be high. Advertisements proclaiming the advantages of infant formula have influenced many mothers overseas to change from the traditional breast-feeding to the use of "modern" infant bottle-feeding.

Because the formula must be mixed with water, poverty-stricken mothers of infants in Africa, Asia, and Latin America unwittingly expose their babies to water-borne diseases to which they have not yet developed an immunity. Lacking pure water and often being unaware of the risks they run, mothers use any available water, most of which is contaminated. Being poor, these mothers may also dilute the formula below the recommended standards, causing infants to suffer or die from malnutrition. UNICEF has estimated that with emphasis on the proper use of infant formula and increased breast-feeding, one million infant lives could be saved in Third World countries.

During the early 1980s, the World Health Organization (WHO) and UNICEF drew up a code of conduct for transnationals that sell infant formula in Third World countries. This was in partial response to a worldwide boycott of Nestle products over the export of infant formula in the early 1980s led by the Institutional Chain of the Infant Formula Action Coalition (INFACT), which finally brought Nestle Corporation to its knees and had a major effect on the marketing of infant formula by other corporations. The WHO and UNICEF codes contained provisions that all labels should warn users about the product's improper use. The code also limited free promotional supplies and prohibited direct consumer advertising, gifts to doctors, and hospital promotional distributions.

In 1988, American Home Products/Wyeth was the target of the group Action for Corporate Accountability over their marketing practices which endangered infant health. In many developing countries the corporation encouraged new mothers to forgo breast-feeding by distributing free infant formula through hospitals. Wyeth's booklet for mothers in Taiwan featured a full-page picture of a white mother bottle-feeding a fat baby, presumably with Wyeth's infant formula. Bristol-Myers has distributed literature containing code violations to mothers in the Dominican Republic, Mexico, Taiwan, and other Third World countries.

A new development occurred on October 4, 1987, the fourth anniversary of the end of the Nestle boycott, when Action for Corporate Accountability announced a new boycott of Nestle Corporation and also American Home Products. It was charged that these corporations continued to violate WHO and UNICEF marketing regulations for infant formula in the Third World. The "donation" of infant formula supplies to hospitals and maternity wards is not charitable, according to Dr. Rajanand, a Bombay professor of pediatrics: "The purpose of the industry in bringing the formula to hospitals is to induce sales. This is their one and only purpose."[22]

Exploitation of the Land

Increasingly more land in the underdeveloped countries is being used for greater quantities of export food products that proportionately fewer people in their home countries can afford. Africa now supplies Europe not only with traditional products like palm, peanut, and copra oils but also fresh fruits, vegetables, and even beef. Mexico and countries of Latin America ship many of these products, as well as winter luxury foods such as strawberries, asparagus, and flowers to the United States. Vital tropical forests are being cut down to make land available for growing these exportable products.

Agribusiness is large-scale corporate agricultural production and processing; a corporation may control all the production, processing, storage, and marketing of an agricultural commodity. In developing countries, agribusinesses, including large plantation and lumbering operations, are largely concentrated in rubber, bananas, pineapple, sugar, palm and other oils, coconuts (copra), tea, cattle, lumber, and various luxury items such as cut flowers and fresh fruits. American corporations have long dominated banana agribusinesses in Central America (for example, United Fruit Company) and rubber in Liberia (Firestone). U.S. conglomerate Gulf and Western dominates sugar production and processing in the Dominican Republic where it controls 8 percent of all cultivated land.

The evidence suggests that Third World agribusinesses, with their huge plantations and ranch lands, frequently help to destroy the local food crop production and employment patterns in the host country. They do little to satisfy local demand for increased food supplies. Nearly all agribusiness products are exported to the industrialized Western nations that pay far more for products than can the local market buyers. Costa Rica, for example, has increased its beef exports to North America by 92 percent in recent years, and this increase has been accompanied by a 26 percent decline in local meat consumption. In Colombia, a hectare of land used to raise carnations for export brings a million pesos a year, while wheat or corn raised there would bring only 12,500 pesos. Consequently, Colombia, like most other Latin American countries, must use its scarce foreign exchange to import wheat. Giant agribusinesses like General Foods, Ralston Purina, Quaker Oats, Swift, and Armour also process and export great quantities of high-protein products like fish meal that could well be used in the host country for human consumption but is used instead to feed America's 35 million dogs and 30 million cats. One expert on world hunger, Susan George, has put it this way: "Any rich mongrel or pampered puss is a better customer for agribusiness than a poor human being. Little has changed since William Hazlitt, replying to Parson Malthus in 1807, stated that the dogs and horses of the rich eat up the food of the children of the poor."[23]

Corporate agribusinesses cloak their activities in the false claims that they are benefiting the ordinary people of the host country. They claim that the people who work for them and the poor as a whole are better off economically. This is often clearly incorrect, as an International Union of Foodworkers' report for the 1974 World Food Conference stated: "There are great numbers of agribusiness workers whose low salaries, substandard housing, poor health and squalid working conditions are such that hunger, malnutrition and under-nourishment for them and for their families are commonplace." Clergy and Laity Concerned, a prominent social activist group, charged in 1977 that Del Monte "has benefited greatly from martial law in the Philippines. [Ferdinand] Marcos has exempted much of the agricultural land owned by foreign corporations from his 'land reform' program and has banned strikes by workers on agribusiness plantations. . . . Del Monte's operations in the Philippines [are] evidence that hunger and poverty are the darker side of corporate profits." Gulf and Western workers in the Dominican Republic, for example, used to receive extremely low wages; only if they work for the corporation at least 48 years do they become eligible for pensions, which are only worth about $6 a month.

Conversion of forest to grazing and crop land is by far the leading cause of tropical deforestation. Agribusiness connected with providing the industrialized world with beef, rubber and palm oil, and lumber derived from operations like those of Weyerhauser has greatly contributed to the destruction of the tropical rain forests and their giant centuries-old trees. By 1980, almost 40 percent of the world's tropical forests had been destroyed.[24] According to FAO estimates, for 1981-1985, every year over 27 million acres of the developing world's tropical rain forests were destroyed.[25] Some scientists predict the almost total destruction of these giant forests within the next 50 years or so.

Demand for inexpensive beef for fast-food outlets has been one of the primary factors contributing to the destruction of these rain forests. A little over two decades ago, the United States imported only 2,000 tons of beef a year. By 1980, however, beef imports had risen to over 100,000 tons. Meat from grain-fed American beef cattle is far more costly than the tougher, leaner beef that comes from Central and South America. There cattle feed on grass that, in many cases, has replaced the rain forest. This cheaper beef is a plentiful source for the hamburgers, hot dogs, tacos and frozen TV dinners that have helped make the fast-food industry the most rapidly growing segment in the giant U.S. food business. McDonald's, however, advertises that its hamburgers are made from "100 percent pure American beef." Because of these heavy demands, beef production in many developing countries has doubled; over the past 20 years, beef exports from Costa Rica, Guatemala, and Honduras have tripled. Environmentalists Paul and Anne Ehrlich have commented on this situation:

The rainforests are being sacrificed to keep up the flow of meat destined almost exclusively to be hamburgers served by fast-food chains. Beef can be produced at very low cost in poor countries because of the availability of cheap labor and cheap land ("useless" rainforest). Grass-fed beef can be raised in Latin America at a quarter the price at which it can be raised in Colorado. Although imports from Latin America only amount to 1 or 2 percent of U.S. beef consumption, they cut a nickel or so off the price of a hamburger. Ironically, though, while more than a quarter of all Central American forests have been destroyed in the past twenty years to produce beef for the United States, per-capita consumption of beef in Central American nations has dropped steadily.[26]

When once these rain forests are destroyed to provide cattle-raising and other agribusiness lands, a century or more may be required for them to regenerate. The tropical rainforests play an essential role as filters for the Earth's atmosphere. Without them, excessive soil erosion also results, producing increased river silt and flooding. The destruction of the rain forests, furthermore, endangers half the world's 10 million species of plants and animals, which have long made these forests their home. Too much deforestation might even change the world's climate, potentially causing a "greenhouse effect." After the rain forest is gone, all that may be left will be plantations of pasture land for fast-food beef and fast-growing softwood trees which are ground up to make toilet paper.

Exploitation of the People

Pope John Paul II's third encyclical of 1981 took aim at the transnationals that have built up vast "empires" throughout the world today. The pope claimed that large corporations are contributing to the ever-widening disproportion between the incomes of the rich and poor nations. As the developed countries put the highest possible prices on their products and at the same time try to fix the lowest possible prices for raw materials or semi-manufactured goods, they create a wide gap between the rich and poor countries' national incomes. The pope cautioned that "workers' rights must come ahead of profits" in the poor countries.

U.S. transnational corporations have been in the process of moving many of their manufacturing facilities to the newly developing countries since the time of the Korean War. Third World countries have encouraged these moves in the belief that the introduction of the plants add to industrial growth, increase their people's employment opportunities and, at the same time, decrease their dependence on imports from the developed countries. The U.S. multinationals have different motives, however: cheaper wages, lower employee benefits, less stringent health and safety standards, and a more open labor market. Corporations have been enticed into plant relocations in Third World countries that offer them the right to import raw materials, plant components, and equipment duty-free, and give them tax holidays of up to 20 years. Corporations that do not want to relocate their plants directly can often work out attractive subcontracting arrangements in the Third World.

Most of the work done in Third World countries is labor intensive. For example, Southeast Asia's semiconductor factories of U.S. giants like National Semiconductor, Texas Instruments, and Motorola are part of a "global assembly line" that stretches half way around the world. In much of this labor-intensive work, silicon wafers which are made in New Jersey are shipped to Southeast Asian countries where they are cut into tiny chips, then bonded by the workers to circuit boards. With their Third World operations, Levi Strauss, Blue Bell, and other conglomerates, including subsidiaries of General Mills and Gulf and Western, have cornered a fifth of the U.S. clothing market. Rockport shoes are made in Taiwan, Perry Ellis "American Series" slacks are made in Mauritius, Bell telephones come from Singapore and Taiwan, and Spalding's "Official NBA" basketballs are manufactured in Korea.

Much Third World production involves "outward processing." Workers in U.S. plants design and cut the goods, which are then shipped to Mexico and Central American countries for processing. From there they are re-imported for final finishing and packaging in the United States. In this roundabout manner, corporations save import duties on the finished garments, paying duty only on the value added. This process has seriously hurt American workers' jobs. In planning their moves, the multinationals often carefully choose those countries in which labor unions are nonexistent or weak, or countries that are so dominated by a right-wing or military government that they can safely pay low wages and operate with minimal worker safety regulations. The AFL-CIO News stated in 1988 that: "Aided by favorable tariff breaks, hundreds of American firms have migrated to Mexico. . . . In the past decade alone, American firms have invested $2 billion on assembly plants just across the border, shipping products back into this country at such a pace that they account for nearly 20 percent of Mexico's $3.5 billion annual trade surplus with the United States." At 900 of these "maquiladoras," some 300,000 women and girls work for wages of 30 to 75 cents an hour.

Even though American multinationals claim that they are contributing to the development of these poor countries, their primary goal is to obtain cheap labor. The average worker in the United States in 1988 received $13.90 an hour; in South Korea, it was only $2.45; and in Taiwan, $2.71. The average hourly wage paid in the semiconductor industry in the United States in 1982 was $5.92; in Hong Kong it was $1.15; in Singapore, $.79; in Malaysia and the Philippines, $.48; and in Indonesia, $.19. Fringe benefits are correspondingly low, and there is little or no protection for them from trade unions, which are often banned or their right to strike limited. For example, Philippine President Ferdinand Marcos, in 1982, outlawed all strikes in the U.S.-dominated semiconductor industry. Over and over, reports have circulated that as soon as a worker protest begins over pay or working conditions in South Korea, Indonesia, Thailand, or Taiwan, for example, carloads of police and government officials descend on the plant to put down the demonstration.

Those who work for American corporations operating in Third World countries often have to tolerate appalling working conditions. They may work 12-hour days, and although toxic fumes and dangerous liquids may be present, workers, unlike those in the United States, are usually not required to wear protective clothing, gloves, or face masks. Women working in the intensive semiconductor plants bend over microscopes all day, and if they develop severe eye ailments, as they commonly do, and thus become unable to work, they have no alternatives except to retire or face dismissal.[27] There is usually no workers' compensation. The health of textile and garment workers, who are primarily women, is often endangered by U.S. multinational overseas garment and textile affiliates. Two experts on this problem have stated:

> The firms, generally local subcontractors to large U.S. (and European) chains such as Sears and J.C. Penney, show little concern for the health of their employees. Some of the worst conditions have been documented in South Korea. . . . Workers are packed into poorly-lit rooms where summer temperatures rise above 100 degrees Fahrenheit. Textile dust and lint, which can cause brown-lung disease, fill the air. The dampness that is so useful in preserving thread causes rheumatism and arthritis among the workers.[28]

Union Carbide makes Eveready batteries in Indonesia. The employee working conditions that an American journalist found in Union Carbide's Indonesian plant in 1981 would never be tolerated in the United States.[29] The company had failed, for example, to warn workers about the dangers of carbon black, which is used in battery manufacturing. It contains mercury and contaminates the environment in and around the plant. As late as 1981, both male and female employees in the highly dangerous chemical mixing room generally worked 16 hours a day.

Most American multinationals that move abroad to reduce labor costs prefer to hire women for detailed assembly-line work. They work for even less money than men and it is easier to exploit them. In Haiti, for example, where nearly all the baseballs sold in the United States are made, thousands of women perform the final operation for four major U.S. companies in producing a baseball whose parts are sent in from the United States. U.S. Rawlings Sporting Goods Company, the chief manufacturer of baseballs in Haiti, also has a monopoly on all balls used by the National and American baseball leagues.[30] Rawlings pays its workers, most of whom are female, about $2.75 a day for producing 30 to 40 baseballs—about 7 to 9 cents a ball. In the United States, Rawlings sells the baseballs for about $4, almost 50 times what it pays the Haitians to make them.

Multinationals prefer hiring women workers not only because they cost less but because they find them generally more docile than men. Women are more easy to press into boring, repetitive assembly-line work for the low wages the multinationals offer. Women are far less likely to present problems than young males. Even when they do try to press for higher pay or better working conditions, Third World governments often support the multinational's opposition to their demands. One astute observer pointed out that East Asian governments "have taken measures to make their country's women more attractive as potential employees by ensuring that they will not resist demands made on them by foreign firms."[31] The governments sometimes use repressive means to keep women workers in line. During one 5-month labor dispute in Control Data's Korean plant in 1982, the unionized, all-female assembly-line workers were preparing to leave their Seoul plant when the guards shut and locked the gate.[32] Security guards and male supervisory personnel severely beat some of them, causing some pregnant women to miscarry. In another case, when women workers in a U.S. Guatemalan jeans and jacket factory drew up a list of complaints about low piecework wages and lack of overtime pay, the plant manager reported to local authorities that he was being harassed by "communists." When the women reported for work the following day, they found the factory surrounded by a heavily armed contingent of military police. The so called communist organizers were identified and fired. Similar episodes have occurred in the Philippines, the Dominican Republic, South Korea, and elsewhere in the Third World.

U.S. transnational corporations often operate on the assumption that the poorer and more malnourished the people, the more likely they are to spend a disproportionate amount of their income on a luxury item. If a profit is to be made through creating a demand, corporations do not stop to consider at whose expense they will make their profit. In many parts of the world, for example, poor rural families will sell a few eggs and a chicken to buy Coke soft drinks, even though their children lack protein; and poor city people may buy American processed baby foods when they could have prepared their own at little cost.

Partly because of decreasing domestic sales, the United States has also become a major partner in the increased promotion, sale, and consumption of death-dealing cigarettes in the very parts of the world where malnutrition and hunger are most prevalent. The cigarette manufacturers have been highly successful. By the early 1980s, according to the World Health Organization, the total consumption of cigarettes in the Third World was already increasing by an average of more than 3 percent a year. According to the World Health Organization, this is primarily due to the aggressive advertising campaigns conducted by "unscrupulous tobacco industries." Of the approximately 600 billion U.S. cigarettes made in 1988, 100 billion went overseas, and half of these to the Far East. As Surgeon General Koop pointed out, "I don't think we as citizens can continue to tolerate exporting disease, disability and death." Moreover, the United States cannot hope to get worldwide cooperation in its fight against drugs, according to Representative Chester Atkins (D-Mass.), "when we have a drug our own government says is addictive, and is killing us, and we are spreading that drug overseas." Representative Mel Levine (D-Calif.) said: "The message we are sending is that Asian lungs are more expendable than American lungs."

Even though American cigarettes cost far more in these developing countries than the local brands, the aggressive advertising campaigns for American brands have greatly boosted their sales. U.S. tobacco companies have responded to awakening concern in developed countries over the link between smoking, cancer, and heart disease by launching an all-out sales assault on potential Third World and Asiatic consumers. Generally many youths there prefer to smoke American brands because the advertisements link them to modernity and prestige. In almost all these countries, the infamous Marlboro cowboy lures youths into feeling they are part of the American West: "Come to Where the Flavor is . . . Marlboro Country." Marlboro is now the world's largest selling cigarette, particularly among the young, with sales that total more than $3.8 million worldwide. According to a 1983 report, the tar and nicotine content of U.S. cigarettes sold in the Third World is often twice the level of identical brands sold in the United States.[35] Throughout the Third World, labels of health hazards on cigarette packages are the exception rather than the rule.

The issue of exporting American cigarettes to Asiatic countries came to a head in 1989. On grounds of "unfair trade discrimination," the U.S. Cigarette Export Association persuaded the government to intimidate Japan, Korea, and Taiwan with threatened economic sanctions when each of these countries had sought to keep out American cigarettes. In 1989, however, Thailand put up a stiffer resistance and enlisted U.S. anti-smoking groups such as the American Heart Association, the American Cancer Society, and others to help out with congressional testimony. Although Thailand has a state-run cigarette monopoly, the Thais feared that the clever advertising of U.S. cigarette companies would induce more of their people to smoke. In addition to forcing Thailand to admit the cigarettes, the cigarette association demanded the right to advertise on Thai TV, which bans all such advertising on health grounds.

As a consequence of callous corporate behavior by American tobacco corporations, four U.S. congressmen joined together in 1989 to introduce a bill to (1) forbid American companies to advertise overseas in ways that are prohibited here; (2) prevent our country from threatening trade sanctions against countries that are unwilling to allow the promotion of cigarettes; and (3) force cigarettes sold abroad to carry the same warning labels they carry here.

Exploitation of the Country

Mexican President Jose Portillo, in an address before the United Nations General Assembly in 1983, said that transnational corporations exhibit a "pattern of domination" over many developing countries that endangers the country's sovereignty over their economic progress, and their very existence as a national state. Through corrupt and often illegal practices, the transnationals interfere to support regimes that maintain conditions favorable to their own activities, or they may endeavor to strengthen their ties to whichever potential ally in the country might provide conditions most suitable to their needs.

In many cases, U.S. transnationals have exhibited an almost total disregard for the political well-being of the people of the Third World. American transnationals have done extensive business with such nefarious regimes as that of Iran's Shah Riza Pahlavi and with Central American dictators like Nicaragua's Anastasio Somoza. In Chile, ITT helped to topple the democratically elected president, Salvador Allende. ITT presumably then got the man it wanted, Augusto Pinochet, a long-ruling, right-wing military dictator who helped the company get what it wanted. U.S. multinationals have long played a major role in the financial as well as the policy control of Central America. Two multinational corporations, Standard Brands and United Fruit, have largely dominated the economy of Honduras, one of the poorest countries in Latin America, where bananas make up the bulk of export earnings. The multinationals have demonstrated their power most effectively when they have feared their profits being reduced or when they have suspected that their business interests might be nationalized. For example, during the early 1950s under the regime of the newly elected democratic Guatemalan president Jacobo Arbenz, the government raised property taxes, encouraged unions, and initiated a land reform program. These changes seriously concerned the large land-holding United Fruit Company, and it unjustly accused the government of being part of an international communist conspiracy. In fact, the communists actually played only a minor role in the Arbenz coalition government. United Fruit, because of its desire to protect its power and assets, pressured Washington to take drastic action in Guatemala. With the threat of U.S. military intervention and the help of the Central Intelligence Agency (CIA), in an operation code named "Operation Success," the Arbenz coalition government fell. For many years following the coup, Guatemala suffered from right-wing military dictatorships dedicated to backing the wealthy landowners and the United Fruit Company. Only in 1986 was Guatemala once again able to install a democratic government. Long ago, the famed Marine Corps General Smedley Butler explained this policy of government intervention in the Third World to protect corporate interests:

> I spent 33 years . . . being a high-class muscleman for big business, for
> Wall Street and the bankers. . . . I helped purify Nicaragua for the

international house of Brown Brothers in 1909-1912. I helped make Mexico and especially Tampico safe for American oil interests in 1916. I brought light to the Dominican Republic for American sugar interests in 1916. I helped make Haiti and Cuba a decent place for the National City Bank boys to collect revenue in. I helped in the rape of half a dozen Central American republics for the benefit of Wall Street.[37]

For most of the blacks (who make up the bulk of South Africa's population), their share of the country is like that in the developing world; for the whites it is not. For many years the highly visible presence of U.S. corporations and their subsidiaries in South Africa has drawn tremendous opposition from anti-apartheid activists. At its peak, U.S. corporations accounted for more than 20 percent of all direct foreign investment in South Africa. U.S. petroleum corporations controlled about 40 percent of all petroleum sales. In 1982, U.S. corporate investments in South Africa totaled $14.6 billion, about 70 percent of them coming from 10 large corporations, including Ford, General Motors, General Electric, U.S. Steel, Goodyear, Caltex, and Mobil Oil.

Nearly all U.S. corporations operating in South Africa eventually signed and generally practiced the American-derived Sullivan Principles which require them not to discriminate in the workplace. However, their continuing presence there gave a corporate blessing from the United States to an unjust system. In the United States, mounting pressures for American corporate divestment in South Africa came from liberal groups, churches, investors, and others. As a result, the U.S. Congress in 1986 passed a law, overriding a veto by President Reagan, that prohibited further private investments in South Africa and banned the import of certain materials. Many U.S. corporations had already pulled out of the country, but as of 1989 a number of large U.S. corporations were still operating there. Among the largest remaining companies were Goodyear Tire and Rubber, International Paper, Johnson and Johnson, United Technologies, and Caltex Petroleum. Also, according to *Fortune,* corporations still operating there but planning to leave were Mobil, RJR Nabisco, Control Data, NCR, and Hewlett-Packard.[38] As corporations pull out of South Africa, however, they leave a foot in the door: some of their operations generally continue under South African ownership. Other corporations have actually improved their profit margins by selling through low-overhead distributors and through licensing agreements. South Africans can still buy CBS records, Levi jeans, and U.S.

automobiles, even though the corporations behind these products no longer operate in their country. The real pressures that precipitated the withdrawal of U.S. corporations from South Africa came from social action groups and the Congress. Corporate moral scruples about apartheid were never involved. Instead, the people and the government of the United States had to intervene.

Notes

1. Dan Kurzman, *A Killing Wind* (New York: McGraw Hill, 1987); and David Weir, *The Bhopal Syndrome* (San Francisco: Sierra Club Books, 1987).

2. See Russell Mokhiber, *Corporate Crime and Violence: Big Business Power and the Abuse of the Public Trust* (San Francisco: Sierra Club Books, 1988) pp. 86-96.

3. Mokhiber, *Corporate Crime and Violence.*

4. Amie Street, "Nicaragua Cites Pennwalt," *Multinational Monitor* 2 (May 1981): 25; and Bob Wyrick, "Chemical Plant's Poison Inflames a Nation," *Newsday*, December 21, 1981.

5. Bob Wyrick, "How Job Conditions Led to a Worker's Death," *Newsday*, December 17, 1981.

6. Herman Rebhan, "Labor Battles Exports," *Multinational Monitor* (March 1980): 6.

7. Bob Wyrick, "Asbestos Plant Imperils Village in India," *Newsday*, December 16, 1981.

8. Wyrick, "Asbestos Plant Imperils Village."

9. Amy Goodman, "The Case Against Depo-Provera," *Multinational Monitor* (February/March 1985): 3-15.

10. John Braithwaite, *Corporate Crime in the Pharmaceutical Industry* (London: Routledge and Kegan Paul, 1984), pp. 257-65.

11. Milton Silverman, Philip R. Lee, and Mia Lydecker, *Prescriptions for Death: The Drugging of the Third World* (Berkeley: University of California Press, 1982), p. 10.

12. Silverman, Lee, and Lydecker, *Prescriptions for Death.*

13. Cited in James E. Coleman, *The Criminal Elite: The Sociology of White Collar Crime* (New York: St. Martin's Press, 1985), p. 46.

14. Silverman, Lee, and Lydecker, *Prescriptions for Death*, p. 108.

15. *Wall Street Journal*, May 15, 1986.

16. Mokhiber, *Corporate Crime and Violence*, p. 185.

17. David Weir and Mark Schapiro, *Circle of Poison: Pesticides and People in a Hungry World* (San Francisco: Institute for Food Development and Policy, 1981), pp. 77-78.

18. Ibid., p. 11.

19. "Pesticides and Pills: For Export Only," Public Broadcasting System radio broadcast, October 5 and 7, 1982.

20. Weir and Schapiro, *Circle of Poison*, p. 17.

21. Weir and Schapiro, *Circle of Poison*, p. 29.

22. *Multinational Monitor* 9, no. 9 (September 1988): 4.

23. Susan George, *How the Other Half Dies: The Real Reasons for World Hunger* (Totowa, N.J.: Rowman and Allanheld, 1977), p. 146.

24. Ellen Hosmer, "Paradise Lost: The Ravaged Rainforest," *Multinational Monitor* 8, no. 6 (June 1987).

25. Sandra Postel, "Protecting Forests," in Lester R. Brown et al., *State of the World, 1984: A Worldwatch Institute Report on Progress Toward a Sustainable Society* (New York: W. W. Norton, 1985), pp. 74-79.

26. Paul Ehrlich and Anne Ehrlich, *Extinction: The Causes and Consequences of the Disappearance of Species* (New York: Random House, 1981), pp. 163-64.

27. Rachel Grossman, "Bitter Wages: Women in East Asia's Semi-Conductor Plants," *Multinational Monitor* 1 (March 1980): 9.

28. Annette Fuentes and Barbara Ehrenreich, *Women in the Global Factory* (Boston: South End Press, 1984), p. 21.

29. Wyrick, "How Job Conditions Led to a Worker's Death."

30. Allan Ebert-Miner, "How Rawlings Uses Haitian Women to Spin Profits Off U.S. Baseball Sales," *Multinational Monitor* 3 (August 1982): 11-12.

31. Grossman, "Bitter Wages."

32. Matthew Rothschild, "Women Beat Up at Control Data, Korea," *Multinational Monitor* 3 (September 1982): 14-16.

33. Fuentes and Ehrenreich, *Women in the Global Factory,* p. 35.

34. *Christian Science Monitor,* February 2, 1989.

35. John Cavanagh and Joy Hackel, "Turning the World into 'Marlboro Country,' " *Guardian,* April 13, 1983.

36. Paul Sigmund, *Multinationals in Latin America: The Politics of Nationalization* (Madison: University of Wisconsin Press, 1980).

37. Quoted in *Washington Spectator,* January 15, 1988.

38. *Fortune,* April 24, 1989.

DISCUSSION:
Moonshiners

When the new world's first saloon opened its doors in Boston in 1625, the king's agents were there to impose excise taxes (Barleycorn, 1975, p. 117). The first rebellion in U.S. history, which took place while George Washington was still the first president, was an uprising in western Massachusetts by farmers who resented taxes on whisky (Slaughter, 1986). Illicit enterprises developed in response to liquor restrictions and prohibitions throughout history. Social subsystems developed that served the essential functions of production, distribution, consumption, socialization, social control, participation, and mutual support (Potter, 1994). OC in the southern United States developed its own unique flavor. However, illegal liquor production was a lucrative illicit enterprise in many places.

According to the federal agency responsible for enforcing liquor taxes in the United States, the Internal Revenue Service, moonshining was a cancer, and moonshiners well-organized peddlers of poison. There were production specialists, transportation specialists, distribution specialists, and financial specialists. By its illegitimacy, moonshining avoided many of the problems that any legitimate business must face. Quality control was of no concern. Trade unions among its workers were nonexistent. Social security taxes were not paid; income taxes were not withheld. No minimum wage, paid vacations, or standard work week was provided. Cleanliness and sanitation were unknown. No reports were made. Trucks carried no company names. Sample testings of moonshine consistently revealed heavy concentrations of lead salts because of the use of automobile radiators for condensers in stills. "Rotgut" recipes may have included lye, rubbing alcohol, and other toxins to speed fermentation. Children born to moonshine-drinking mothers often had serious deformities. A high rate of heart damage was reported in chronic moonshine drinkers. Conceivably, hundreds of leaded liquor fatalities were unreported as such each year (Licensed Beverage Industry, 1966, 1974; U.S. Department of Health and Human Services, 1992).

Potter (1994) pointed out that the integral role and usefulness of moonshiners in communities and societies guaranteed their success despite the risks. In certain regions, moonshining operations were tenacious and well integrated in the culture. When the 18th Amendment to the U.S. Constitution prohibited the manufacture, sale, and transportation of intoxicating liquors in 1920, the market for illegal distillers was expanded immensely. Those already involved built up their businesses, and many other entrepreneurs were attracted to moonshining.

During the Prohibition Era of the 1920s, Chicago was said to be the most corrupt city in the United States. A huge tenement network of alcohol cookers grew up there. Gangsters shipped over Sicilian families and set them up with a cooker each. The raw alcohol was collected each week: taken to the gang's warehouse and cut, flavored, colored, bottled, and labeled; and sold as whiskey and gin. Gangsters were said to gross $150,000 per month from this operation (Allsop, 1961, p. 76).

The repeal of Prohibition did not mean the end of moonshiners. For example, in 1994, taxes in Canada led to a boom in smuggled alcohol (Fennell, 1994). The supply of illegal alcohol will continue when a market develops for cheaper alcohol or liquor that is difficult to get legally. A significant deterrent is the accessibility of legal liquor. Shortage or absence of legal outlets lures moonshiners. The highest number of seizures of moonshining stills occurred in the southeastern region of the United States known as the "moonshine belt," where many districts are "dry" or prohibit the sale of liquor (Licensed Beverage Industry, 1966).

The notion of restricting alcohol use represents a fundamental contradiction in the social order. It represents a conflict between those who would drink liquor and those who would stop them. The era of Prohibition in the United States was a time of deep corruption and crime.

President Hoover stated in 1929, "If the law is wrong, its rigid enforcement is the surest guarantee of its repeal" (quoted in Woodiwiss, 1988, p. 30). As a result of the strict enforcement of this widely unsupported law, there were by that time more than 40,000 liquor law offenders in federal prison (Woodiwiss, 1988). Hypocrisy was endemic. People grew accustomed to dealing with illegal markets. Organized production and distribution outstripped organized enforcement. Lawlessness was widespread.

From 1950 through 1965, the estimated output of moonshine in the United States, according to Internal Revenue Service information, was a river of about 1 billion gallons. Moonshine represented a federal, state, and local tax loss of more than $12 billion (Licensed Beverage Industry, 1966, p. 6). The subculture of moonshiners is the living reminder of the contradiction of prohibition. Illegal production is the inevitable response to restrictions of illicit substances. Perhaps the lesson of history is that the greater the restriction, the greater the value of illicit enterprise. Yet the philosophy of prohibition persists when all evidence shows that this approach maximizes the harm that illicit substances can do to society (Woodiwiss, 1988).

2

The Political Economy
of Mountain Dew

Wilbur R. Miller

Chapter 2 (pp. 15-39) of *Revenuers and Moonshiners,*
by Wilbur R. Miller (Chapel Hill: University of North
Carolina Press, 1991)

As the southern black and the white supremacist began to fade from
national attention as Reconstruction wound down in the middle 1870s,
a new southern figure moved toward center stage. This was the Appalachian moonshiner, more often called a "blockader" by his neighbors
because he distilled corn whiskey or fruit brandy without paying the
federal tax and "ran the blockade" of revenue officers to sell his product.
To the local-color novelists and journalists who became popular after the
Civil War, the moonshiner seemed to typify all that made Appalachia
different from the rest of the nation. He became a standard literary
character representing the outlaw as a rugged individualist or victim of
historical processes beyond his comprehension or control. In more modern terms, southern moonshiners resembled Eric Hobsbawm's "primitive rebels" and "social bandits" on American soil. They were rebels,
supported by their neighbors but not politically organized. They were
outlaws but only because a distant central government "criminalized"

part of their way of life by imposing a tax on home-distilled whiskey they had produced for generations. Novel readers may have seen moonshiners as colorful, and modern scholars may have perceived them as participants in "archaic" social movements, but to the federal government they were less colorful than costly because of their tax evasion and shooting at revenue officers attempting to suppress their illegal activity. By 1876 most of the work of district attorneys and marshals in Appalachia was revenue cases, in Georgia amounting to four-fifths of federal prosecutions.[1]

Although illicit distillation occurred in regions as diverse as Utah Territory and Brooklyn,[2] moonshining was concentrated in the mountains and foothills of the southern Appalachians and neighboring Piedmont areas. One of the blockaders' strongholds was in the Blue Ridge border areas of eastern Tennessee, western North and South Carolina, and northern Georgia. Another concentration was in the Cumberlands of eastern Kentucky, West Virginia, and western Virginia. The Ozarks of Missouri and Arkansas contributed their share, along with the hills of northern Alabama and Mississippi. In 1891 the Appalachian region accounted for 68 percent of the nation's cases of selling liquor without a license and 77 percent of the cases of illicit distilling, better known as moonshining.[3] . . .

[By 1890,] living on smaller farms or landless, many mountain people became poorer and less able to rely on their own resources. Cash was scarce. . . . During the later nineteenth century, mountain people's need for cash increased because manufactured goods began to supplement and then to supplant homemade products. Although they often could revert to old ways in an emergency, people began buying such things as matches, commercial dyes and printed cloth, and kerosene lamps (without chimneys, which broke in transit over the rough trails). Sometimes they even purchased cornmeal if they had a bad crop or if their farm was too small to supply the family. . . . Local property taxes, low but rising in areas where outsiders were buying land for timber or minerals or where railroads were being built, also required cash payment, and many people had trouble raising the money.[4]

For mountain families who wished to remain on their land, marketing farm products was increasingly necessary to acquire cash. In some areas, though, marketing was restricted by the geographical barriers that hampered many highlanders' economic opportunities. In Union County, Georgia, the people "raise a few hogs, a little wheat, and make the bulk of their crop in corn. There is no market near them, and when the years accounts are cast up they find themselves with enough bread and meat but without a cent of money." Mountaineers sometimes did not fare well when they could reach the markets. In Burke County, North Carolina, farmers living ten miles from the railroad saw half the price of their corn eaten up by shipping costs, making them "poorer every year." After traveling two days to town, highlanders encountered worldly derision of their "quaint costumes and grotesque teams" and purchasers' demands that they "'take in trade' something they do not want." Some mountaineers raised turkeys and hogs, which they drove to market, but they did not always get good prices because the animals lost weight on the trek. One agricultural product, though, always commanded a ready market and could be easily transported on a mule—mountain dew.[5]

Whiskey or brandy could indeed bring in more cash than most farmers ever saw, particularly if the tax bite were avoided. A mule able to carry only 4 bushels of corn could pack whiskey equivalent to 24 bushels. If the mountaineer had a team and wagon with access to a road, he could haul about 20 bushels of corn on a long journey to market, where he could get $10 for his load. If he converted his corn into liquor, he could carry the equivalent of 40 bushels, 120 gallons of whiskey. In the 1890s his whiskey without a revenue stamp would bring at least $150. Those who could not afford the investment in distillation equipment could barter their corn for whiskey made by their more industrious neighbors, who would accept 3 bushels of cornmeal as the price of a gallon of their whiskey ($1.10) in 1881.[6]

Contemporaries disagreed about the profitability of moonshining. A. H. Brooks, a veteran revenuer, argued that only a few men made money as blockaders. He thought that the typical moonshiner was "a very poor miserable man, who drinks up a good deal of the profits." Another experienced revenue officer, though, asserted that moonshining was highly profitable: the blockader "can make money by running an illicit distillery, and *money* and *fun* are above all, the articles he is seeking for in this life." A journalist was more precise about the economics of illicit distilling. Giving the figure of $1.10 to $1.20 per gallon of moonshine in a good market in 1901, he also concluded that wildcatting could be profitable. The average size still could produce 80 gallons a week, giving a seasonal income of $90 per week in cash or barter. Deducting $20 for materials such as the corn, the moonshiner could earn $70 a week during the distilling season. As in any risky business, success in moonshining probably depended on the distiller's skill, ambition, and ability to market his product. For those willing to take the risks, there was money in corn juice.[7]

Lack of markets for other farm products was the most common contemporary explanation for moonshining, and modern writers repeat it as part of the image of blockaders as victims of mountain isolation. Durwood Dunn, however, argues that other ways to supplement farm income were available, at least in Cades Cove, that would help sustain a family. He says that making whiskey was "an easy way out," implying agreement with the revenuer's view that moonshiners sought the most money for the least work. It is clear that mountaineers turned to wildcat distilling for diverse reasons, more complex than either simple need for cash or entrepreneurial quest for profits.[8]

Some moonshiners were not seeking an alternative marketable product or looking toward the profits of blockading. A few were most interested in the whiskey itself. Daniel A. Tompkins, North Carolina's textile industry pioneer, met an old wildcatter on the road who said he made money, but "I drinked up the profit and more too and had to quit." Other people seem to have taken a turn at the still for short-term, specific purposes. According to a mountaineer, some farmers made brush whiskey to pay local property taxes, meeting one obligation by evading another. One moonshiner, Samson, told a sympathetic reporter that he was not "making this whiskey to speculate on." Instead he was only making enough to buy books and shoes so his three children could attend school and "get a little taste of education." A mountain woman told visitors that "thar's some things you rally want money fur," but "how kin we kerry the corn to barter when thar is no road?" "Thar is a way—" she hinted, and predicted that next time the visitors came she would have a chair and frock for the baby. These people were not really "moonshiners," but individuals who borrowed somebody else's apparatus or used their own still only occasionally to do a little stilling to raise money for specific purposes.[9]

Some blockaders may have been "just a simple-minded countryman, who makes whisky instead of selling eggs and butter," like Tallulah's John Crawford, a thirty-eight-year-old farmer with seven children who signed with an x when he was tried for distilling, working at an illicit still, and illegally selling liquor at both wholesale and retail in 1881. Samuel Cantrell, tried in 1890, appears in the 1900 census of Tallulah as a tenant farmer aged forty-four with six children. Other Tallulah moonshiners were fairly substantial members of their communities. James Tilley, a farmer aged forty-three with six children, was able to pay the expenses of travel from Atlanta, where he was tried, to serve his term in the Hall County jail at Gainesville, closer to home in Tallulah. In 1881 Cicero Blalock, a young man of thirty-three, pled guilty to moonshining and served three months in the Hall County jail. Although he declared himself too poor to pay the $200 fine, a few years later he was serving as Rabun County tax collector, and in 1900 he was living in Tallulah as a fifty-two-year-old farmer who owned his land and headed a family of seven children. Just as it is difficult to delineate a typical mountaineer, it is hard to describe a typical moonshiner: he could be a simple farmer; he might be a social outcast like the distillers of Chestnut Flats, Cades Cove; but he could also be a solid, respected citizen.[10]

General circumstances or specific needs of mountaineers' lives pushed some people toward illicit distilling. Others, in true entrepreneurial fashion, saw the opportunities in selling blockade whiskey to thirsty lumberjacks, miners, and millhands. Industrialization was a "pull" factor for many moonshiners. Some regions in the mountains witnessed the sudden growth of company towns or new cities like Middlesborough, Kentucky, which increased from sixty valley farmers to five thousand people between 1883 and 1889. Older communities also expanded, like Asheville, North Carolina, a tourist center and rail hub that grew from two thousand residents in 1880 to ten thousand in 1890. Whether rude camps in the woods or cities with all the modern amenities, these towns attracted whiskey drinkers who both patronized legal saloons and drank moonshine white lightning. Some company bosses outlawed saloons. The closed company towns, supplied by a single store, did not provide markets for local farmers' produce. They did, though, unintentionally provide customers for blockaders. The new elite of managers and professionals whose careers were tied to industrial development looked down upon the mountaineers and strove to improve the quality of life and moral tone of the towns. They often championed local option prohibition to suppress the rowdiness for which some places became notorious. In doing so, they helped reduce public tolerance of drinking and moonshiners, but if successful in drying up the towns, they also opened a wider market for blockaders.[11]

The blockader, rooted in the rural culture of the mountains, often made a successful and profitable transition to the modern world. Moonshiners entered their trade for different reasons, some choosing it for lack of alternatives, others seeing opportunities in making mountain dew. However diverse their motivations, most had to be risk takers skilled in a complex art.

Illicit distillation was by no means easy work, especially when carried on in secret at risk of arrest and destruction or confiscation of moonshiners' stills. "Blockadin' is the hardest work a man ever done," a mountaineer recalled, "and hit's wearin' on a feller's narves. Fust chance I git, I'm a goin' ter quit!" Illicit distillers had to haul bushels of corn up mountainsides and whiskey down, spending long nights in unheated still-houses always alert for betrayal. Moonshiners usually located their stills in crude log shelters near the heads of the coves or hollows formed by swift mountain streams that provided the cold water necessary for their operations. Hidden by trees or almost impenetrable mountain laurel and reached by paths known to only a few people, stills were usually safe from prying eyes. As the government accelerated its enforcement of the revenue laws in the later seventies, blockaders installed their stills so they could be easily carried off on the first warning of an impending raid. Many a posse reached a still-house to find everything but the valuable still itself.[12]

Some ingenious moonshiners developed unusual hiding places for their operations. Caves under riverbanks were favorites. One old North Carolina distiller, Charles Folias, often seemed to disappear into the ground just as revenue officers were about to apprehend him. He in fact ran into a tunnel leading to the cave where his still was hidden. One day, however, he encountered a nest of rattlesnakes in his tunnel: if he went forward he would be bitten; if he backed out he would be arrested. He gave up, telling the revenuers that he "was forced to surrender on account of the infernal snakes inside, and you deserve no credit for it." Another cave operation was more elaborate. It could be reached only by an underwater entrance beneath the riverbank and was accidentally discovered by a revenuer searching the island where he suspected a still was located. The cave had originally been a hideout for deserters from the Confederate army during the Civil War. One of the most complex hiding places, beyond the means of most moonshiners, was disguised as a blacksmith's shop. The bellows were used to fan the flames under the still, and water was brought in through underground pipes. Urban illicit distillers could operate disguised as legitimate businesses, but this elaborate arrangement was unique in the mountains. Finally, the Reverend

Baylus Hamrick, a Baptist minister, operated a still hidden in the basement of his own house. Such arrangements evaded detection for many years.[13]

Mountain dew required several weeks of processing from harvested corn to final product, the work usually of two or three persons who shared the $15 to $30 investment in a copper still and worm. Sometimes a single person would work a crude still consisting of half a barrel turned upside down over a soap kettle; the copper tubing for the worm was the only purchase necessary. Distillation began with sprouting the unground corn: warm water was poured over the ears for about three days, draining out through a hole in the bottom of the barrel. When two-inch sprouts appeared, converting the starch into sugar, the corn was ready to be dried and ground into meal. The blockader or a friend who owned a small "tub mill," producing one-half to two bushels of meal per day, carried on this operation. Pouring boiling water over the meal converted it into "sweet mash," which was allowed to stand for two or three days. If rye was available, rye malt, prepared like the cornmeal, was added to hasten fermentation, which took eight to ten days and required maintenance of a constant temperature without a thermometer. A skilled distiller could tell the proper degree of fermentation by the sound in the barrel; it was at perfection when the bubbling resembled rain drumming on a roof or a slice of pork frying in the pan. The result was "sour mash," the liquid portion of which was called "beer," alcoholic and "sour enough to make a pig squeal." This beer was then poured into the still, which had an enclosed copper cap and spiral tube, the worm. This worm was surrounded by a watertight barrel or box through which cold water was kept running. Stills consequently had to be located near flowing streams. The moonshiner built a fire under the still, often within a stone furnace surrounding the pot to prevent heat loss. The heat caused the alcohol in the beer to vaporize and then condense into a liquid again while passing through the cold worm. The spirits, at this stage impure "singlings," drained into a receiving tub or barrel.

A second distillation was necessary to remove the water and oils remaining in the singlings. With a fire at lower temperature, the process of boiling, vaporizing, and condensing was repeated to produce "doublings." This stage was delicate and required skill and experience: if distillation were too brief, the liquor would be sour and weak; if too long, pure alcohol. The final result was a clear whiskey, ready for immediate consumption without aging.[14]

Mountain dew varied in strength and taste according to the distiller's skill. A Kentucky revenuer "heard it estimated" that three-fourths of the whiskey consumed in his district was moonshine "considered much better" than legal whiskey. A newspaper reporter who tasted the Tallulah district's product described it as "somewhat thicker than the regular article, and is less firey. It tastes fairly well, although it has a flavor suggestive of fallen leaves." Another writer considered moonshine "raw and fiery to the civilized palate, with a faint smoky aroma." Though harsh, it was pure, since "its makers know none of the arts of adultera- tion." Not all outsiders agreed about the quality of brush whiskey. An 1867 writer condemned moonshine whiskey as "nearly all *very bad*," because of mountaineers' adulteration of the liquor with buckeye tree pods to give a "bead," or bubbles that appeared when the whiskey was shaken, an indication of proof. Twenty years later another writer de- scribed moonshine as "a vile production, repulsive in taste and smell," resembling diluted pure alcohol. Finally, a reporter's personal experi- ence of the effects of Rabun County, Georgia, moonshine in 1885: "The instant he has swallowed the stuff he feels as if he were sunburned all over, his head begins to buzz as if a hive of bees had swarmed there, when he closes his eyes, he sees six hundred million torch-light proces- sions all charging at him, ten abreast, and when he opens his eyes the light blinds him and everything seems dancing about." After passing out, this particular novice took forty-eight hours to sober up. Some of these descriptions fit a beverage called "mountain dew," but others are more appropriate to concoctions denominated "white lightnin'," "bust- head," "pop-skull," "white mule" (because of the kick), "red eye," "forty- rod" (the distance the stuff makes one run before passing out), or "bumblings" (from the noise in a drinker's head, as described above).[15]

Mountain people were not necessarily heavy drinkers, as many were too poor to afford regular consumption of even locally made whiskey: "In drinking, as in everything else, this is the Land of Do Without," the early twentieth-century chronicler of mountain life Horace Kephart declared. "Comparatively few highlanders see liquor oftener than once or twice a month." Charles Dudley Warner said that travelers who had read about moonshining would be disappointed in the sobriety of moun- tain people near Boone, North Carolina. Nineteenth-century writers pictured mountaineers as drinkers but rarely drunkards. In some com- munities like Cades Cove, churchgoing farmers condemned drinking, especially public or social drinking.

Alcohol became a problem at home when drunken men abused wives and children. More conspicuously, drinking led to violence when men got drunk at large public gatherings outside of their own communities. "Corn squeezins" were an essential element in gatherings of men at barbecues, political rallies, court sessions (after adjournment of the grand jury), dances, or parties. Whiskey contributed to the fights that sometimes marred such occasions. Young men, often landless and foot-loose, made up a volatile group in some mountain communities. Their sense of honor could be a chip on their shoulders, and they routinely carried pistols or knives. They were sensitive to personal slights, and whiskey dissolved their inhibitions. They sometimes released them, as at Christmas, in shooting up the settlement with little harm, but at other times in deadly fights with rivals. The dangerous effects of whiskey were very apparent to people near Morganton, North Carolina. In 1885 drunken young men disrupted services in Mountain Grove Church; Charles York stabbed his brother John to death in a drunken rage; and at Glen Alpine Station a crowd from the country with "new apple-jack holding sway" became rowdy, "shooting, cursing and cutting up generally" with a homicide as a result. In Dahlonega, Georgia, the election for constable of the Yahoola district in 1873 was accompanied by "a considerable quan-tity of spirits . . . which, of course, caused some rowing" climaxed by a stabbing. Next year three drunken young men "conducted themselves so badly" at a church meeting that it was broken up. The local editor denounced whiskey drinking and carrying of concealed weapons as "two curses which should be put down, and that speedily." In Kentucky's Harlan County a man attempting to kill his son-in-law in a drunken fight over a card game shot and killed his own wife and brother when they tried to interfere. A local jury held that the killing was an accident. In some areas, people seem to have tolerated drinking sprees as a release of energy, despite sometimes unfortunate results. Rising temperance sentiment in the later nineteenth century reduced this tolerance, but some mountaineers defied churchgoers and retained their old attitudes toward liquor.[16]

Blockaders developed clever ways of reaching their customers, often their immediate neighbors. Sometimes they hid a jug and cup in a brush heap; the customer would leave his money in the cup after taking his drink. Another method was use of "bell trees" or hollow trunks, known only to local regulars: after the customer left his money and rang the bell in the log, he could return a short time later to find a cup of mountain dew. Such marketing of course depended on local people's trust of each other. Less secretive moonshiners placed fresh-cut laurel branches in the road on Saturday afternoons. Local men knew that following the direction of the branches led to the distiller himself dispensing from his jug.

Some blockaders sought wider markets, hauling their ten-gallon kegs out of the mountains on mule-drawn sledges. One group of North Carolina moonshiners sold to bootleggers who filled jugs slung over the back of their horse and then dispensed the liquor into containers that tippling valley farmers left near the road along with the requisite cash. Other wildcatters marketed their product directly from their wagon, usually hiding the liquor under apples or other produce, to customers in valley towns or to drovers who passed by on the way to market.[17]

Some moonshiners took advantage of modernization, particularly the railroads, to expand their operations. A judge confidently predicted that "a railway through these wildernesses would cure illicit distilling" by bringing farmers closer to markets, but sometimes the cure helped spread the problem. Railway networks enlarged the market for enterprising distillers. In the early twentieth century the station platform at Traumfest, North Carolina, was often stacked with jugs of "vinegar" that exuded "a powerful alcoholic smell." An 1889 map of a moonshine district near Pruitton in Lauderdale County, Alabama, revealed a railroad and two long-distance roads not far from the still sites. Some moonshiners clearly had one foot in the mountains' traditional culture, but the other was in the modern world that was increasingly penetrating the Appalachians.[18]

Moonshining, like mountain farming, was often a family business. In lists of persons arrested during raids, the same surname frequently appears. Raiders in South Carolina in February and March 1877 netted two Taylors, two Turners, two Trammels, two Pittmans, two Quinns, and three different Turners. A Georgia sweep in 1875 brought in two Brandts, two Bennetts, two Greens, and three Scotts. An 1879 Kentucky raid landed four Johnsons and two Ferrells; North Carolina revenuers captured four Yorks in 1877. Four members of the Ramsey family, immigrants from Kentucky, were arrested in Arkansas in the 1890s. One party of raiders had warrants for ten members of the same family; they were thwarted by a seven-year-old girl, niece of the patriarch, who ran ahead to warn the distillers. Harrison Gibson of Kentucky and his five sons, along with two sons-in-law, became wealthy after stilling for several years around the turn of the century.[19]

Most moonshiners were white men. There were a few black blockaders: two were captured in an 1876 South Carolina raid; one was arrested in Virginia in 1879; and three in South Carolina in 1885. A black woman in Elbert County, Georgia, operated a still with a white partner. The white woman confessed that she had been moonshining for several years, but the revenuers let her go because she had a small baby with her. The black woman, though, "had to tramp the usual road paved for the violator of the revenue laws." Revenuers surprised another integrated still in Georgia in 1891. The white blockaders surrendered, but the blacks "were game" and "met the enemy with a volley of distillery refuse." The possemen, their clothes saturated and stinking, finally closed in and captured the resisters, except old Simon Turnipseed, who was caught only after an officer fired at him. Blacks were more likely to be hired as laborers by larger white operators than to have their own stills. However, by the turn of the century in North Carolina, blacks were becoming more important as blockaders, making up about one-fourth of the state's moonshiners. As among whites, a black preacher could sometimes preach at a service while his associates sold his own "wild cat" to the congregation. The most common black violation of the revenue laws was retailing without payment of special tax, which meant peddling half pints or pints of whiskey from jugs at "Negro frolics" or meetings.[20]

Since moonshining was a family business, women were often supporters of their menfolk. They sometimes met the revenuers at the door of their houses, pretending ignorance of their husband's, father's, or brother's whereabouts. When they did give information, a revenuer found it "wholly unreliable as regards the locality of the distilleries." Sometimes they had the important responsibility of delaying the officers while the men escaped, or they gave warning themselves of the revenuers' approach. In Georgia, women yelled, cursed, and blew horns as a raiding party rode through a valley. "*I never in my life,*" a deputy exclaimed, "*heard so much profanity and filthy language as was incessantly thrown in our faces by the women, wives and daughters of the distillers.*" South Carolina women "gave a peculiar shout or warning, which seemed to arouse the whole neighborhood," and raiders were soon under fire. An inexperienced deputy was forced to withdraw under the onslaught of a sturdy mountain woman, who gave him a thorough tongue-lashing and pummeled him with her fists. One moonshiner's wife, who was "caught and brought down from the hills" after her husband's death, was the "wildest thing" a Sunday-school teacher and her valley neighbors had ever seen. They discovered that she had brought her husband's still, undoubtedly her most valuable possession, hidden in the bedclothes.[21]

Some women went even farther for their men. Susan Van Meter, "a dashing young widow" from Kentucky, was arrested in 1881 for shooting at a deputy marshal trying to arrest her lover. The judge asked if she meant to kill him, perhaps chivalrously offering her an escape, but she replied: "Of course I tried to kill him, and am only sorry that I failed. He was after John . . . , and I knew he would catch him; and I love John well enough to die for him." A few months earlier she had jumped from a second-story window in her nightgown, running two miles to warn John that a posse was after him.[22]

A few women were moonshiners themselves. Lucy McClure, kin in spirit to Susan, had been sought for eight years "as one of the most persistent and daring of West Virginia's moonshiners." Twenty-four years old, she was "a young athletic woman of great nerve and presence of mind, she was a fine rifle and revolver shot, and rode a beautiful sorrel horse, which has many a time saved her." Mollie Miller of Tennessee may have been less dashing, but she was a deadly opponent of the revenuers. She was first noticed during a raid on her father's still, in which three revenuers were killed and the rest retreated under heavy fire. During a later raid, guided by a man who "had a grudge against" him, Sam Miller died. A few days later the marshal received a coffin with the informer's body. Mollie went on to become a leader of Polk County moonshiners, credited with the deaths of three revenuers and four or five informers. She was arrested only once but received a light sentence because of weak evidence. After construction of a railroad that reached Mollie's domain, the officers were able to break up her gang; Mollie retired, occasionally being summoned to Chattanooga to appear as a witness. After collecting her fees, she walked sixty miles to her home. She died in bed. Tennessee was also home to Betsy M., a "moonshineress" who allegedly weighed 600 pounds. Seated on a low bed, she dispensed mountain dew to whomever came her way. She was unmolested by revenuers, supposedly not only because she was determined to resist but because her great weight made it impossible to force her to travel against her will over the rugged three miles to the nearest wagon road. Near her house were the graves of several sons, some of whom had been killed in revenue raids, others in a local feud. Betsy was a Melungeon, "an olive-skinned people of corn-whiskey renown" who had lived in Hancock County, Tennessee, for generations. Mrs. Henderson of Habersham County, Georgia, distilled for twenty years. When she was arrested she explained that she had been accused of killing her husband and sold liquor to pay the lawyers working to exonerate her. Melinda Turner, a fifty-year-old widow, was colorful in a folksy way. Living in an isolated, one-room cabin high on a mountainside in White County, Georgia, she said that "I have made whisky since my old man died, . . . and I guess I'll make it till I go whar he is. . . . I'm as good a hand to make the corn-juice as you ever laid eyes on in your borned days." Taken to the Atlanta jail, she described the city, which she was seeing for the first time in her life, as so noisy that she "couldn't hear her ears." Nancy McCoy Hatfield Phillips, a McCoy who first married a Hatfield and, later, Frank Phillips, a bitter enemy of the family, joined her husband in helping support the family by selling moonshine. One woman, Bettie Smith of Fentress County, Tennessee, was allegedly the author of "that wild and stirring romance, 'The Blue-Headed Sapsucker, or the Rock Where the Juice Ran Out.' " Her trial was the occasion for probably apocryphal banter about Bettie's age and her explanation of how and to whom she sold her whiskey: "Some time ago a party of gentlemen came out into my neighborhood to hunt deer. The party got out of whiskey, but found it difficult to buy any. After a while I told a man if he would put his jug down on a dollar and go away, he might when he came back, find the jug full of whiskey." The judge asked, "Would you know the man?" "Oh yes, sir," the sprightly woman responded, "I recognized him in a moment. You are the man, judge." Some women in the mountain South aided and protected their men in the moonshine business, and occasionally they took a hand in producing wildcat whiskey themselves.[23]

Blockaders were always prepared to satisfy their neighbors' or more distant customers' thirst for something stronger than pure mountain water. Moonshiners were often in a better position than most mountaineers to experience benefits from industrialization. They were quick to take advantage of expanding markets in camps and company towns and gained new recruits from farmers needing cash for specific purchases or payments or tempted by the profits from mountain dew. They fit Gordon McKinney's general description of entrepreneurs: "The more enterprising secured capital and started their own businesses utilizing the resources of the mountains." Moonshiners' capital investment was their still; their resources, the corn and clear, cold water of mountain streams.[24]

Increasingly over the years, though, modernization cost them the support or tacit sympathy of solid citizens, especially in the towns, who were embracing the nineteenth century's moral attitudes toward liquor. Revenuers, of course, were another agent of modernization whom blockaders did not welcome. Change, as often, led to conflict.[25]

Notes

1. Henry D. Shapiro, *Appalachia on Our Mind: The Southern Mountains and Mountaineers in the American Consciousness, 1870-1920* (Chapel Hill: University of North Carolina Press, 1978), pp. 104-5; E. J. Hobsbawm, *Primitive Rebels: Studies in Archaic Forms of Social Movement in the 19th and 20th Centuries* (New York: W. W. Norton, 1959), chaps. 1-2; for application of Hobsbawm's and other social scientists' theories to moonshiner resistance, see William F. Holmes, "Moonshining and Collective Violence: Georgia, 1889-1905," *Journal of American History* 67 (Dec. 1980): 589-611. Amos Akerman to E. Pierrepont, Atty. Gen., Feb. 22, 1876, SC, Ga.

2. Internal revenue records report moonshining in Utah, Indiana, Illinois, Ohio, Pennsylvania, Florida, Texas, New Hampshire, and the cities of Chicago, New Orleans, Brooklyn, Troy, and Poughkeepsie, New York.

3. *Annual Report, Commissioner of Internal Revenue, 1891*, HED 4, 52d Cong., 1st sess., pp. 44-46 (table).

4. Edward King, "The Great South: Among the Mountains of Western North Carolina," *Scribner's Monthly* 7 (Mar. 1874): 536-37; William G. Frost, "Our Contemporary Ancestors in the Southern Mountains," *Atlantic Monthly* 83 (Mar. 1899): 312; James L. Allen, "Through Cumberland Gap on Horseback," *Harpers New Monthly Magazine* 73 (June 1886): 58; Charles D. Warner, "Comments on Kentucky," *Harper's New Monthly Magazine* 78 (Jan. 1889): 269 (my italics); Altina L. Waller, *Feud: Hatfields, McCoys, and Social Change in Appalachia, 1860-1900* (Chapel Hill: University of North Carolina Press, 1988), pp. 43-44 (an example of increasing land values).

5. Young E. Allison, "Moonshine Men," *Southern Bivouac* 5 (Feb. 1887): 531-32; *Atlanta Constitution*, May 19, 1880 (Union County), Aug. 31, 1890, and Feb. 12, 1893 (hogs and turkeys); *Morganton Star*, Sept. 18, 1885 (Burke); M. L. White, *A History of the Life of Amos Owens, the Noted Blockader, of Cherry Mountain, N.C.* (Shelby, N.C.: Cleveland Star Job Print, 1901), p. 10.

6. William L. Downward, *Dictionary of the History of the American Brewing and Distilling Industry* (Westport, Conn.: Greenwood, 1980), p. xxi; Henry M. Wiltse, *The Moonshiners* (Chattanooga, Tenn.: Times Publishing Co., 1895), pp. 208-9.

7. "Testimony . . . Revenue in the Sixth District of N.C.," testimony of A. H. Brooks, Revenue Agent, p. 136; George Wesley Atkinson, *After the Moonshiners, by One of the Raiders* (Wheeling, W. Va.: Frew and Campbell, 1881), pp. 24, 14-15; Samuel G. Blythe, "Raiding Moonshiners," *Munsey's Magazine* 25 (June 1901): 420.

8. Durwood Dunn, *Cades Cove: The Life and Death of a Southern Appalachian Community, 1818-1937* (Knoxville: University of Tennessee Press, 1988), p. 233.

9. Daniel Tompkins to Hal, Aug. 12, 1883, Tompkins Papers, photocopy courtesy Duke University Library; Francis Lynde, "The Moonshiners of Fact," *Lippincott's Magazine*

57 (Jan. 1896): 70; Atkinson, *After the Moonshiners*, p. 15; Horace Kephart, *Our Southern Highlanders* (New York: Outing, 1913), p. 121 (all on taxes); *Atlanta Constitution*, Aug. 10, 1896; Rebecca Harding Davis, "By-Paths in the Mountains, III," *Harper's New Monthly Magazine* 61 (Sept. 1880): 535. Since dialect has been quoted here for the first time, a comment on its use in this book is appropriate. Nineteenth-century writers used dialect to heighten the impression of mountaineers' quaintness and isolation. Some of the dialect may be accurate transcription; other quotations are what journalists thought mountaineers should sound like. Since I am neither a native of the mountain South nor an expert in American speech patterns, my safest course is simply to record all the spellings as they appeared in the original source.

10. *Atlanta Constitution*, Dec. 18, 1896; on social status of moonshiners generally, see Cratis D. Williams, "The Southern Mountaineer in Fact and Fiction" (Ph.D. dissertation, New York University, 1961), p. 113, drawing from a study conducted during the prohibition era. Though prohibition made moonshine a bigger business, I think that many nineteenth-century moonshiners could also be described as substantial citizens. For Crawford, see Records of the U.S. District Court, Northern Georgia, Record Group 21, National Archives, Atlanta Branch, box 94, case no. 4496 (March Term 1881), and no. 38 in the 1880 census; Cantrell was in box 208, case no. 8755 (March Term 1890) and no. 60 in the 1900 census; Tilley, box 97, case no. 4588 (March Term 1881), and no. 57 in the 1880 census. For Blalock information, see District Court Records, box 98, case no. 4650 (March Term 1881); Andrew Jackson Ritchie, *Sketches of Rabun County History* (Foote and Davies, [1948]), p. 300, and 1900 census (where he is household number one). The Blalock family had a small settlement named after them in northwestern Rabun County.

11. Kephart, *Our Southern Highlanders*, pp. 187-89; John Gaventa, *Power and Powerlessness: Quiescence and Rebellion in an Appalachian Valley* (Urbana: University of Illinois Press, 1980), p. 56; Ronald D. Eller, *Miners, Millhands, and Mountaineers: The Industrialization of the Appalachian South, 1880-1930* (Knoxville: University of Tennessee Press, 1982), pp. 101, 186-87, 234-35; Jacquelyn D. Hall, James Leloudis, Robert Korstad, Mary Murphy, Lu Ann Jones, and Christopher B. Daly, *Like a Family: The Making of a Southern Cotton Mill World* (Chapel Hill: University of North Carolina Press, 1987), pp. 164-65, 132; Gordon B. McKinney, *Southern Mountain Republicans, 1865-1900: Politics and the Appalachian Community* (Chapel Hill: University of North Carolina Press, 1978), p. 129. For discussion of impact of prohibition, see chaps. 7 and 8 of this book.

12. Kephart, *Our Southern Highlanders*, p. 140; T. N. Cooper, Coll., N.C., to Raum, Feb. 15, 1883, LR, box 894 (portable stills).

13. *New York Times*, Sept. 29, 1882 (Folias); Jan. 7, 1895 (underwater); O. H. Blocken, Rev. Agt., to Raum, Aug. 4, 1880, LR, box 911 (blacksmith); *New York Times*, Apr. 14, 1895 (minister).

14. Kephart, *Our Southern Highlanders*, pp. 128, 132-36; Esther Kellner, *Moonshine: Its History and Folklore* (Indianapolis: Bobbs-Merrill, 1971), pp. 56-60. The methods described here are the simplest and most traditional. Refinements introduced in the twentieth century included a "thump keg" or doubler located between the still and worm through which the hot vapor passed with great buildup of heat, amounting to a second distillation. This saved the step of doubling in the original still. Another timesaving step was use of sugar instead of sprouted corn to begin fermentation. Real old-timers scoffed at such corner cutting, which did not produce true corn juice. For details on newer methods, see Jess Carr, *The*

Second Oldest Profession: An Informal History of Moonshining in America (Englewood Cliffs, N.J.: Prentice Hall), pp. 98-104.

15. J. Olney, Rev. Agt., to Raum, May 14, 1877, LR, box 910; *New York Times*, May 17, 1888; Lynde, "Moonshiners of Fact," pp. 72-73; A. H. Guernsey, "Illicit Distillation of Liquors," *Harper's Weekly* 11 (Dec. 7, 1867): 773 (taste); Allison, "Moonshine Men," p. 534 (adulteration); Donald A. Baine, "Among the Moonshiners," *Dixie* 1 (Aug. 1885): 12-13 (effects). The arrival of state prohibition encouraged more widespread adulteration of moonshine (Kephart, *Our Southern Highlanders*, pp. 88-89).

16. Kephart, *Our Southern Highlanders*, p. 138 (quotation); Charles D. Warner, "On Horseback," *Atlantic Monthly* 56 (July-Oct. 1885): 99 (quotation); Lynde, "Moonshiners of Fact," p. 73. On condemnation of drinking, see Dunn, *Cades Cove*, pp. 193-94, 233. For young men, see Waller, *Feud*, pp. 94-97; on violent effects of whiskey drinking, see Williams, "The Southern Mountaineer," pp. 104, 352-56; William L. Montell, *Killings: Folk Justice in the Upper South* (Lexington: University Press of Kentucky, 1986), p. 158; *Morganton Star*, June 26, 1885; May 29, 1885; Sept. 25, 1885; *Dahlonega Mountain Signal*, Feb. 13, 1873; Aug. 29, 1874; Apr. 18, 1879; Warner, "Comments on Kentucky."

17. John C. Campbell, *The Southern Highlander and His Homeland* (New York: Russell Sage Foundation, 1921), p. 109; Margaret W. Morley, *The Carolina Mountains* (Boston: Houghton Mifflin, 1913), p. 216 (sales methods); Guernsey, "Illicit Distillation," p. 773 (sledges); Wilbur G. Zeigler and Ben Grosscup, *The Heart of the Alleghenies; or, Western North Carolina* (Raleigh: A. Williams, 1883), pp. 362-64.

18. Kephart, *Our Southern Highlanders*, p. 130 (markets); Davis, "By-Paths," p. 535; Morley, *Carolina Mountains*, p. 213 (vinegar); map drawn by Deputy Collector W. W. Colquitt, in W. H. Chapman, Rev. Agt., to Commissioner, Dec. 7, 1889, MLR, box 914.

19. J. W. Corsbie, Dep. Coll., N.C., in J. Wagner, Rev. Agt., to Raum, May 18, 1877, "Enforcement of Internal Revenue Laws: . . . Report of the Commissioner of Internal Revenue . . . to Explain the Necessity For Employment of Armed Men . . . ," *HED* 62, 46th Cong., 2d sess. (1880), p. 93 (describing a family settlement); Lieut. J. M. McDougall, 7th Cav., to Asst. Adj. Gen., Dept. South, Feb. 6, 1875, 831 AGO '75 (Ga. list); Lieut. J. Anderson, 18th Inf., to Cmdg. Officer, Feb. 21, Mar. 5, 1877, 1343, 1394 AGO '77 (two S.C. lists); J. F. Buckner, Coll., Ky., to Raum, Jan. 22, 1879, "Enforcement of Internal Revenue Laws," p. 78 (Ky. list); J. J. Mott, Coll., N.C., to Raum, Dec. 10, 1877, ibid., p. 102 (N.C. list); Isaac Stapleton, *Moonshiners in Arkansas* (Independence, Mo.: Zion's Printing and Publishing Co., 1948), p. 45 (Ramseys); Wiltse, *Moonshiners*, p. 121 (ten); Gerald Carson, *The Social History of Bourbon: An Unhurried Account of Our Star-Spangled American Drink* (New York: Dodd, Mead, 1963), pp. 110-11 (Gibsons).

20. Lt. W. S. Patten, 18th Inf., to Post Adj., June 21, 1876, 3629 AGO '76; D. J. Lewis, Dep. Marshal, to J. L. Lewis, Marshal, Feb. 2, 1879, in J. L. Lewis to Atty. Gen., Feb. 5, 1879, SC Va.; J. L. Black, Dep. Coll., S.C., to D. F. Bradley, Coll., Nov. 20, 1885, in Bradley to Commissioner, Dec. 1, 1885, LR, box 889; *Dahlonega Mountain Signal*, Aug. 14, 1875 (partners); *Atlanta Constitution*, Dec. 13, 1891; *Charlotte Observer*, Nov. 30, 1902 (black moonshiners); White, *A History*, p. 10 (preacher); W. H. Brawley, Dist. Judge, S.C., to Atty. Gen., Apr. 3, 1895, DJ 1661 '94, box 74 (selling).

21. J. A. George, Dep. Coll., Ga., to Raum, Apr. 28, 1877, LR, box 897 (ignorance and warnings); J. A. Cooper, Coll., Tenn., to Raum, July 6, 1877, "Enforcement of Internal Revenue Laws," p. 111 (unreliable information); W. O. H. Shepard, Dep. Coll., to A. Clark,

Coll., Ga., Apr. 9, 1880, in Clark to Raum, Apr. 15, 1880, LR, box 891 (cursing) (original italics); H. H. Jillson, Dep. Coll., to E. M. Brayton, Coll., S.C., Aug. 23, 1877, "Enforcement of Internal Revenue Laws," p. 183 (shout); Wiltse, *Moonshiners,* pp. 120-21 (fists); Olive D. Campbell Diary, Nov. 20, 1908, p. 37, typescript, Southern Historical Collection, University of North Carolina (wife).

22. Atkinson, *After the Moonshiners,* pp. 158-59 (Van Meter).

23. *New York Times,* Oct. 15, 1891 (McClure); *Cincinnati Enquirer,* n.d., quoted in *Internal Revenue Record and Customs Journal,* June 4, 1894, p. 175 (Miller); Wiltse, *Moonshiners,* pp. 65-68; Joseph E. Dabney, *Mountain Spirits: A Chronicle of Corn Whiskey from King James' Ulster Plantation to America's Appalachians and the Moonshine Life* (New York: Scribners, 1974), pp. 137-39 (Betsy), 128-29 (Henderson); *New York Times,* Mar. 18, 1893 (Turner); Waller, *Feud,* p. 241 (Phillips); Jasper, Ga., *Piedmont Republican,* Sept. 19, 1891, copied from *Arkansaw Traveler* [sic] (Smith; courtesy of Robert S. Davis, Jr.).

24. McKinney, *Southern Mountain Republicans,* p. 126.

25. Ibid., chap. 7, on modernization as increasing the level of violence in the mountains.

PART

II

ETHNICITY
AND TRADITION

There is a growing body of evidence indicating that organized crime groups evolve around specific illicit activities, rather than the opposite.

Albanese (1996, p. 9)

In some other studies of OC, researchers and investigators fell into the "ethnicity trap." Instead of focusing on criminal opportunities and the crimes themselves, they identified gangs by ethnicity or location. Such a viewpoint was too narrow. It also promoted stereotyping by policymakers and enforcers. With efforts to control OC focused on one ethnic group or subculture, countless others were free to evolve in secret, sometimes without restriction.

Yet the factor of ethnicity cannot be ignored in any valid study of OC. The trap involves looking at some ethnic or cultural characteristics as criminogenic and as having explanatory power in understanding OC. Such a perspective is backwards because, as Albanese pointed out, the crime precedes ethnicity. In other words, as a response to criminal opportunities, organizations develop that often involve people familiar to one another with a shared history. Although their shared history contributes common behaviors to the members' daily activities, other behaviors evolve that are based on the criminal activities that were the group's fundamental organizing principles. Members of ethnic OC groups may enjoy traditional cultural foods, stories, and beliefs in common, but what brought them together was their criminal activities. As a result of those activities, the ethnic OC group also evolved other patterns and beliefs that were outside the tradition of the culture. Gang traits helped set the group apart and provided them with an identity separate from their common ethnic heritage. Rather than viewing ethnic traits as causes of OC, this book focuses on a common ethnic background among group members as a response to the prevailing conditions in which OC exists.

OC groups necessarily exist in a world of secrecy. An examination of many types of secret societies by Mackenzie (1967) provided a view of some common characteristics that survived from primitive to modern times. He found that almost all of the clandestine groups were hierarchical in structure, with an elaborate system of ranks with high-sounding names. Regalia and meeting places were given strange names. Separated from the wider community in which they flourished, secret societies further differentiated themselves by self-contained and self-consistent environments.

Another means of holding the group together is a specially created story of its origins that takes on the qualities of a legend. Many secret societies lay claim to ancient origins. A great deal of emphasis is placed on the ritual of initiation ceremonies. A clear dividing line is drawn between the initiated and the uninitiated. The ceremony is meant to transport the initiate out of a mundane world into a new kind of fellowship. Elaborate and often fearful oaths bind the members to secrecy. The initiate subscribes to such oaths only because of beliefs that they are binding by some deep and powerful sanction and that personal integrity depends on maintaining full and unquestioning membership with the group (Mackenzie, 1967).

OC groups may be tied by bonds of culture and ethnicity for several reasons. In a common culture, there are traditional codes of allegiance and honor that idealize the gangster relationship. In a common history, there are shared rituals that take on special significance of love and fear among gangsters. A shared language, outside the language of the dominant culture, is valuable for expediting crime and maintaining secrecy. A common culture also provides a system of personal control into which members are socialized at an early age, so that its power is strong and lasting. Strong internal control or discipline can more easily be enforced in gangs with a shared heritage of dominance and submission. Finally, an ethnic subculture makes an excellent recruitment base that keeps the gang healthy and growing (Goodson & Olson, 1995).

Waves of refugees and immigrants provide cover and concealment, as well as a pool of recruits for OC. Because immigrants are fearful of law enforcement, they are reluctant to cooperate with the police. Historically, the police have not provided the same level of service to immigrant neighborhoods (Goodson & Olson, 1995, p. 88). The market for illegal Chinese immigrants was said to have earned billions of dollars for OC. Smuggling immigrants is a growth industry, less risky than and almost as lucrative as drug trafficking (McDonald, 1997).

The section of a city where Asian migrants reside is commonly known as Chinatown, even if many of the residents are Korean or Vietnamese or from other Asian countries. Some authors have called Chinatowns in the United States "criminogenic" (Huey Long Song & Huripz, 1995). However, other authors have examined Chinese OC in Hong Kong that developed in the mid-1800s. The depth and corruption that exist there do not involve only migrants (Chin, 1996). There has also been a rise in crime in mainland China since the 1980s (Ma, 1995). However, victimization patterns of Asian gangs in the United States are different from those found in Asia because of the status of Chinese migrants, the difference in the legal institutions, and the different types of relationships formed by residents of U.S. Chinatowns. Crime patterns reflect social contradictions at many levels, and in many places, they are not confined to ethnic enclaves.

DISCUSSION:
Chinese Gangs

Chinese gangs are reported to be the largest importers of heroin in the United States (Martin & Romano, 1992) and continue to be responsible for a great proportion of the heroin entering Canada as well (CISC, 1996). Chinese gangs in triad secret societies extend more than 2,000 years and are deeply rooted in Chinese culture. In the past, membership in a Chinese triad involved being bound in a network of social relations based on the ideas of history, mythology, and legend. Five core norms have been identified as central to the gang's organization: loyalty, righteousness, nationalism, secrecy, and brotherhood. Triad members showed total commitment to these values, regardless of the social ramifications of their actions (Chin, 1995; Myers, 1996).

Chinese gangs in the late 1980s and 1990s have primarily become enterprises interested in making money. Evidence suggests that a new generation of Chinese criminals has emerged that is much more likely to infiltrate the larger society than in the past because of money laundering and white-collar crime. They are wealthy, sophisticated, and well connected. They are not committed to strong subcultural values and can assemble quickly when criminal opportunities arise and dissolve a criminal operation immediately on its completion (Chin, 1996).

OC groups smuggling Chinese into the United States are said to be organized as "task forces" rather than as families. That is to say, members form small groups that assemble to perform a particular piece of work. This organizational structure is highly responsive to changing sociological and market changes and constraints (Zhang & Gaylord, 1996). The image of membership in Chinese secret societies that has emerged from investigation is fluid and mobile rather than fixed and traditional (Chin, 1990).

3

Gang Characteristics

Ko-lin Chin

Chapter 6 (pp. 100-124) of *Chinatown Gangs,* by Ko-Lin Chin (New York: Oxford University Press, 1996)

Attributes of Gang Members

Newspaper accounts and government reports on Chinese gangs usually focus on gang activities and ignore the social structure of gangs and the background of the people involved in gang activities. In only one study, conducted in San Francisco by the Institute of Scientific Analysis (Joe, 1993, 1994; Toy, 1992a, 1992b), were a substantial number of Chinese gang members interviewed for the purpose of examining their age, country of origin, education, family background, and other vital demographic and socioeconomic characteristics.

Sex

My study indicates that gang membership is restricted to males, which reconfirms the findings of Toy (1992a) and Joe (1994) on Chicago gangs in San Francisco. According to my male subjects, females are not considered for gang membership. They possess little knowledge of and have no interest in male criminal activities. Nevertheless, many young Korean and Chinese females do hang out with members of Chinese gangs in New York City. Asked about her role in extortion activity, a female subject replied: "I do not get involved. If I am with them while they are collecting money from a store, I stay outside the store."

Some subjects, both male and female, indicated that women are asked to leave when men begin to discuss gang business. They also stated that females are discouraged and dissuaded from learning about gang activities and structure.

Most young women become associated with Chinese gangs through male gang members with whom they attend school. Females with problems at school or at home may find affiliation with gangs appealing because the gangs provide money, food, and a place to stay for females who are seeking sanctuary from school or from home. Some young women find hanging out with gang members fun; others become affiliated with gang members because they like the protection gangs provide. Gang affiliation makes the young women perceive themselves as desirable or important, and the females who hang out with gang members typically boast about their affiliation with the gangs.

Although fun, excitement, and power are associated with hanging around with gang members, the respondents recognized that doing so could also be dangerous because the women could be sexually exploited. According to a female subject, only those who are steady girlfriends of gang leaders are immune from rape by gang members. Another female respondent indicated that once, while visiting a nightclub, she was drugged by male gang members with whom she hung out. She believes that if she had not left the premises before losing control, she would have been raped. Still another female subject revealed that she always took her drink with her when she went to the restroom so it could not be spiked while she was away. Also, women gang associates were susceptible to rape if they violated certain gang rules or dated members of a rival gang. A male gang member attested to this by saying that women who ignored gang rules would be "served," meaning they would be raped by one or more gang members.

Little is known about whether females affiliates of Chinese gangs are forced to work in prostitution houses. None of the eight female subjects interviewed was being coerced into working as a prostitute. However, one subject indicated that gang leaders would assign females who were considered promiscuous to work in Chinatown massage parlors owned by the gang.

A female subject summed up her ambivalent feelings about being affiliated with gang members: "They [gang members] could be fun, and they could be dangerous. When you are with them, you get someone to back you up. People help each other out. However, you get sick of it too."

Another female subject attempted to leave a gang by seeking help from her parents. She went to stay in Hong Kong temporarily, but later rejoined the gang because, as she put it, she missed them:

> Girls can't go out with members from other groups. Also, boys are not supposed to tell girls anything about the gang. These things bother me. However, girls want to be popular. If you hear Canal Boys [Born-to-Kill], the top gang, girls like to be known to be with them. If I was offered to choose again, I wouldn't want to be in it. I don't want to spend the rest of my life like this. I want to meet more friends, but they won't trust me if I get to know others. They keep doing the same routine. It's like a waste of time. I want to go to college. A lot of kids I know, they are dropping out [of the gang]. I want to have a future. Last year, I really hated them. I asked my parents to send me to Hong Kong. I was with them for four years. However, after staying away from them for a while, I really missed them. I eventually came back and hung out with them again.

Females are not considered gang members, but they nevertheless play an important role in a gang's daily activities. Some women are asked to carry guns for males because females are less likely to be searched when stopped by police. Also, females often work as the "eyes and ears" of the gangs because they are not ordinarily criminally suspect, and they may hang out with more than one gang. For example, as one female subject observed: "Girls can be really important because we can do things without being detected. That is, we are less noticeable. For example, we often go check out places [for rival gang members or police officers] for our boys."

Also, the girlfriends of gang leaders become the "elder sisters" of ordinary gang members, and they are obliged to look after the male gang members, especially when the leaders are on the run or imprisoned.

Age

Many law enforcement authorities claim that Chinese gang members are usually older than African American or Hispanic gang members (Bresler, 1981; Posner, 1988). A police officer who worked in Manhattan's Chinatown indicated that labeling Chinese gangs as youth gangs is not appropriate because most gang members are in their late 20s and early 30s (Chin, 1986). He insisted that gangs in Chinatown should be viewed as adult gangs.

My study does not support this observation. The average age of the 62 gang members who participated in my study was approximately 19 years. The majority (82%) were 20 years old or younger, and about one in three were 18 years old. Only three subjects were in their late 20s or older. Most of the Chinese gang members who participated in this study were teenagers rather than adults; however, I did not interview any high-level gang leaders, and it is probable that the leaders may be older than their followers. Joe (1994) also found that most Chinese gang members in San Francisco were teenagers. My research suggests that Chinese gang members are not normally older than members of other ethnic gangs (Conly, Kelly, Mahanna, & Warner, 1993; Los Angeles County District Attorney, 1992).

Country of Origin and Ethnicity

The media often describe Chinese gangs as immigrant gangs, which implies that it is mainly foreign-born Chinese who join the gangs (Rice, 1977). For example, the 25 Ghost Shadows members convicted for racketeering activities in 1985 were all born abroad (Polsky, 1985). The majority of the gang members in my study were immigrants. However, more than one-third of them were born in America. Joe (1994) also found that there are a substantial number of American-born Chinese in San Francisco's Chinese gangs. It is possible that, while mainly young immigrants joined Chinese gangs in the 1960s and 1970s, more and more American-born Chinese were lured into them in the 1980s and 1990s. Thus, theories on Chinese gangs' formation would be flawed if they ignored the possibility that a growing number of American-born Chinese are joining gangs.

Among foreign-born subjects, most were born in either Hong Kong or China. The rest came from Vietnam, Taiwan, Korea, or Cambodia.

Subjects born in Korea were all Koreans, whereas subjects from Vietnam and Cambodia included Chinese, Vietnamese, and Cambodians. The average number of years the foreign-born subjects had been in America was 9.3, which indicates that most were not recent immigrants. This was also the case for members of San Francisco's Chinese gangs—their average length of stay in America, according to Joe (1994), was 10.8 years.

In terms of ethnicity, most subjects (68%) identified themselves as Cantonese or Toisanese. . . . This finding is not unusual because most immigrants from Hong Kong declare themselves as Cantonese and the Cantonese are the most dominant Chinese group in the United States (Zhou, 1992).

Over the past ten years, throughout the United States, there has been a noticeable increase in gang involvement among adolescents from Vietnam, Laos, Cambodia, Taiwan, the Philippines, China, and Korea (Badey, 1988; Butterfield, 1985; Vigil & Yun, 1990). In southern California, young immigrants from Vietnam, Laos, and Cambodia have been very active in gang activities (Butterfield, 1985). Two relatively new gangs in New York City, the Green Dragons and the Fuk Ching, were founded in the 1980s by Fujianese youths from China (Dannen, 1992). While ethnic differences within Chinese gangs appear to be fading, Chinese gangs are interested in recruiting mainly Asian youths. The more powerful gangs, such as the Flying Dragons and the Fuk Ching, now have factions consisting of mainly Korean or Fujianese teenagers, and the Born-to-Kill gang is made up predominantly of Vietnamese or Vietnamese-Chinese (English, 1995). Of the 62 male subjects in my study, only one was white. . . .

Education and Employment

Among the 62 subjects in my study, 38 (61%) were either full- or part-time college or high-school students. . . . Only a few stated that they spoke English poorly (10%) or read and wrote English inadequately (8% and 7%, respectively). In light of these findings, the contention by some observers that most Chinese adolescents enter gangs because of language barriers should be re-examined. Most (87%) had a 10th grade or higher educational level. . . . Among the 14 subjects who indicated that they had some college education, only two were not attending college at the time the interviews were conducted.

Contact with the Criminal Justice System

About half the subjects stated they had been arrested at least once, . . . mostly for minor crimes, and most were released without being imprisoned. During the interviews, several subjects jokingly referred to their arrests as being "invited to the precinct to sip tea." Only nine subjects (15%) were ever incarcerated. Their prison terms ranged from one to three years. Only a few of those arrested had been put on probation.

Family Background

The study found no evidence to support the hypothesis proposed by Posner (1988) that many Chinese gang members are living in America without their parents. Only three subjects indicated that either one or both parents were absent.

Only one subject stated that his parents were born in the United States. The average length of stay in the United States for the subjects' fathers was 14.7 years, and for the subjects' mothers, 14.4 years. . . . According to Joe (1994), the average length of stay in the United States for the parents of San Francisco's Chinese gang members was also about 14 years.

Like the members of other ethnic gangs, most Chinese gang members in my study were from working-class families. Only one subject's father and three subjects' mothers were professionals. Most subjects' parents either worked in restaurants or in garment factories. Three subjects stated that their mothers had attended college, and 10 subjects reported that their fathers had attended college.

Most of the subjects lived with their parents (73%). Only seven subjects lived in "gang houses." I found no evidence to support the contention that young Chinese gang members are under the constant authority and control of gang leaders or tong elders. The majority of them still live with their parents and are under the guidance (to the extent that adolescents ever are) of their parents.

Most subjects (65%) stated that they either occasionally or rarely saw their parents. Sung (1977) found that most immigrant parents work long hours in restaurants and garment factories and have little time for their children. More than half of the subjects (54%) indicated that they got along with their parents. And most (76%) said that their parents did not understand them. It is apparent that most subjects did not have a satisfactory relationship with their parents. However, it is not clear whether their dissatisfaction led them to join gangs or if their involvement in gang activities generated unhappy parent-child relationships.

Profiles

Profiles of two deceased gang leaders are provided here to bring the human element to the discussion of the characteristics of Chinese gang members. These brief case histories are constructed from newspaper and magazine articles.

Michael Chen

Before he was killed in 1982, Michael Chen was a leader of the Flying Dragons. Chen, a Cantonese, was born in China in 1950. When he was 13 years old, he immigrated to New York City from Hong Kong with his mother and a sister. There they joined his father, who had left China when his mother was pregnant with Chen. After his arrival, Chen worked as a delivery boy for a Chinese restaurant in upper Manhattan while attending Seward Park High School, near Chinatown. After his graduation from high school, Chen attended college briefly. Chen's father earned his living as a taxi driver.

In 1976, Chen was arrested in Queens for homicide, but the charges were dismissed. The following year, he was indicted in the slayings of two members of the rival Ghost Shadows during a brazen shoot-out in the crowded Pagoda Theater on East Broadway in Manhattan's Chinatown. However, he was later acquitted. Chen, who was known as "The Scientist" because of his "cool" and patient ways, rose to become the leader of the Flying Dragons in the late 1970s. He owned three expensive sports cars and dressed only in designer clothes. He was considered to be extremely good to his parents and especially affectionate toward his grandmother. Chen had a reputation for being polite and never seemed outrageous or rude. He did not drink, smoke, or gamble, and was generous toward others (Breslin, 1983). He did, however, have a weakness for women.

On March 13, 1982, Chen's body was found on the ground floor of the Hip Sing Credit Union, which was located across the street from the Hip Sing Association on Pell Street (Weiss, 1983). He was apparently murdered with a handgun. According to various sources, Chen received a telephone call in the early morning. He left his apartment, which was above the Hip Sing Credit Union, and showed up at a coffee shop adjacent to the credit union. Neighbors heard the gun shots, but none bothered to call the police. No suspect was arrested, and the case has never been solved. The police theorize that the killing was carried out by people whom Chen knew well because he would not have gotten out of bed at that time to meet strangers. The fact that the credit union where Chen's body was found was operated by the Hip Sing Association, an organization affiliated with the Flying Dragons, also led law enforcement authorities to speculate that the murder was at least sanctioned by the Hip Sing.

Chen thought of himself as a businessman and had invested in a nightclub in Flushing, Queens, and a meat market and a paper supply house in Manhattan. Before his demise, he allegedly told his friends he was contemplating completely disassociating himself from the gangland of Chinatown and transforming himself into a respectable businessman.

Andy Liang

Andy Liang was a member of the Fuk Ching gang and later a leader of the Tung On gang. Liang's family immigrated to the United States in 1982 from Guangdong, China. Liang was born in 1963. He attended school briefly after his arrival in America, but quit when he had trouble following the academic demands and joined the Fuk Ching gang. Liang's family, which consisted of his parents and a younger sister, lived in an apartment on Eldridge Street, in Manhattan's Chinatown. His parents worked long hours in garment factories to make ends meet.

Liang was in a car with two other Fuk Ching members in September 1985 when three men opened fire on them. One of the other Fuk Ching gang members in the car was killed. Liang's criminal record included a conviction for assault in 1985 in Brooklyn, for which he was put on probation, and a conviction for robbery in 1986 in midtown Manhattan, for which he was put on probation for five years. In 1986, Liang's 12-year-old sister was strangled to death by a deranged neighbor. In April 1987, Liang was shot three times on East Broadway by members of the Flying Dragons. He recovered from this attack only to be shot and killed on Division Street in June 1988 by a prominent Chinatown businessman. When the police arrived at the scene, they found Liang had been shot 19 times. The businessman was later acquitted on the grounds that he had been acting in self-defense (Fraser, 1991). Before his death, Liang had been living in a Tung On gang apartment located at the headquarters of the Tsung Tsin Association. The gang was providing protection to a gambling establishment within the building.

Entering and Leaving Gangs

Although the reasons for and social processes of recruitment and induction into African American and Hispanic gangs have been extensively studied by social scientists, little empirical work has been done on the movement of Asian youths into gangs. Chin (1990) hypothesizes that Chinese youths participate in delinquent behavior because they are unable to cope with problems they face in school, their families, and the community. Their transformation from delinquents to gang members is propelled by their association with adult crime groups and the internalization of the norms and values of the triad subculture. According to Toy (1992a), young Asians in San Francisco join gangs mainly because they need protection or because they grow up into the gangs. Song, Dombrink, and Geis (1992) theorize that Chinese youths are involved in gang activities because of identity crises and negative reactions from law enforcement authorities. Many official reports and popular books on Chinese gangs charge that young people in Chinatown join gangs mainly because they are lured by the opportunity to make money (Posner, 1988; U.S. Department of Justice, 1985, 1988).

In this study, most respondents gave more than one reason for becoming gang members. The top five reasons, in order of importance, were money, protection, fun, brotherhood, and power/status. . . .

Half of the 62 subjects mentioned making money as one of the primary reasons for joining a gang. They were impressed by the amount of money gang leaders appeared to have and were excited by their generosity with money. The would-be gang members knew that by becoming a gang member they would be able to make at least some money by watching the streets or protecting gambling houses. Moreover, they were aware of the gangs' pervasive involvement in extortion and related crimes involving businesses in the community. One subject asserted that gang activity was "all about making money." Studies of other ethnic gangs also suggest that financial incentives are one of the most important factors in the decision to enter a gang (Jankowski, 1991; Padilla, 1992; Taylor, 1990).

The second most often cited reason for entering a gang was self-protection. Many subjects joined gangs because they were frequently attacked by schoolmates, who may or may not have been gang members. The subjects found that hanging out with members of a Chinese gang was the most effective way to deter such attacks. One subject explained that he joined a Chinese gang because it offered him much-needed protection:

> I was attacked by black or Hispanic schoolmates several times. The teachers never listened to my side of the story. They stole my sports jacket, and they insulted me with racial slurs. My friends always came to help. I needed their friendship for self-protection. So I joined them.

Fun and brotherhood were also mentioned as major reasons that gangs were appealing to the subjects. One respondent said he joined a gang simply because he was asked to "play": "My friends knew some [Flying] Dragons. My friends asked me whether I would like to *po* [hang out] together and play, and do some dark society thing. I said, 'OK.' "

Power/status was another reason many Chinese subjects gave for joining gangs. The respondents realized that being a gang member signified power and status, and this translated into the power to approach Chinese businesspeople for money and favors. Being a gang member also involved being feared by ordinary Chinatown residents, and gang members had the opportunity to be affiliated with some of the most powerful figures in the community.

Sex, women, excitement, school problems, and family problems were also mentioned by subjects as reasons for involvement in gangs. Only two subjects mentioned drug use as a reason for joining a gang. According to Fagan's study (1989), African Americans and Hispanics join gangs for the following reasons: material incentives, recreation, a place of refuge and camouflage, physical protection, rebellion, and commitment to community. It appears that Chinese youths join gangs for reasons that are not dissimilar to those of youths from other ethnic groups.

Recruitment and Membership

It is not known how Chinese gangs recruit new members. Almost all the respondents in this study stated that they joined gangs voluntarily. Only one felt that he was somehow pressed to join. Over the past 25 years, there have been reports in local newspapers that adolescents were forced to join gangs in Chinatown ("Gang Members," 1980). According to these reports, those who refused the invitation were severely beaten by gang recruiters. I found no evidence to substantiate these reports. One subject revealed that the intensity of his gang's recruitment depended on how many members were arrested: "If some brothers are arrested, we recruit more often, like every two months. Otherwise, once every six months."

Although the initiation ceremonies of triad societies are well documented (Booth, 1991; Morgan, 1960), little is known about how adolescents are inducted into Chinese gangs in the United States. Chin (1990) found that the Flying Dragons' initiation ceremony is similar to that of the triad societies. For example, new members have to take oaths, drink wine mixed with the blood of other new recruits, and pay tribute to *Guan Gong*. A member of the Flying Dragons described the initiation ceremony:

> At the initiation ceremony, I had to take oaths, bow to the gods, and drink wine mixed with blood. Two *dai lo*s [big brothers] and two uncles [tong members who play the role of middlemen between the tong and the gang] were present at the ceremony. After the ritual, one of the uncles gave me a *hung bao* with cash inside and congratulated me: "Now you are part of the family."

Another gang member also indicated that he was asked to take oaths when he joined: "I had to take the gang oaths. The ceremony was performed inside a restaurant."

However, not all Chinese gangs conduct an initiation ceremony. It seems that the non-tong-affiliated gangs are less likely to carry out initiation ceremonies than are gangs that are affiliated with tongs. According to a subject who was a member of the non-tong-affiliated White Tigers gang: "I became a member by accepting their invitation. We went to a restaurant and celebrated. There was no initiation ceremony. We just drank together until we got drunk."

Another subject, a member of the non-tong-affiliated Born-to-Kill, confirmed the former's claim: "For Vietnamese, there was no ceremony. They introduced us to other members. We do not have a formal initiation ceremony."

Most subjects were extremely proud of their membership in a Chinese gang, at least initially. When asked how he felt after joining the Flying Dragons, a subject replied excitedly: "I felt very good, very powerful, very resourceful."

Dissociating: Reasons and Processes

My study suggests that membership in a Chinese gang does not last for life. Members did drop out of the gangs and did not experience retaliation from their peers for their actions. The reasons for leaving most often mentioned by those subjects who stated that they had left the gangs (n = 32, or about half of the sample) included being urged to leave by family members, seeing other members get into trouble, being arrested, seeing members of the same gang being killed, and deciding to go back to school. . . . Of the 32 former gang members in the sample, at the time of the interviews, 14 had left the gang less than a year ago, 8 had dropped out of the gang for one to two years, and the rest had dissociated from the gang for about three years. The average length of gang membership for the former gang members was about two years; and for the active gang members, it was about three years.

Some left the gangs because their family members were deeply concerned and anxious about their involvement in gang activities. In some cases, parents, siblings, or girlfriends urged the subjects to leave. In other cases, family members sent the subjects away, either abroad or out-of-state, so they could avoid gang peers. One subject indicated that he finally left his gang when his mother threatened to kill herself if he continued his gang association.

Some decided to leave their gangs because they had seen too many fellow gang members get into trouble with the law. One left because his *dai lo* was sent to jail. One street-level leader said he quit because his followers were constantly being arrested for getting into fights and he simply did not want to be bothered by these incidents anymore.

Some dropped out of the gangs after being arrested by police. For some of the respondents, being arrested amounted to what Garfinkel

(1956) called a "degradation ceremony." Certain youths came to realize the risk of being incarcerated and decided that being a gang member was not worth it, especially when they found out that their *dai lo* might not bail them out if they were arrested. One member put it this way:

> Because my friends got into trouble with the law, we were running into a cage. It was like a cycle. You bailed out someone with money collected from protection rackets, you got caught, you had to pay more. A friend of mine was caught and needed $3,500 for bail. *Dai lo* said he didn't have the money. Then I told myself, "Forget about it. What's the point in being a member of the gang."

Others left their gangs after they witnessed close friends being killed. Under such circumstances, they either felt guilty for their friends' deaths or feared they might be murdered too. One subject gave the following account of his decision to leave his gang:

> A friend of mine was dancing with a girl from another gang. A guy pulled the girl away from my friend. We assumed he was a Tung On. We approached him and asked, "Who the hell are you?" He said, "If you want to know, we'll go outside." That's when we got outside. They had three guys. They had people outside carrying weapons. This guy shot at my friend. My friend was dying in my arms. We all left the scene before the police arrived. I still feel guilty for leaving my friend there to die. He might have survived if I had stayed there with him. I still have nightmares about the incident and see him in these dreams. I saw many other friends get killed. It's not worth it. Because they died for stupid reasons, like over a girl. After my close friend was killed, I was pretty determined to leave.

Still others left because they eventually came to realize that being a gang member was not as glorious as they thought before joining. They became disillusioned when they found that gang leaders were not really concerned for their well-being and that close friends may kill one another over money or women. They said there was no "righteousness" among gang peers and, after a while, extorting money from merchants could be not very glamorous. According to a subject:

> I felt like I had the potential to do something else. I felt that the life of a gangster was not glorious anymore. It is a way of life that is filthy and

corrupt. Also, there were so many intergang fights. The gangs only know how to victimize their own people. It is really disgusting.

Another subject decided to leave because he realized that his gang activity was becoming more and more serious.

At the beginning, it was a lot of fun. However, later I found that this was a dead end. I committed some minor crimes, such as extortion and protecting gambling places, after I joined the gang. Later on, I began to get involved in serious crimes, such as assault and home-invasion robbery. It got more and more risky.

Leaving the gangs was not that difficult for most subjects. Most dropped out simply by not showing up at the gangs' hangouts. Their gang peers may have called them at home or at their beeper numbers, but if they ignored the calls, they were left alone after a while.

Some talked to their *dai los* about their decision to leave. They often said they wanted to go back to school or were tired of being a gang member. Interestingly, more often than not, their *dai los* were supportive and urged them to study hard. One said: "I talked to my *dai lo* that I was fed up with it. College is good for me. My *dai lo* said, 'Be a good kid.' It was fine with him."

However, a few were threatened when their *dai lo* or gang peers found out they planned to leave the gang. One subject was able to leave only because his elder brother was himself a senior member of the gang and was able to get him out: "I was just an ordinary member. I left Chinatown for about four months. My elder brother talked to someone. My brother was also a gang member. He said it wasn't an easy task. We were threatened."

Some were subjected to extortion by their gangs, and some were even assaulted. One subject said: "I had to pay thousands of dollars to my gang before they let me leave. I saved that money for many years from gang activities, so I didn't mind paying them."

On the basis of what former gang members had to say about their experiences in dissociating themselves from their gangs, it appears that the level of difficulty a gang member had in extricating himself depended on the rank he held in the gang, how much he knew about the gang, and whether he intended to join another gang, as well as what particular gang he belonged to, what his leader was like, and what reasons he cited for leaving. If the subject was an ordinary gang member who knew very little about his gang's involvement in more serious crime, he would be able to leave relatively easily. If, on the other hand, the subject was a senior gang member and had an intimate knowledge of gang activities and membership, he might not be allowed to leave his gang readily (Ng & Tharp, 1983).

Structural Characteristics . . .

According to law enforcement authorities, Chinese gangs are better organized than other ethnic gangs because they are closely associated with adult crime groups and are more involved in profit-generating criminal activities, such as extortion, the smuggling of aliens, gambling, and prostitution, which require the gangs to function as units with their own specific tasks (U.S. Department of Justice, 1988; U.S. Senate, 1992). Steady income from these illegal activities also enables Chinese gang leaders to enjoy control of their members, to restrain members from involvement in reckless violence, and to stabilize the hierarchical structure of the gangs. In brief, people in the law enforcement community generally agree that all Chinese gangs are "organized gangs" similar to Cloward and Ohlin's (1960) "criminal gangs," Spergel's (1964) "racket gangs," and Taylor's (1990) "corporate gangs."

Although there are official law enforcement assumptions about Chinese gang structure there are no empirical data on the size, infrastructure, norms, and values of Chinese gangs. In the following sections, I will try to shed some light on the structure of Chinese gangs, by analyzing the information from my interviews with former and active gang members.

Size

The New York City Police Department's Asian Gang Intelligence Unit, which operates out of the Fifth Precinct, in Manhattan's Chinatown, can only guess at the size of the major gangs in their area. And Intelligence Division detectives who cover the entire city believe that a gang's size is not stable but that it is fluid and is built around a hard core of 20 to 30 members.

I asked the subjects in my study about gang size. Most were either reluctant to answer the question or not sure how many members actually belonged to their gang. Other studies have also found that gang members generally do not know how many people belong to their gangs at a given time (Yablonsky, 1970). Those in my study who volunteered an estimation were not consistent in their assessments of gang size. Nevertheless, I think it is worthwhile to present what they said about the size of their gangs.

A member of the Ghost Shadows said there were 70 to 80 active members in his gang, including those who were active in Queens. A subject who belonged to the Born-to-Kill (BTK) thought that there were some 150 core and 70 peripheral members in his gang. Another BTK member estimated that there were 300 members in his gang. A member of the Flying Dragons said his gang had about 200 members. A youth belonging to the Taiwan Brotherhood revealed that there were 12 to 15 core members and 40 to 50 peripheral members in his group. A member of the White Tigers said his gang had 10 core members and 20 to 30 peripheral members.

After examining the data from the questionnaires and taking into consideration the information collected from informal talks with the subjects, we can safely say that there are hard-core and peripheral members in all the Chinese gangs in New York City. The smaller gangs such as the White Tigers, Green Dragons, Taiwan Brotherhood, and Golden Star appear to have a maximum of 20 core members and 50 peripheral members. Major gangs such as the Ghost Shadows, Flying Dragons, Tung On, Fuk Ching, and Born-to-Kill may have fewer than 100 core members and an unknown number of peripheral members. The number of members in a particular gang might change dramatically, especially when a gang is indicted by federal prosecutors as a racketeering enterprise or has been glamorized in the media after committing a reckless violent crime and attracts thrill seekers.

Faction and Clique

How cohesive are Chinese gangs? Are Chinese gangs monolithic organizations or coalitions of age-graded groups? These are important questions that need to be answered before we can fully understand the structure of Chinese gangs and the junction that violence plays in them.

A unique aspect of Chinese gang structure is the prevalence of various factions within it—this is especially true of gangs based in Manhattan's Chinatown. For example, the Flying Dragons have six factions—three in Manhattan and three in Queens. Each of the three groups in Manhattan occupies a street—namely, Pell, the Bowery, and Grand. The Pell Street group consists of mainly American-born Chinese, and the other two groups are made up of predominantly Cantonese youths. The three Flying Dragons factions in Queens are the Chinese Flying Dragons, the Korean Flying Dragons, and the Grand Street faction in Flushing. Like the Flying Dragons, the Ghost Shadows have three groups in Manhattan's Chinatown—namely, the Mott, Bayard, and Mulberry factions. Each reigns in those particular streets in the Chinese community. The same is true for the Born-to-Kill, the Tung On, and the Fuk Ching. This study did not find factions among gangs based in Queens and Brooklyn.

According to my respondents, rivalry among factions is common. This is confirmed by the media in their many reports on incidents of intragang violence. The Pell and the Grand factions (Manhattan) of the Flying Dragons are often in conflict with each other. In 1991, a member of the Grand faction was shot and killed by a member of the Pell faction. According to a member of the Grand faction, he was not allowed to appear in Pell Street. If he had to go there, he was obliged to inform the Pell group through his *dai lo* so that his coming and going would not be a surprise. Likewise, factional killings are not unusual among the Ghost Shadows. In 1991, there was a shooting between two factions of the Ghost Shadows, and an innocent bystander was killed by a stray bullet (Steinberg, 1991). In 1985, an outburst of violent activities among two rival groups of the Tung On shocked the Chinese community (Ibert, 1985). My data strongly suggest that there is little cooperation among the various factions of a Chinese gang and that these factions or subgroups can be considered gangs in and of themselves.

In New York City's Chinese gangs, each faction may consist of two or more cliques. Like other ethnic gangs (Los Angeles County District Attorney, 1992), Chinese gangs depend on cliques as their basic building blocks. However, Chinese gang cliques are not formed according to age, as Hagedorn (1988) found was the case with Milwaukee's non-Asian gangs, but rather are headed by clique leaders who have executive authority at the street level. The relationship between a clique leader and his followers is probably the strongest relationship within the hierarchy of a Chinese gang, regardless of whether or not the gang has factions. Cliques that belong to a faction may compete with one another for the attention of the faction leader, but their relationship appears to be much more cordial than the relationship between factions.

My data suggest that non-tong-affiliated gangs appear to be more cohesive than tong-affiliated gangs. This may be because non-tong-affiliated gangs are smaller and lack competing factions. Because there are more direct interactions among members of non-tong-affiliated gangs, there are fewer intragang conflicts than there are in tong-affiliated gangs. Also because smaller amounts of money are at stake, there tends to be less friction. In tong-affiliated gangs, cooperation among factions is almost nonexistent; however, as has been noted, cliques within a faction seem to be able to coexist rather peacefully.

Affiliation with Adult Organizations

According to local and federal authorities, certain Chinese gangs in San Francisco and New York City are closely associated with adult organizations known as tongs. Those Chinese gangs function as "street muscle" for the tongs, performing such tasks as guarding gambling clubs and massage parlors sanctioned by the adult group, collecting debts for gambling clubs, protecting the territory of the adult organization from outsiders, and occasionally working as couriers for heroin trafficking groups (U.S. Department of Justice, 1985, 1988; U.S. Senate, 1992). According to the authorities, those Chinese gangs are tightly controlled by tongs, there is an alliance between those gangs and the tongs, and the tong-affiliated gangs are better organized and tend to be more involved in income-generating criminal activities than non-tong-affiliated gangs (Bresler, 1981; Posner, 1988; Kinkead, 1992).

Other observers, mainly researchers in California and Canada, have claimed that gangs are only loosely affiliated with tongs and that tongs exert little or no control over gangs . . . (Dubro, 1992; Joe, 1994; Toy, 1992b).

. . . I found that with the exception of the Born-to-Kill, the major Manhattan-based Chinese gangs are affiliated with certain adult organizations. Certain tong members who are known as *ah kung* (grandfather) or *shuk foo* (uncle) serve as mentors for the gang members and play the role of liaison between tongs and gangs. During the interviews, gang members often talked about those mentors with respect and fear. When asked how he viewed the *ah kung* of his gang, a subject exclaimed, "*ah kung* is very ferocious, very powerful, very capable."

I found that most tong-affiliated gangs have more than one principal or primary leader. For example, the Flying Dragons have two or more *dai dai lo*s (big big brothers), who are very close to certain officers or members of the Hip Sing Association. These *dai dai lo*s control the various factions of the gang. Each faction has a *dai lo* (big brother) and one or more street-level *dai lo*s (clique leader) who are known as *yee lo* (second brother) or *saam lo* (third brother). Each street-level *dai lo* is in charge of several *ma jai*s (little horses) or *leng jai*s (little kids).

The *dai dai lo*s take orders from one or more *ah kung*s or *shuk foo*s. The *dai dai lo*s then convey orders to the *dai lo*s, who in turn relay them to the *yee lo*s or *saam lo*s, and the latter provide instructions and orders to the *ma jai*s or *leng jai*s. Most instructions from the *ah kung*s to the gangs have to do with collecting gambling debts and protecting gambling dens and prostitution houses in the tong's territory. I did not find the *ah kung*s or *shuk foo*s to be actively involved in commanding gang members to commit violent crimes or participate in international crimes such as heroin trafficking or the smuggling of aliens. According to the subjects in my study, the only connection between tongs and gangs appears to be around gambling debt collection. Two subjects made the following comments about the tong-gang connection:

> We rarely take orders from the affiliated-tong, unless someone owes gambling debts to the tong or certain gambling places. We go collect the money for them. We hang out at the adult organization's building and play mahjong in their gambling places. The uncle will tell the *dai lo* what to do.

The *ma jai*s [ordinary gang members] seem to have little knowledge of their faction *dai lo*s, nor of the *dai dai lo*s, *ah kung*s, or *shuk foo*s. They take orders only from their immediate leader, who is the street-level *dai lo*. They are instructed by gang leaders not to ask questions about the leadership structure. Likewise, the street-level *dai lo*s are only familiar with their immediate leaders—*dai lo*s or *ah kung*s. Thus, there is evidence that tong-affiliated Chinese gangs are hierarchical. Ordinary gang members may meet those above their immediate leaders only during their initiation ceremony. . . .

. . . Some *dai dai lo*s are also officers of the affiliated tong. Before his arrest for heroin trafficking, a *dai dai lo* of the Flying Dragons was elected national manager of the Hip Sing Association, an important position within the organization. When the gang leader was robbed of $40,000 in cash and shot by unknown assailants at an attorney's office in Chinatown, the Hip Sing Association posted a $10,000 reward for information that might lead to solving the case. Likewise, the highest leaders of the Ghost Shadows and the Tung On gangs have, at times, served as officers of their affiliated adult organizations. Some ordinary gang members also join the affiliated tongs, but it is not clear why some do and others do not.

On occasion, the relationship between tongs and gangs is established not only through formal appointments but also by means of family ties. For example, in the late 1980s and early 1990s, leadership of the On Leong Merchant Association and the Ghost Shadows gang was believed to be controlled by three brothers. J. Caleb Boggs III, staff counsel to the Senate's Permanent Subcommittee on Investigations, testified:

> The president of the On Leong Association is Wing Wah Chan. Wah was previously New York Chapter President until his brother, Wing Yueng Chan, resigned as national president in April, 1989. A third brother, Wing Lok Chan, aka "Lok Jai," is the main leader of the affiliated Ghost Shadows gang. (U.S. Senate, 1992, p. 67)

Likewise, the younger brother of the president of the Tung On Association was alleged to be a former leader of the Tung On gang (Meskil, 1989). . . .

Territory

Every Chinese gang in New York City maneuvers in its own territory. When subjects were asked whether their gangs had a territory, all but one answered negatively. Manhattan's Chinatown is divided into several gang turfs, and each gang normally controls two or three blocks. . . . The gang territories in Queens and Brooklyn are more spread out, with the Green Dragons in control of Jackson Heights and Elmhurst, the White Tigers and the Taiwan Brotherhood in control of Flushing, and the Golden Star in control of Brooklyn.

Tong-affiliated gangs usually claim those streets belonging to the adult organization with which they are associated. For example, the

Ghost Shadows' major territory is Mott and Bayard Streets, and it is no coincidence that the adult organization affiliated with the Ghost Shadows, the On Leong Association, also reigns in these two streets. Likewise, the Hip Sing Association is located on Pell Street, and the Flying Dragons, the gang affiliated with the Hip Sing, has a strong hold on Pell Street. Since most Chinatown gangs have more than one faction, each faction normally occupies one block.

Division of Labor

According to my survey of Chinese gang members, some gangs, especially those not affiliated with a tong, have no distinctive division of labor. Members are considered by the *dai lo* and among themselves as equals. In the non-tong-affiliated gangs, members are collectively involved in extortion, fighting, and other activities. In the tong-affiliated gangs, however, there is some division of labor, and certain members are assigned by the *dai lo* to be street watchers, debt collectors, protection money collectors, or enforcers. Members of tong-affiliated gangs do not have the ready access to their *dai lo*s that members of non-tong-affiliated gangs do, possibly because tong-affiliated gangs are in general much larger.

Gang Lifespan

. . . Of the 15 gangs [investigated], only five have dissolved. The Continentals, the first and only gang of American-born Chinese, disappeared from Chinatown quickly because it could not compete with gangs of predominantly foreign-born Chinese, such as the Ghost Shadows and the Flying Dragons. The Continentals' inability to integrate with a tong also diminished its status within the community. The Ching Yee became obsolete after two members were brutally murdered by a rival gang. The White Eagles collapsed because the gang was expelled from Mott Street by the On Leong Association and replaced by the Ghost Shadows. After several of its leaders were ambushed on Mott Street by the Ghost Shadows, the Black Eagles gang also faded from Chinatown. The Kam Lun gang lasted less than a year because of the downfall of the affiliated Kam Lun Association, which was ruthlessly attacked by a rival group. The Ghost Shadows and the Flying Dragons, two gangs that control the core areas of Chinatown, have existed for more than a quarter of a century. They are deeply entrenched in the community because of their affiliation with two of the most powerful community associations. As long as the tongs remain in control of Chinatown and the gangs are able to maintain good relationships with the tongs, it is unlikely they will be removed from the community.

Norms and Rules

According to subcultural theorists, a gang represents a subcultural group with its own norms and values (Cohen, 1955; Miller, 1958; Wolfgang & Ferracuti, 1982). Research has shown that certain gang norms are similar to the norms prevalent in the gang's underclass community. Chin (1990) proposed that a specific system of norms and values is closely followed by Chinese gang members. He concluded that the norms and values of the Chinese secret societies, triads, tongs, and gangs are compatible with and shared by members of a Chinese criminal subculture historically and popularly known as *jiang hu,* or the "dark society." In order to understand the behavioral patterns of gang members, their coping mechanisms, and the sources of gang conflicts and tensions, it is important to examine some of the norms and values that characterize and define the gangs.

Some of the norms and rules most often mentioned by my subjects were:

- Do not go to another gang's or another faction's territory without good reason or the permission of your *dai lo.*
- Do not look for trouble, especially by engaging in street fighting or reckless shootings.
- Do not betray your gang—do not leak information about your gang to outsiders, especially when you are arrested and interrogated by police.
- Do not threaten store owners when they refuse to pay protection or extortion money—you should know how to collect the money without threats or the use of force.
- Do not hang out with members of rival gangs.
- Do not use drugs.
- Do not become involved in heroin dealing.
- Listen to the *dai lo* and follow his instructions carefully.

- If you see members of another gang on your turf, beat them up.
- Respect the *ah kung*s.
- Do not kill anyone who belongs to the same gang.
- Do not flirt with another member's girlfriend.
- Do not ask too many questions about gang business.

A member who violates these norms and rules might be punished by his peers or *dai lo*, either lightly or severely. He could be physically assaulted or killed. One subject had the following to say about punishment for violators: "If you break the rules, you get beat up. I saw a lot [of this sort of punishment]. Like if you did something wrong, you have to light up a cigarette and have to burn your arm or palm. The *dai lo* may get his follower killed if the latter joins a rival gang."

When asked why and how certain members are promoted and become leaders, my subjects cited the following qualities or conditions that are considered by primary gang leaders and tong members as essential for leadership. Leaders must:

- Be able to recruit many followers
- Be good at dealing with business owners—that is, be capable of collecting money from merchants in the territory regularly without using threats and violence
- Possess a stable source of income (either legitimate or illegitimate) and be generous with money
- Be willing and capable of negotiating with rival gang leaders when there are intergang or intragang conflicts
- Have good relationships with elders of the affiliated tong
- Be trusted by the primary leader
- Have guts and be aggressive
- Know how to make money
- Be low-key
- Be good at interpersonal relationships in general

When someone is promoted and becomes a leader, that does not mean the position is permanent. On some occasions, a *dai lo* might be either forced to leave the gang or killed. One subject provided a chilling account of promotion and demotion within his gang:

If a *dai lo* got killed or jailed, someone will be promoted. In this situation, everybody has an equal chance of being promoted. However, even after one is promoted as a leader, he may be disliked by *shuk foo*. If that's the case, *shuk foo* could put him [the *dai lo*] up at the altar [meaning, have him killed]. *Shuk foo* is a very ferocious person. He makes the decision.

Nevertheless, according to the data collected from the gang study and my years of observation of the development of Chinatown gangs in New York City, gang leadership is relatively stable. Several well-known *dai dai lo*s have been able to remain in power for many years. Very rarely has a *dai dai lo* or a faction *dai lo* been disposed of by the affiliated tong or by their followers.

Summary

In examining the data collected from Chinese gang members in New York City, I found few differences between members of Chinese gangs and members of other ethnic gangs. Members of Chinatown gangs, like members of gangs in the black and Hispanic communities, are predominantly underclass adolescents who enter the gangs for material gain, protection, power, and excitement. Also, the average length of membership of Chinese gang members appears to be similar to that of members of other ethnic gangs. There is no evidence to suggest that once a Chinese youth enters a gang, he will be unable to dissociate himself from the gang or be forced to remain in the gang for a prolonged period of time.

The connection between street gangs and adult organizations is a structural aspect of Chinese gangs that is different from that of other ethnic gangs. Although some researchers have found black and Hispanic gangs to have been affiliated with adult groups at one time or another (Moore, 1978; Vigil, 1988), the relationships appeared to be less permanent and pervasive than such relationships in the Chinese community. However, the gang-tong linkage does not seem to tighten gang cohesion, and in this respect there is little difference between Chinese gangs and other ethnic gangs.

My findings do not support the assertion made by some observers that a well-organized, monolithic, hierarchical criminal cartel, sometimes referred to as the "Chinese Mafia," exists in the United States and in many other nations. Secret societies, triads, tongs, and gangs are alleged to be the building blocks of this organization. My findings also do not support the notion that a chain of command exists among these various crime groups or that they coordinate with one another routinely in international crimes such as heroin trafficking, money laundering, and the smuggling of aliens. Instead, my data suggest that in most cases gangs are not controlled by tongs. Rather, the gangs work for tongs and adult crime groups on an ad hoc basis. Furthermore, gang cohesion is strained by the lack of cooperation among the various factions of a specific gang.

An important aspect of Chinese gang structure is the existence of a small number of tong members who serve as mentors for tong-affiliated gangs. According to my subjects, these mentors, who are called *ah kung* or *shuk foo,* appear to play an important role as criminal middlemen in connecting the tongs and the gangs, and in providing gang leaders and ordinary gang members with guidance in developing and nurturing criminal careers within the Chinese community. The law-enforcement community appears to know very little about these tong members, and as a result, most of them remain immune to prosecution. Most officers of the tongs are not *ah kungs,* and some of the *ah kungs* may not even be listed as tong officers. Ordinary gang members do not have access to the *ah kungs,* which makes the task of identifying and prosecuting the *ah kungs* all the more difficult.

References

Badey, J. (1988). *Dragons and tigers.* Loomis, CA: Palmer Enterprises.

Booth, M. (1991). *The triads.* New York: St. Martin's.

Bresler, F. (1981). *The Chinese mafia.* New York: Stein & Day.

Breslin, J. (1983, March 15). The toughest gangster on Pell Street. *New York Daily News,* p. 4.

Butterfield, F. (1985, January 21). The shifting picture of crime by U.S. Vietnamese. *New York Times,* p. A1.

Chin, K. (1986). *Chinese triad societies, tongs, organized crime, and street gangs in Asia and the United States.* Unpublished doctoral dissertation, University of Pennsylvania.

Chin, K. (1990). *Chinese subculture and criminality.* Westport, CT: Greenwood.

Cloward, R. A., & Ohlin, L. E. (1960). *Delinquency and opportunity.* New York: Free Press.

Cohen, A. (1955). *Delinquent boys.* New York: Free Press.

Conly, C., Kelly, P., Mahanna, P., & Warner, L. (1993). *Street gangs: Current knowledge and strategies*. Washington, DC: Government Printing Office.

Dannen, F. (1992, November 16). Revenge of the Green Dragons. *New Yorker*, pp. 76-99.

Dubro, J. (1992). *Dragons of crime: Inside the Asian underworld*. Markham, Ontario: Octopus.

English, T. (1995, February). Slaving away: Chinese illegals oppressed at home, exploited here. *Smithsonian*, pp. 12-14.

Fagan, J. (1989). The social organization of drug use and drug dealing among urban gangs. *Criminology, 27*, 633-667.

Fraser, C. G. (1991, July 5). 18-shot killing a defense act, a jury decides. *New York Times*, p. B3.

Gang members assaulted a youth after he refused to join them. (1980, November 4). *World Journal*, p. 24.

Garfinkel, H. (1956, March). Conditions of successful degradation ceremonies. *American Journal of Sociology, 61*, 420-424.

Hagedorn, J. (1988). *People and folks*. Chicago: Lakeview.

Ibert, D. (1985, May 27). Gang attacks spread fear in Chinatown. *Bergen Record*, p. A27.

Jankowski, M. S. (1991). *Islands in the streets*. Berkeley: University of California Press.

Joe, K. (1993). Getting into the gang: Methodological issues in studying ethnic gangs. In M. De La Rosa & J. Adrados (Eds.), *Drug abuse among minority youth: Methodological issues and recent research advances* (NIDA Monograph Series 130). Washington, DC: Government Printing Office.

Joe, K. (1994). The new criminal conspiracy? Asian gangs and organized crime in San Francisco. *Journal of Research in Crime and Delinquency, 31*, 390-415.

Kinkead, G. (1992). *Chinatown*. New York: HarperCollins.

Los Angeles County District Attorney. (1992). *Gangs, crime and violence in Los Angeles*. Los Angeles: District Attorney's Office.

Meskil, P. (1989, February 5). In the eye of the storm. *New York Daily News Magazine*, pp. 10-16.

Miller, W. (1958). Lower class culture as a generating milieu of gang delinquency. *Journal of Social Issues, 14*, 5-19.

Moore, J. (1978). *Homeboys*. Philadelphia: Temple University Press.

Morgan, W. P. (1960). *Triad societies in Hong Kong*. Hong Kong: Government Press.

Ng, D., & Tharp, P. (1983, March 7). Chinese gang war claims new victim. *New York Post*, p. 4.

Padilla, F. (1992). *The gang as an American enterprise*. New Brunswick, NJ: Rutgers University Press.

Polsky, C. (1985, February 19). Feds: Chinatown indictments target modern "Black Hand." *New York Newsday*, p. 3.

Posner, G. (1988). *Warlords of crime.* New York: McGraw-Hill.

Song, J. H., Dombrink, J., & Geis, G. (1992). Lost in the melting pot: Asian youth gangs in the United States. *Gang Journal, 1*(1), 1-12.

Spergel, I. (1964). *Racketville, slumtown, haulburg.* Chicago: University of Chicago Press.

Steinberg, J. (1991, July 6). Tourist in car killed as she chances upon Chinatown gunfight. *New York Times,* p. L23.

Sung, B. (1977). *Gangs in New York's Chinatown* (Monograph No. 6). New York: City College of New York, Department of Asian Studies.

Taylor, C. (1990). *Dangerous society.* East Lansing: Michigan State University Press.

Toy, C. (1992a). Coming out to play: Reasons to join and participate in Asian gangs. *Gang Journal, 1*(1), 13-29.

Toy, C. (1992b). A short history of Asian gangs in San Francisco. *Justice Quarterly, 9,* 647-665.

U.S. Department of Justice. (1985). *Oriental organized crime: A report of a research project conducted by the Organized Crime Section, Federal Bureau of Investigation, Criminal Investigative Division.* Washington, DC: Government Printing Office.

U.S. Department of Justice. (1988). *Report on Asian organized crime, Criminal Division.* Washington, DC: Government Printing Office.

U.S. Senate. (1992). *Asian organized crime: Hearing before the Permanent Subcommittee on Investigations of the Committee on Governmental Affairs.* Washington, DC: Government Printing Office.

Vigil, D. (1988). *Barrio gangs.* Austin: University of Texas Press.

Vigil, D., & Yun, S. (1990). Vietnamese youth gangs in Southern California. In R. Huff (Ed.), *Gangs in America.* Newbury Park, CA: Sage.

Weiss, M. (1983, March 14). Chinatown gang leader shot dead. *New York Daily News,* p. 5.

Wolfgang, M., & Ferracuti, F. (1982). *The subculture of violence.* Beverly Hills, CA: Sage.

Yablonsky, L. (1970). *The violent gang.* Baltimore: Penguin.

Zhou, M. (1992). *Chinatown: The socioeconomic potential of an urban enclave.* Philadelphia: Temple University Press.

DISCUSSION:
The Yakuza

Since the 1950s, the Yakuza have become so wealthy, diversified, and omnipresent in Japanese society that their agenda is virtually indistinguishable from that of the national government. There is a strong symbiotic relationship between the two. The Japanese Yakuza constitute a parallel universe running beneath virtually every institution and industry in the nation. They are known as the *Boryokodan*, which means "the violent ones," to the Japanese National Police Agency. The official membership of Boryokodan groups in Japan was estimated at well over 80,000, but criminal associates may make up more than 10 times that number (U.S. Senate, 1992).

The father-child relationship between boss and soldier is the fundamental building block of Yakuza groups (Seymour, 1996). Despite radical changes in other aspects of the organization, that mentor/teacher/patron/ *sensei* role remains essential to the group. The strong bonds that result from this relationship are legendary. With this relationship in place, gangsters are loyal and committed and have accepted a pattern of dominance that is deeply embedded in their very identities.

Even so, the Yakuza are in the midst of a transformation. Their structured world of tattoos, finger cutting, and total obedience is in danger of obsolescence. Japan's gangsters have recently discovered that the criminal world of the late 20th century does not require dogma, chivalry, or absolute loyalty. Instead, the times call for sophistication, cunning, and adventurous scheming. An entire generation of Japanese mobsters has passed away. The new model is not the top-down, tightly knit group once identified as Yakuza. Members now come to the group through gangs of street punks and hot rodders. Fast profits and plentiful handguns have become a standard of power in the Japanese underworld.

The Yakuza move between underworld and upperworld with a fluidity that derives from a long tradition of corruption. Current U.S. law enforcement sources state that their major concern about Japanese crime is money laundering (U.S. Senate, 1992). Their concern has been aroused by large-scale real estate purchases by unknown Japanese organizations. Upscale properties in Hawaii, California, and Nevada have been taken over by Japanese interests. The source of the money is impossible to trace.

While law enforcement focuses on real estate transactions and paper trails, the effect of Yakuza pressure on the international stock market has been given no more than incidental examination. Nor has there been a thorough study of the impact of the Yakuza on international money markets. Although many writers described the Yakuza as known and operating out in the open in Japan, very little has been established about their operations in the Americas.

In the past, Japanese learned to live with the Yakuza and keep the peace. They provided a certain public harmony, but that social contract may be breaking down (Kaplan & Dubro, 1986, p. 281). Law enforcement efforts in Japan traditionally worked with the Yakuza more than against it. Often police raids against Yakuza headquarters or investigations of crime scenes were "face saving" rather than serious enforcement efforts. Police attacks on one Yakuza gang were staged for the benefit of another Yakuza mob. Corruption reached to the very top. How the present-day Yakuza relates with authorities is a significant question. Vaksberg (1991) explained that, with new economic conditions and accumulated wealth, an OC group is likely to turn itself into a normal participant in the economic system (p. 264). Perhaps the reason there is so little serious examination of the Yakuza in the Americas is that it is virtually indistinguishable from legitimate enterprise.

4

North America: Foothold on the Mainland

David E. Kaplan
Alec Dubro

Chapter 9 (pp. 241-269) of *Yakuza: The Explosive Account of Japan's Criminal Underworld,* by David E. Kaplan and Alec Dubro (Reading, MA: Addison-Wesley, 1986)

In 1975, an unusual gangster film starring Robert Mitchum and Japanese actor Ken Takakura opened in the United States to a generally indifferent audience. The unconvincing plot, the strange and highly stylized Japanese acting, and the exotic setting didn't send Americans flocking to the box office. But viewers were probably amused by the outlandish and anachronistic swordplay, and found the finger-cutting sequences both compelling and gruesome. In any case, the movie, entitled simply *The Yakuza,* enjoyed a short run to nearly empty houses. It deserved better. It still plays occasionally on late-night television, but in 1975 Americans neither knew nor cared about the subject matter—Japanese organized crime.

By the early 1980s, that began to change. Americans other than Hawaiians slowly became aware of the Yakuza through the news media, and indirectly because of the new posture of U.S. law enforcement. Press reports of official statements about the Yakuza conveyed a note of panic, with headlines like "Japanese Organized Criminals Invading West," and "FBI Chief Warns of Japanese Crime Ring."

A number of top Washington law enforcement officials, including Attorney General William French Smith and FBI chief William Webster, warned on several occasions that the Yakuza presented a threat to the nation that warranted swift action. Partly as a response to this clamor, members of the Reagan administration decided to include the Yakuza in the agenda of the President's Commission on Organized Crime, formally created in July 1983. Some previous legislative panels, like the Kefauver and McLellan Senate committees, had a discernible impact on organized crime by putting pressure on law enforcement and increasing citizen awareness. But the Reagan commission was the first to acknowledge the fact that organized crime is changing, and that it is no longer the exclusive domain of the mafia, if ever it was.

California authorities recognized this change rather early, owing perhaps to the weak position of traditional Italian syndicates in that state. In the 1980s, state authorities paid less attention to the Italian groups and more to the "nontraditional" gangs, which include everyone else. In its 1981 report to the legislature, the California Bureau of Organized Crime and Criminal Intelligence (BOCCI) devoted as much space to Israeli, Vietnamese, and Japanese groups as to the Mafia. Three years later, it was clear that this broader version of organized crime was firmly entrenched on the national level, and that it included the Yakuza.

In its initial public hearing, held in November 1983, the President's commission devoted its agenda to the direction and scope of American organized crime, and Smith, Webster, and Drug Enforcement Administration chief Francis Mullen urged new strategies for dealing with its changing structure.

The second public hearing, in New York in March 1984, focused on money laundering, a requisite task of all organized crime groups in and out of the United States, including the Yakuza. Cash, according to commission director James Harmon, is the "life-support system without which organized crime cannot exist." The commission discovered that the money to be laundered for the $80 billion annual U.S. drug trade, for example, comes from all points of the compass—East Asia as well as Latin America—and many U.S. bankers have been only too willing to oblige organized crime.

Finally, in its third hearing, held on October 25, 1984, the commission gathered in New York to address the issue of Asian organized crime, and the Yakuza was to occupy one-third of the agenda. Certainly, the attention was justified. Verifiable police reports placed Yakuza from Roanoke, Virginia, to Arizona to Seattle. The Yakuza were highly involved in the Japanese tourist industry, were smuggling guns and pornography out of the country, allying themselves with American gangsters and gamblers, and laundering funds. They were, in short, getting well entrenched in America, and it was time to place them under closer scrutiny.

The first witness called before the President's commission appeared shrouded in a black robe and hood, looking somewhat like a *ninja*. He was led across the floor of the high-ceilinged, columned hall to a seat behind a screen that shielded him from the press and audience. Chief Counsel Harmon then revealed to the commission and audience that the man was an oyabun, or leader, in a major Japanese organized crime gang.

The twelve commission members present listened carefully as the witness described tattooing and yubitsume, or ritual finger-cutting, and provided a graphic recounting of how that painful act is accomplished. "The actual procedure is to take . . . what they in Japanese Yakuza call a little silver knife—on a table—and you pull it towards you and bend over and your body weight will snap your finger off. . . . The finger that is severed is put in a small bottle with alcohol and your name is written on it and it is sent to whoever you're repenting to as a sign that you are sorry."

The nameless oyabun also elaborated on the organizational charts of the Yamaguchi-gumi and Sumiyoshi-rengo that the commission had provided, and explained how the Yakuza are active in his own specialty, economic crime. Gangsters in Japan, he told the panel, try to find companies in financial trouble, and engage in a number of schemes to take them over. Through bogus notes and threats to company officials and creditors, they would assume control of the ailing business, sell off the assets, and profit from the failure.

This Yakuza had personally run high-stakes card games two or three times a month in Japan. Because of his status, he retained 40 percent of the profits, which amounted to from $40,000 to $60,000. After expenses, he realized about $16,000 per game. Money, though, had to be passed up to the very highest echelons: Yakuza leaders maintained control through money, and lower members rose by passing it on. Nonetheless, said the witness, "I would say that I lived a very good life, probably equivalent to the presidency of a company employing three hundred to five hundred people."

Later in the day, another hooded witness made an appearance. Also a Japanese national, this anonymous informant had been a U.S. resident for ten years, and he described Yakuza activity in New York. Card games, with stakes in the many thousands of dollars, were being run by a combination of Yakuza, Yakuza associates, and Italian-American hoodlums. The customers were both Japanese nationals and Japanese-Americans. He believed that the Italians, who wore guns and sold stolen goods at the games, were actually in charge of the action.

Less dramatic than the hooded witnesses, perhaps, but equally revealing was the testimony of three American policemen, all knowledgeable in the workings of the Yakuza in the U.S.: Inspector John McKenna of the San Francisco Police Department; Detective George Min of the Los Angeles Police Department; and Bernard Ching of the Honolulu Police Department. The three intelligence cops described in brief how the Yakuza were gaining crucial footholds in their respective communities.

Bernard Ching described the Hawaiian Yakuza scene in much the same terms he had used to reporters nearly three years earlier: gun smuggling, prostitution, pornography, extortion, and drugs. What was new to some observers, however, was the admission that Yakuza activity was not confined to the islands. Detective Min of Los Angeles presented an impressive list of Yakuza activities in the large Japanese communities of southern California. "I have seen many crimes instituted by the Yakuza," he told the panel. "We have cases of homicide, prison escape, gun smuggling, money laundering...." Inspector McKenna, for his part, added that the SFPD had identified members of the Sumiyoshi-rengo in the San Francisco area. He believed that a pattern of intimidation and extortion existed within the Japanese business community.

None of the testimony by police, and little by the witnesses—except the finger-cutting and other exotic Japanese customs—was particularly startling crime news. Activities from money laundering to murder are, of course, the basic stuff of organized crime. No, the news was that it was Japanese, and it was occurring both in Japan and in the United States, and it contradicted popularly held beliefs. The public, to the extent that they thought about it at all, believed that the Japanese had virtually no crime problem, and that Japanese-Americans were the most law-abiding of citizens. Now, the issue of Yakuza coming to America would stir up some ugly ghosts from the past. . .

The Cotton Connection

Early in the 1930s, some Japanese in America were drawn to the narcotics trade for the simple reason that the Japanese Empire, in its conquest of East Asia, had acquired much of the opium, morphine, and heroin business there. Connections between the drug distributors in Asia and America were logical and fairly easily made.

Harry J. Anslinger, the crusading chief of the U.S. Bureau of Narcotics for much of its existence, commented that in the pre [-World War II] years, "We would not be far short of the mark if we said that ninety percent of all the illicit 'white drugs' of the world are of Japanese origin, manufactured in the Japanese Concession of Tientsin, around Tientsin, in and around Dairen, or in other cities of Manchuria, Jehol, and occupied China, and this always . . . under Japanese supervision." Unfortunately, a good deal of prewar propaganda colored evaluations of Japanese criminal activity, but even if Anslinger exaggerated by two or three times the percentage of Japanese-manufactured narcotics, that still left a lot of white drugs. And some of them found their way into the United States.

The Bureau of Narcotics began to notice Japanese morphine, called "cotton morphine" because of its appearance, as early as 1932, just one year after the Japanese takeover of Manchuria. The following year, the grave concern voiced by the bureau began to show signs of justification, although the quantities seized were still rather small. Japanese were arrested with cotton morphine in Tacoma, Washington; Portland, Oregon; and Hawaii. All the arrests involved Japanese residents of America. In Portland, four tins seized in a February 24, 1933, raid bore the label "Japan Pharmaceutical Establishment" and contained morphine hydrochloride. The other arrests involved a similar type of morphine.

For the next five or six years, there were numerous arrests of Japanese passengers and crew members of steamships, most sailing under Japanese flags. They brought in morphine, heroin, and sometimes even cocaine, a drug obviously made not in Tientsin, but in South America. There were also functioning American distribution networks, headed by Japanese.

In April of 1935, California authorities arrested Fujiyuki Motomura, a major San Pedro drug trafficker, with over $5000 worth of cocaine and morphine, about 10 pounds in those days. Police believed that Motomura was tied to an additional 50 pounds of drugs found elsewhere in southern California. The following year, California authorities again made a major arrest when state narcotics police in Los Angeles arrested Toshiyoshi Nagai for attempting to sell 5 pounds of morphine to undercover officers. Nagai told the prospective buyers that his brother owned a morphine factory in Japan and that he, Toshiyoshi, could supply any amount the buyers wanted. The smugglers were apparently using a number of routes, most of them successful; in 1938, the American representative at the Geneva drug conference told the assembled officials that 650 kilos of heroin from Japan had been captured by American agents on the West Coast. Using the usual law enforcement formula of ten to one—for every pound or kilo seized, police assume that ten get through—the Japanese may have accounted for some 6500 kilos of heroin in the period described.

In addition to their own operations, the Japanese were responsible for supplying huge amounts of heroin to the biggest drug rings in the United States. These gangs at the time were under the control of Jewish and Italian gangsters, operating all over the country. In San Francisco, for instance, mobster Mario Balestreri, successor to the mob run by "Black Tony" Parmagini, decided to increase his take and buy directly from the producers. He sent his men to purchase from Japanese dealers in Kobe, Japan, and Shanghai, China, then in Japanese hands.

In 1939, police discovered that two of Louis "Lepke" Buchalter's lieutenants, Yanis Tsounias and George Mexis, had fled to the Japanese Concession at Tientsin and set up a heroin operation. The two were shipping enough to the United States to supply 10,000 addicts for a year, according to the Bureau of Narcotics.

The Japanese connection, of course, ceased to operate in the United States after December 7, 1941. Japanese and Korean drug dealers continued to work in the occupied territories of Asia, and a substantial body of evidence indicates that the Japanese were responsible for spreading, or at least maintaining, a very high level of narcotic addiction, particularly among the Chinese.

The Japanese also had their hand in gambling in the United States, although here it was controlled by resident Japanese for the most part.

By 1910 there were over 70,000 people of Japanese descent in the United States, with at least a third of those living in and around Los Angeles. The center of Japanese activity in the United States was in the downtown L.A. community of Little Tokyo. And controlling all the gambling, as well as other aspects of the community, was the Tokyo Club, situated atop a three-story building at Jackson Street and Central Avenue.

Although it was based in Los Angeles, the Tokyo Club had branches—or more correctly, franchises—all over the West, from Seattle to the Mexican border. The bulk of the operation was in California, with eight Tokyo Clubs in the Central Valley alone. It was a very successful operation. In the 1920s, it counted a profit of more than $1 million a year, a considerable sum in those days. Because it held the biggest accumulation of capital in the Japanese community, the Tokyo club functioned as a bank as well. It also supported sports teams and lined the pockets of police and city officials.

The men who ran the Tokyo Club were businessmen-gangsters. Recalls Howard M. Imazeki, the retired editor of the San Francisco Japanese-American daily *Hokubei Mainichi*, "We didn't call them Yakuza then, but now I think that's probably what they were." Power struggles frequently occurred within the club, sometimes erupting into gunfire. Wrote criminologist Isami Waugh, "In the case of insubordination and disobedience Club President Itatani was severe in meting out the penalty: he sent his gang of powerful burly men to take care of these rebels in the Chicago gangland manner. . . In two or three extreme cases, so the grapevine reported, men were actually murdered and their bodies were disposed of so well that even the police detection failed."

The gangsters who ran the Tokyo Club and the drug smuggling rings were interned along with the rest of the Japanese population early in 1942. Like the Yakuza in Japan, many of them appeared to harbor ultranationalist sentiments. Openly rightist Japanese in the camps were sent to a special section at the camp in Tule Lake, California, and many of these were repatriated to Japan after the war. There have been no follow-up studies on the Tokyo Club leaders, but it's more than possible that many of them returned to their ancestral land. In any case, after the Tokyo Club closed its doors in 1941, it never reopened.

With the criminal leadership gone, and the post-internment community far too traumatized to engage in open lawlessness, organized crime in the postwar Japanese community was at a virtual standstill. Study after study reported a phenomenally low arrest rate among Americans of Japanese ancestry through the 1950s and 1960s. Gambling did not disappear, of course, and the Japanese were part of the poker clubs that made their appearance in the Los Angeles suburb of Gardena, but these were legalized operations. It was, according to Los Angeles police, not until the late 1960s that Japanese-Hawaiian gamblers drifted over from the islands and began to set up illegal bookmaking operations.

Southern California Yakuza

Los Angeles today has a lot to attract the Yakuza. Beside the climate, the money, and the glamour, Los Angeles has the largest Japanese community on the mainland. All told, over 200,000 people of Japanese descent reside in the L.A. area. More than 99 percent of these have no connection with the underworld, but a growing number of Yakuza have slipped into the Japanese community here, and some are doing quite well.

One of them, Tetsuo "Leo" Orii, runs the club Niji, a modern-day successor to the Tokyo Club. A hostess bar that offers an assortment of barely dressed Asian and [Western] women as companions, Niji caters mostly to businessmen from Japan. Orii has been involved in various business ventures in and around Los Angeles, and at least one police intelligence report called him "the most influential figure of the Japanese organized crime faction" in the city.

Orii is quite open and respectful of his links with the Yakuza. "I've entertained the oyabun of Sumiyoshi when they come here," he boasts. "We are brothers of the same family. When the chief of Sumiyoshi came to the U.S., he stayed at my house. They come to my bar."

Orii says he joined the Yakuza at age sixteen, and spent the next ten years fighting his way through prison and the tough Sumiyoshi-rengo gangs that dominate much of Tokyo. He made a name for himself by extorting money out of college kids in Tokyo's busy Ginza district. But, he says, after a decade with the Yakuza, he'd had enough. "The only way out was to leave Japan, but I'm still in. They won't let you out."

So, young Tetsuo arrived in America, went into legitimate business, and claims he kept up his unbreakable link with the Yakuza only by putting up oyabun at his Pacific Palisades home. Even if he wanted to, he says, he could not be a real Yakuza in America. He admits there is some Yakuza activity in Hawaii, but not on the mainland. "Yakuza are not into California because it's not profitable," he argues. "They can make twice as much money in Japan. They can't speak English very well, so they go where the Japanese are."

The problem, maintains Orii, is the police. The LAPD's Asian Task Force, he says, picks on him because "they need to show a reason for their existence." Most gangsters, of course, like to claim that they are simply honest citizens who just happen to have a few shady associates. Orii, however, got caught. In 1975 he and his partner, Tomonao Miyashiro, a.k.a. Tony Kawada, were arrested and convicted of shaking down a Japanese businessman. LAPD brought charges of conspiracy, extortion, kidnapping, and assault with a deadly weapon against Miyashiro, who tried to shoot the victim. Orii, apparently not present at the shooting, was charged only with attempted extortion.

Orii is only one individual in a rather large, fluid group of Yakuza-connected Japanese in the Los Angeles area. Members of this group allegedly engage in racketeering and investment scams. Names appear and reappear on various watch lines, but there have been few arrests.

It has remained for police intelligence to piece together what the Yakuza are up to. The most definitive statement comes from BOCCI, an arm of the California Department of Justice. In its 1981 annual report, BOCCI assessed the Yakuza:

> Law enforcement authorities have noted during the past several years that a number of Japanese organized crime members have immigrated from Japan and are now residing in the San Francisco and Los Angeles areas. There are approximately 50 gang members and associates now living in California.
>
> Law enforcement sources indicate that Japanese organized crime groups are operating tour agencies, Japanese gift shops and night clubs. Their criminal activities include extortion of Japanese businesses, harassment of Japanese tourists, prostitution, gun and pornography smuggling, narcotics distribution and laundering money.

For deeply held cultural reasons, and because they are strangers in the United States, Japanese nationals here are extremely reluctant to talk with American police about their troubles with the gangsters. Victims of Yakuza shakedowns will most likely just suffer the loss and try to forget it. One group in Los Angeles that has tried hard to break through this barrier is the LAPD's Asian Task Force. Criticized by some as a public relations outfit, the Task Force has indeed put a lot of effort into simply maintaining a presence in the various Asian communities in Los Angeles, including the Japanese. One problem in dealing with the Yakuza is that they have yet to cause as much trouble as America's Chinese or Vietnamese gangs, and therefore do not lead police to spend the time or money to pursue them.

Nonetheless, as the exploits of Orii's partner, Miyashiro, demonstrated, the Yakuza in California are not necessarily delicate in their tactics. A pair of unsolved crimes, reminiscent of the Tokyo club killings of fifty years earlier, is evidence that the Yakuza have to be taken seriously. Two Asian male bodies found in remote parts of southern California, one in a shallow grave near Oxnard on the coast north of L.A., and a second found near Castaic Lake in the Angeles National Forest, pointed strongly to Yakuza skulduggery. "We never could identify the bodies," said LAPD Detective George Min, "but one was heavily tattooed, and the other was also believed to be Yakuza."

In February of 1984, a Japanese murder victim was positively identified by police and was also believed to be the victim of Yakuza violence. Hiroshi Eto, reportedly running from massive gambling debts in Japan, had been found strangled in his room at the Los Angeles Hilton. A Japanese newspaper reported that Eto, a "dating club" operator, had heavily insured his life with an American carrier prior to his leaving Tokyo. Upon Eto's death, a Taiwanese male stood to collect about $315,000 in yen in what is by now a standard, and gruesome, Yakuza method of collecting back debts. Some Yakuza in L.A. apparently make their living as hit men for this and similar tasks.

Beyond the shakedowns and outright murders, the Yakuza's principal activity in southern California is money laundering, a very difficult operation for police to detect. Here, as in Hawaii and elsewhere, the easiest, most efficient money laundry is a high-volume cash business, such as a bar, restaurant, or gift shop. But the Yakuza are also investing in noncash businesses in the Los Angeles area, according to Detective George Min. As in Japan, construction companies are a favorite of the gangs, and the LAPD has kept watch over a number of Japanese-owned firms. As officials in Hawaii noted, though, law enforcement can trace money back to Japan and run into a stone wall. "Japanese bankers," said one Honolulu official, "are like Swiss bankers. They reveal nothing." . . .

The West Coast Sex Trade

Although Japanese newsweeklies frequently feature nude photos of young women, hard-core pornography is outlawed in Japan. The demand is filled, then, from overseas countries, including the United States. Similarly, live women are imported from the United States to Japan, either with their consent or, as often, through subterfuge and trickery. The so-called white slave trade from the United States isn't comparable to trade in women that exists between Thailand or the Philippines and Japan, but it exists and shows no sign of abating. The reason is simple: novelty.

Tokyo-based journalist Jean Sather, in her investigation of the problem, found that American women hold a special attraction for Japanese men. . . .

. . . The Yakuza, naturally, are only too willing to attempt to cash in on the market, but they have a problem: few Yakuza speak English well enough to entice women to come to Japan. They have, therefore, tended to operate through fronts or paid agents on the West Coast. According to various police reports, these agents usually obtain women by placing ads for singers and dancers in the entertainment press, publications such as L.A.'s *Drama-logue* and *Music Connection*. These have listings for "cattle-call" drama auditions, as well as for seamier performances, such as nude modeling and porno pictures. The ads by talent agents are designed to appeal to the starving actress or singer.

What happens to the women in Japan varies, but not much. Instead of straight jobs as singers or dancers, the women are expected to add tasks ranging from "hostessing" in bars to outright prostitution. As *Playgirl* magazine reported, "One American woman told of a club where she was forced to dance nude with half a dozen other women until a mob of audience members swarmed onto the stage and molested the performers. Another described a club where dildos were thrown out randomly to the audience for use on the performers."

Often, no matter what the duties of the woman, she will either not be paid, or be paid far less than she was promised, so that escape from Japan—and even escape from the employer—becomes nearly impossible. One American woman recruited from Los Angeles told her story to the *Japan Times* just hours before she fled Japan. Her stay included two attempted rapes and violations of her contract. Her employer, one Kanji Chiba, "insisted that she relinquish her [return air] ticket for 'safekeeping,' which she did." Even when exploited, the women sometimes cooperate with their exploiters to an unnecessary degree. Said one: "A lot of the mistakes have been mine. You're naive, vulnerable, ambitious, you dream. That's what these people capitalize on—your dreams."

Women who return from what is often a hellish experience in the Yakuza clubs often seek revenge, but usually get little satisfaction. Few of the agents can be located, and the victims have little in the way of legal recourse against those few who can be found. American law holds that the agents must have knowingly sent the women to houses of prostitution, and this is difficult, if not impossible, to prove.

There have been a number of civil suits launched by women against the talent agents. Lisa Petrides of Berkeley, California, answered an ad in the *San Francisco Chronicle* for entertainers. Petrides, who aspired to be a singer, went to an agency in San Francisco for " a very professional audition," and wound up at the Little Club in Tokyo, where her Yakuza bosses insisted that she forget about singing and concentrate on hostessing. She called the agency from Japan, but her old agent refused to help her. When Petrides returned to California, she sued the agency and got a small out-of-court settlement. This agency is still in business.

Another victim of the talent ruse, Kristina Kirstin of Los Angeles, filed a $3.5 million lawsuit in May 1982. She named three defendants; her American agent, its counterpart in Japan, and Alexander Haig, then secretary of state. Haig was charged because Kirstin alleged that the U.S. Embassy in Japan refused to help her when she wished to flee Japan. The embassy, maintained Kirstin, was indifferent to her plight at the Mil Members Club in Kyoto, despite the fact that it was a known Yakuza operation. U.S. officials at the State Department had told her that, by law, she was on her own and they could do nothing.

Even if the State Department were to get actively involved, it is unlikely it could stop the racket. There is simply too much money at stake. Japanese men pay an enormous amount for . . . having sex with a [Western] woman, and the profits to be made are immense. Even in the somewhat tamer area of hostessing, the bars make out handsomely from the presence of [Western] women.

Trying to stem the trade at the American end appears likewise impossible. For one thing, although some victims have stepped forward, most do not. LAPD Detective Fred Clapp, a national expert on the vice trade, estimated that by 1982 the number of victims in the Los Angeles area alone had run into the hundreds. Clapp had, in fact, received over fifty reports from women who had been recruited and deceived through American talent scams, but expressed hopelessness over any attempt to end the trade. "The demand for Caucasian prostitutes," said Clapp, "is so great over there it can't be filled."

The Arming of Japan

When one thinks of the trade in precision machinery between the United States and Japan, the flow seems to be entirely toward the States. But there is one instrument that is entirely an export item from the United States to Japan. Thanks to a combination of high quality, great availability, and minimal legal encumbrances, American firearms are sought and acquired by the Japanese. The distributors, and in this case the customers, of the product are primarily the Yakuza. Americans have competition from various foreign producers, but the Yakuza's most popular second source—the Philippines—also sells a great many American-made weapons. The United States is, in effect, arming the Japanese underworld. . . .

The possibility of such [huge] profits exists largely because of the discrepancy between Japanese and American gun laws. For all practical purposes, guns aren't allowed in Japan, and they are freely permitted in the United States. This, in turn, creates a huge price differential. A pistol that sells legally for $250, a Smith & Wesson Chief's Special, for instance, will command up to ten times that amount in Japan. Ammunition frequently sells for $5 to $12 a bullet there.

For gun buyers, America is a wide-open gun supermarket with only slightly restrictive rules. As one West Coast official of the U.S. Bureau of Alcohol, Tobacco, and Firearms put it, "Most foreign police regard American gun laws as a joke." Japanese laws, however, are anything but a joke.

The idea of a civilian population with easy access to firearms flies in the face of a Japanese tradition that stretches back nearly four centuries. For 200 years, the Japanese conducted a remarkable social experiment by banning all firearms on the islands. It began in the early seventeenth century, largely as a reaction to the cold-bloodedness of combat with firearms, and as a gesture of commitment to the sword, an enduring symbol of honor and stature in Japan. It was also an expeditious way to maintain power in the central government.

As Noel Perrin details in his fascinating book *Giving Up the Gun*, Japan's gunsmiths were summoned to a single city in 1642, forced to work for a government monopoly, and slowly starved out of business. Japan's feudal rulers impounded massive numbers of firearms, and for the next 200 years the development of modern weaponry virtually stopped. When Commodore Perry arrived in 1853, his sailors wryly noted that the Japanese shore batteries defending Tokyo harbor could fit inside and be fired out of their ships' cannons.

A tradition of gun control survived the Industrial Revolution and even World War II. In 1958, the Diet enacted the Firearms and Swords Control Act, which had the effect of making Japan relatively free of handgun murders. In 1980, for instance, 48 people died from handgun wounds in Japan, compared to more than 10,000 in the United States. There are guns in private hands in Japan—881,204 as of 1981—but this official figure is misleading. It include antiques and construction guns (devices for punching holes in concrete) as well as hunting rifles and shotguns. There are virtually no legal handguns at all, except those used by military and police.

To help Japan with its "gun gap," enterprising Japanese have been moving thousands of handguns illegally into Japan in ever-increasing numbers. Guns smuggled into Japan do not go to collectors or to citizens interested in protecting their homes; they go to gangs. A 1981 National Police Agency report noted that 89.5 percent of all handguns seized came from "criminal syndicates." . . .

Americans have been involved in gun smuggling ever since the first days of the postwar firearms ban, and many of these Americans have been military personnel. This is hardly surprising, considering the approximately 48,000 personnel stationed at 118 facilities in Japan. Many of them are bored, lonely, and low on cash, and many have access to stores of American weapons.

The Yakuza have found it convenient to exploit the American military gun pipeline, while also cultivating members of the U.S. merchant marine for the same purposes. The point of contact, suggested a 1980 internal DEA report, is the off-base bars where GIs and others go for drugs, women, and drink. . . .

More recently, the majority of gun shipments to Japan have been handled by civilians rather than military people. Some of the smuggling methods show a great deal of ingenuity. Guns are taken from the United States into Japan in false-bottom bags, inside folk craft articles, in cassette players and travel irons, television cameras, and even inside pineapples, an item commonly carried by Japanese returning from Hawaii. Larger quantities require roomier conveyances, and in 1980 Japanese police discovered five pistols in the gas tank of a British Jensen arriving from the United States. American-built cars are used as well, and it is perhaps not coincidence that Yakuza oyabun are the principal purchasers of imported American cars. . . .

It is a dismal way to alleviate the foreign trade crisis: Japanese gangsters buying American handguns and hiring American entertainers and prostitutes. But the Yakuza, as recent events have shown, are not content simply to buy American. Like good businessmen everywhere, they are investors, and they have expanded activities here mainly because of a strong foothold in their favorite base of operations abroad—tourist trade.

The Tourist:
An Easy Mark

Along with oranges and sinsemilla [marijuana], Japanese tourists ought to be considered lucrative cash crops for the state of California. Some 463,000 Japanese visited the state in 1983, leaving behind hundreds of millions of dollars. Yet most of this booming Japanese tourist industry is a closed system. Tourists typically fly in aboard Japan Air Lines, stay at Japanese-owned hotels, eat in Japanese restaurants, shop at Japanese-owned boutiques, ride about in Japanese tour buses, and patronize Japanese purveyors of drink, guns, and vice. Police suspect Yakuza involvement in a good deal of the racket. In a 1981 report, state investigators noted that the gangs had apparently launched a drive "to dominate the Japanese tourism industry in San Francisco and Los Angeles." The report described a common pattern of accosting cash-laden Japanese tourists and, through deception or intimidation, forcing them to participate in selected tours. . . .

. . . Stuart Eugene "Steve" Conn [is a] . . . fifty-year-old businessman [and] as unlikely an opponent as the Yakuza are apt to find, but Conn has taken on the entire Japanese tour industry. In July 1984, the pugnacious Conn was found by police near . . . Japan Town with bullet holes in his leg and shoulder. From his bed in San Francisco General Hospital, Conn claimed to any who would listen that his assailants were Yakuza.

Police were not entirely convinced. . . . Some thought Conn was attacked by someone with a debt to pay or a grudge to settle. Regardless, the roots of his troubles come from the fact that he decided to compete with the Japanese for some of the tourist yen. Declared Conn angrily, "I'm just trying to make a buck the way our Constitution says I can."

So, Conn opened a gift shop in San Francisco near the downtown area and began selling boutique items. The store—sometimes known as Nikkaido (Upstairs) and sometimes as Sakura (Cherry Blossom)— offered designer clothing and accessories, real and counterfeit. A specialty was Western wear, which for a time the Japanese loved. And, in a separate room in the back, there was a huge selection of pornographic magazines, films, videotapes, and plastic paraphernalia. The operation was typical of Japanese tourist traps up and down the West Coast. . . .

With the apparent enmity of the Japanese tour operators working against him, Conn began to lose money on the store. Suddenly, a savior appeared. Through intermediaries, Conn was introduced to a wealthy and influential Japanese who, he was told, would back the store and put in a word with Japan Air Lines and other tour operators. Conn had never heard the name of his backer before, but was advised it was well known in Japan: Sasakawa. The same Sasakawa with the billions of dollars, the speedboat racing monopoly, the rightist organizations, and the Yakuza ties.

Sasakawa, acting through his son, Takashi, did put some money into the store, but just enough, apparently, to fulfill the terms of his agreement. Conn continued to lose business; he had trouble replenishing his stock and the tour operators failed to come through. Eventually Steve Conn went out of business, complaining to an uncomprehending press that he was the victim of a conspiracy.

Who was responsible for Steve Conn's near-murder? The case was never solved. But clearly, there is a very large amount of money involved in Japanese tourist scams in the West, and no individual or group making that kind of money is about to give it away. If Steve Conn wasn't put out of commission by the Yakuza, his case is a good lesson for anyone with aspirations to muscle in on such a lucrative racket.

The Wrong Side of Japanese Business

While there is no record of eminent rightist Ryoichi Sasakawa ever wanting to own another overpriced, failing gift store, he did lose an immense amount of money in another tourist-related scheme 3000 miles from San Francisco. It was a business deal that called attention to Sasakawa's Yakuza ties in Japan, and that made American law enforcement sit up and take notice.

In 1978, Takashi Sasakawa, Ryoichi's second son, publicly joined with well-known Japanese restauranteur, speedboat racer, and balloonist Hiroaki "Rocky" Aoki to announce plans to lease the aging Shelburne Hotel in Atlantic City and turn it into a casino. The gambling boom was hitting the East Coast, and Sasakawa, for one, wanted to be in on it. Aoki, owner of the famed Benihana chain, felt that a touch of Japan would add some exoticism to the Jersey Shore.

The actual deal was a hopelessly complicated affair involving several paper corporations in both America and Japan, and several hundred million dollars. Of this, Takashi openly owned 47 percent of the enterprise, although no knowledgeable observer believed Takashi was the real investor. His New York attorney asserted to the press that Takashi's father was "far removed from the deal," but few were convinced.

Within months, the U.S. Securities and Exchange Commission charged Takashi Sasakawa and Aoki with insider stock trading. The two men had purchased 60,000 shares of the Hardwicke Company, knowing that they would later engage that company to manage the planned Shelburne Benihana. This move inflated the value of the stock, a patently illegal move. Sasakawa was forced to make restitution to the sellers of the original Hardwicke stock.

The Sasakawas were reportedly quite taken aback with this wrinkle. Ryoichi was used to manipulating stock values for his own profiteering without a peep from the Japanese government. Following that unpleasantness, Sasakawa continued to pump money into the Shelburne project, but without his previous enthusiasm. There were indications that the casino would not fly, and not only because the Securities and Exchange Commission was on his tail. Sasakawa's seedy background had caught up with him. Because of Sasakawa's dossier, American banks refused to "anchor" the project with domestic loans, and New Jersey law enforcement let it be known that any project with the Sasakawa name on it would have a hard time getting a casino license. If New Jersey wanted to keep mob-connected Americans out of Atlantic City, it could hardly open the door to Yakuza-connected Japanese.

Sasakawa's interest in Atlantic City made a good deal of sense, and he brought to it plenty of expertise. The boat-racing czar already knew the gambling business from the ground—or the water—up, and could run large-scale betting operations as well as anyone. Some law enforcement people worried that, had it succeeded, it could have served as the biggest Japanese-owned laundry in the United States, which is why they helped scuttle the deal. When the Sasakawas, Aoki, and the silent partners bailed out—selling their interest to a Philadelphia real estate developer in 1981—they had lost an estimated $27 million. The aging rightist had become quite used to leaving large bundles in the United States, but it must have galled him to involuntarily drop a sum of this magnitude.

Undaunted, in February of 1983, Ryoichi arrived in San Francisco to receive the Linus Pauling Medal for Humanitarianism for his generous donation of $770,000 to the Linus Pauling Institute of Science and Medicine. The man who once called himself "the world's wealthiest fascist" was now out to become the world's greatest philanthropist.

Sasakawa's efforts at self-aggrandizement are boggling. Prior to the black-tie dinner given by the Pauling Institute, he held a luncheon at San Francisco's posh Bohemian Club—which is anything but—and spent the morning giving interviews to the local media. At the luncheon, Sasakawa received the guests bobbing like a buoy in a rough sea and smiling continuously. His publicist, flown out from the giant New York firm of Doremus, told the assembled that Sasakawa was, among other things, a patriot, a man unashamed to love his country and his mother. In fact, Sasakawa erected a statue in Japan of himself carrying his aged mother on his back, but the object of his veneration was less the mother than the bearer.

He also denounces, as he did in San Francisco, accusations of his ultranationalist past and war profiteering as Communist inspired, secure in the knowledge that he has outlived most eyewitnesses. When the authors pointed out to him that U.S. Army documents were quite explicit about his plundering in China, he proclaimed, "I have not exploited one yen or one penny. What I did was to donate several million tuberculosis injections to China." He was equally imaginative in denying any relations with the Yakuza, conveniently forgetting that he had publicly boasted of including the late Yamaguchi boss Kazuo Taoka among his drinking companions.

In spite of Sasakawa's indifferent results in cleaning up Japanese history and his place in it, the grand old kuromaku continues to make a name for himself as a philanthropist and promoter. He has funneled millions through his Japan Shipbuilding Industry Foundation to charities throughout the world. He is the largest private donor to the United Nations and has funded international health centers, Ivy League universities, and even the presidential library of Jimmy Carter, who praised his "good work for peace." As an industrial promoter he has had less success, spending millions in a vain attempt to introduce the Shinkansen, the Bullet Train, to southern California.

Sasakawa's most ambitious giveaway in America is the U.S.-Japan Foundation, headquartered in New York and begun in 1980 with a generous $48 million endowment from Sasakawa. To orchestrate its efforts, the foundation chose as its staff president Richard W. Petree, former political section chief at the U.S. Embassy in Tokyo, and a man accused in the Diet of being an active CIA official. . . . The foundation's original "American Working Group" included such luminaries as Henry Kissinger; Chairman Angier Biddle Duke, former ambassador to four countries and heir to a tobacco fortune; James A. Linen, former president of Time, Inc.; former RCA chairman Robert Sarnoff; and former New York mayor John Lindsay.

The expressed goal of the U.S.-Japan Foundation is to enhance, through grants and education, cooperation between the two countries, primarily of an economic nature. But there is another, more covert goal, and that is to raise the value of Sasakawa's personal stock among the movers and shakers. According to Rocky Aoki, Sasakawa's former business partner, the old ultranationalist is angling for the Nobel Peace Prize, and it appears he is willing to spend almost any amount of money to get it. He has even set up an office in Oslo, Norway, in order to better lobby the Nobel Committee, and in 1985 he was actually nominated for a prize.

Despite all his do-gooding and donating, Sasakawa remains a gambling czar with strong ties to the extreme right in Japan, and with less overt but definite ties to the Yakuza. . . .

Sasakawa is not the only questionable financial figure in the United States to arrive from Japan. An equally worrisome development has evolved in the form of major sokaiya groups [thugs who specialize in disrupting the stock market] arriving at America's doorstep. Sasakawa's clumsy casino attempts and showy humanitarian gestures are easy to see through; the tactics of the sokaiya are considerably more opaque.

On April 21, 1982, the manager of the powerful sokaiya group Rondan Doyukai, a gentleman named Shigeru Kobayashi, attended a stockholders' meeting at the Chase Manhattan bank in New York. Kobayashi sat through Chairman David Rockefeller's opening remarks, and forty minutes of questioning from the floor—undoubtedly fighting the urge to silence the dissenters—and then turned and addressed the crowd. Said Kobayashi: "We represent your stockholders from Japan. I am happy to be here at your general meeting. Now I have the honor of seeing Chairman Rockefeller. . . . He is a great man because he met with His Majesty the Emperor when he visited Japan a couple of years ago, and very few people in Japan can shake hands with the Emperor. I would also like to express my sincere appreciation for your high dividends."

Kobayashi's statement probably amused those stockholders present, but some were also puzzled. Why should Rondon Doyukai send one of its top people to New York merely to flatter the company? Kobayashi later told a Japanese newspaper: "We rode into New York to show them what Japanese sokaiya are. But, just before the meeting, the *Wall Street Journal* carried a sensational article with banner headline saying, 'The Sokaiya are coming, the Sokaiya are coming,' as if the Japanese gangsters were invading the U.S. This raised a stink. We know that the public peace is bad in New York, so we thought we might be eliminated by the Mafia."

Kobayashi somehow avoided a trip to the bottom of the East River, but he needn't have worried in the first place. Nearly six years earlier, in equally violent Los Angeles, another sokaiya group made its appearance. In 1976, according to police sources, fifty Japanese executives filed into one of the ballrooms of the Biltmore Hotel in downtown L.A. They were the top-ranking officers of the largest Japanese corporations operating on the West Coast, and they had come to pay their respects to a group of visiting sokaiya (who had neglected to announce their presence to the press). Police at the same time observed sokaiya Masato Yoshioka making a tour of Los Angeles to present himself at Japanese-owned banks, conglomerates, and securities investment firms, possibly to hit any companies missed at the Biltmore meetings. Although the businesses were reluctant to talk about the incident, information revealed to law enforcement agents that, as in Japan, it was cheaper to pay up than to risk the consequences.

Rondon Doyukai also had made earlier trips to America. They had sent representatives to the 1981 annual meeting of the Bank of America in San Francisco. They were, in the words of corporate secretary John Fauvre, "polite but insistent." The group approached the microphone, said Fauvre, with their own photographer and translator, and introduced themselves with lengthy formality. The sokaiya then did little more than wish the bank good luck, much as Kobayashi would do to Chase Manhattan a year later.

Rondan Doyukai, Japan's largest sokaiya group, has faced the 1982 Japanese crackdown by diversifying. This group, most of whose members all attended one high school in Hiroshima, has invested $232,000 to gain shareholder status in a strategic handful of American and European companies, according to the *Wall Street Journal* report that so terrified Kobayashi. Among those targeted besides Chase and Bank of America were General Motors, IBM, and Dow Chemical.

Other sokaiya operations are underway. Los Angeles and New York City police have discovered that sokaiya-type scandal sheets are being used to extort money from Japanese corporations, and it appears that the sokaiya remain a threat to American branches of Japanese companies, particularly the smaller ones. But it also looms that as Japanese investment capital pours into the United States, and American firms do more and more business with Japanese corporations, American-owned companies, too, may have to deal with the extortion that accompanies so much of Japanese capitalism. It may be subtle at first, but the remarkably versatile and wily sokaiya will surely find a growing international niche within the $85 billion worth of business done annually between the two nations. . . .

PART
III

VIOLENCE

*Stability in the marketplace may be the strongest motive
for controlling individual behavior with violence.*

Smith (1995, p. 18)

In past studies of OC, violence was the element that attracted the greatest attention. Extremes of violence have been seen as a natural part of OC for several reasons. The ability to inflict costly punishments is believed to be an effective form of controlling behavior. Costly punishments in OC may take many forms, but threats and attacks are the most basic. Extortion and protection rackets were some of the earliest forms of OC. As illicit enterprise comes to resemble legitimate business, the threat of physical attack becomes less effective than economic threats and may become outdated. However, that is not to say that OC may become less violent. Costly punishments inflicted by rational organizations may be economic in nature, but to victims, the threat remains to their well-being and livelihoods.

OC is essentially a monopolistic enterprise with the aim of control over the market for whatever illicit goods or services they have for sale. Competition leads to violence as a last resort in a group's drive for control. Violence is also a means of self-protection against the state. Gangsters may view themselves as being at war with the agents of control. Deaths on both sides are inevitable in a war. Violence becomes necessary in illicit markets where there is no state authority (Gambetta, 1995). It may be the gang's only option to protect itself from infiltration or attacks from forces outside the group.

Another form of necessary violence that is prevalent in OC is violence within the group. It is commonly held that internal OC violence is used for two primary purposes. Threats are necessary to enforce the security of the group. Secrecy must be made mandatory, and threats to the integrity of the group must be dealt with severely. To avoid the threat of rebellion, following rules and obeying higher-ups must also be a matter of life and death. Loyalty is essential; failure to live up to the standards of the gang cannot be ignored. For a gang's rules to be effective, they must be enforced, and punishment for disobedience must be swift and severe. Gangsters may have to prove themselves by committing violence as part of their initiation into the group. Violence may also be used within the group to control competition from the outside, including efforts to recruit members from one gang to another (Schlegel, 1987).

The many functions of violence in OC might lead observers to describe it as instrumental: that is, goal-directed violence used as an instrument to reach some organizational end. Violence might be seen as no more than a means. However, there is another role for violence in OC. Expressive violence has no goal but is perpetrated for its own sake. Expressive violence is passionate and personal and comes out of extremes of emotion, such as rage or frustration. Fear is also behind some expressive violence. Following the outburst of violence, the aggressor may temporarily feel relief and release. Although expressive violence may serve no stated purpose of the organization, the emotional ends that it serves for some gangsters may make it frequent or even likely in the insular world of OC. One type of expressive violence may actually serve a purpose for the gang as well as for the gangster. When potential members perpetrate violence to build a reputation and create an identity, these acts may be fulfilling and satisfying personally and may serve the goals of the gang at the same time (Zimbardo, 1985).

DISCUSSION:
The Medellín Cartel

The record of violence achieved by the Medellín cartel in Colombia has never been matched by another OC group. In 1989, at least 63 people were killed by a bomb planted in front of the Colombian Department of Administrative Security. A national airline flight was blown up in mid-flight. More than 30 judges were killed by the cartel in the late 1980s. From 1984 to 1989, the cartel's victims included a minister of justice, supreme court judges, a state police chief, and the leading candidate for president, in addition to thousands of police officers and bystanders. From 1989 to 1990, the cartel declared all-out war against the government, the industrial-political oligarchy, unfriendly journalists, magistrates who enforced laws against drug dealers, and others who had persecuted them in the past. The total war included broadly based attacks on citizens (Lee, 1995). Violence was the cartel's first line of defense to protect trafficking operations from antidrug efforts. Violence undermined national enforcement policies and demoralized the government. The cartel had the wealth and power to challenge the stability of the entire country (Goodson & Olson, 1995).

During the 1990s, Colombia became a "narcodemocracy" (Kerry, 1997). Having built up over more than a decade, the Medellín cartel incorporated the most modern forms of air transport and state-of-the-art communications networks. Enforcement authorities referred to the group as an octopus, and also a hydra, because it was relatively decentralized and amorphous. Key figures were traditionally close relatives, childhood friends, or neighbors. When one member was lost, another was ready to take his place immediately. Studies in Canada found the cartel to be a number of unique organizations, each headed by one distinct trafficker, rather than a large cohesive structure. Understandings worked out with other traffickers simply reduced the cost and the risk of doing business (CISC, 1996). The looseness of the structure made the organization difficult to infiltrate and flexible enough to meet moment-to-moment changes in the cocaine market.

The Medellín gangsters usually lived in fortresslike homes in Colombia and had well-equipped private armies and international connections. Considering the strength of the drug barons, it was logical that terrorists would make alliances with them that would provide revenues and access to weapons. For the cartel, terrorists provided additional small armies for protection, reduced security risks, and a combined force with which to attack the government. The result was called narcoterrorism.

The Medellín drug traffickers became too powerful, too conspicuous, and too greedy. They were involved in politics, sports, public works, and displays of wealth. At the same time, a second group of drug traffickers was gaining control in Colombia. This group, with headquarters in Cali, Colombia, kept a much lower profile and was more intertwined with the existing political and social system within the country. The Cali group included a number of powerful political families, and the level of corruption that spread in their wake reached all the way to the presidency. The evolution of the two groups made the Medellín group all the more visible and an easier target. The Medellín cartel was set upon by government forces with the aid of U.S. technology in the early 1990s. Meanwhile, the lower-profile group in Cali remained relatively intact with substantial influence.

The impact of the drug trade on the country of Colombia has been profound. Considering that the drug sector kept the internal economy in a steady flow of capital, it contributed to the underpinning of the nation's economy. Labor shortages in the agricultural sector resulted from pickers and workers earning better money working with coca and marijuana production. Many of the remote areas invaded by drug traffickers were the homelands for indigenous groups whose ways of life were disrupted and whose homes were displaced. The inflow of capital caused major imbalances in the Colombian financial sector and disturbed the banking system in particular. Black-market dollars, poor loan portfolios, false documentation, huge withdrawals, and other instabilities led to the collapse of a number of financial institutions, a difficult adjustment, and rising inflation. Land values were driven up, and low-cost housing was next to impossible to find (MacDonald, 1988).

The Medellín cartel was an excellent example of multinational systemic crime. The organization was ongoing for more than a decade. The criminal organization stretched across national boundaries and around the globe. It was large, vertically integrated, and involved in the production, supply, and sale of cocaine. The organization included accountants, chemists, lawyers, officials, and enforcement authorities. The leaders of the cartels became major landowners. More than just a criminal enterprise, the cartels set up a veritable state within a state in Colombia.

Martin and Romano (1992) suggested that drug-related systemic violence such as that perpetrated by the Medellín cartel be identified as "drug-related megaviolence" (p. 63). The drug trade, insurgency, and terrorism, with the accompanying demand for illegal arms, all tend to be located in roughly the same areas of the world: Latin America, Southeast and southern Asia, and the Middle East. There is a symbiotic relationship between drugs, terrorism, and arms. In some nations, drug lords penetrate the power structure at all levels. Their influence is felt through the large influx of money they can channel into the political process (U.S. General Accounting Office, 1996). It is a problem shared by all nations of the world.

5

La Comuna Nororiental [The Northeastern Collective]

María Jimena Duzán

Chapter 12 (pp. 194-215) of *Death Beat: A Colombian Journalist's Life Inside the Cocaine War,* by María Jimena Duzán, translated and edited by Peter Eisner (New York: HarperCollins, 1994)

On the hillsides of Medellín, the slum barrios sprout up in a disorganized array, haphazardly devouring the slopes. Life is in constant peril. With periodic torrential rains, pieces of the mountainside sometimes break loose, and mud-slide avalanches can drag an entire neighborhood into the valley below.

One of the barrios perched on the mountainside is known as La Comuna Nororiental—The Northeastern Collective. Streets in La Comuna wind up the steep incline and disintegrate into a mesh of rocky trails and indecipherable labyrinths—a bazaar for drugs, arms trafficking, and assassins. The majority of the fifteen-odd murders committed every day in Medellín take place there too.

In these proletarian barrios over half the population is unemployed. Most of those who work are day laborers or do odd jobs; mothers earn their daily bread as servants in the grand mansions of El Poblado, the section of Medellín where the wealthiest live. But in the slums, nearly half of all high-school students do not graduate (compared with 35 percent in the rest of the city), and 60 percent of the people who live there are squatters who have no legal title to the houses they have built. Whereas statistics show that there are twenty-seven square feet of recreation land per person in Medellín, the figure for La Comuna Nororiental is about one square foot per person.

In these barrios the power of hard cash, the money from drug trafficking, has subverted all the codes of social behavior. Here the name Pablo—it can only mean Pablo Escobar—is spoken with admiration for the sports centers he built and the social programs he promoted, things few traditional politicians have done. In this place where few families include a father; where worshipers venerate the mother, the Virgin and guns; and where the people haphazardly migrated from the countryside to the city, the drug bosses found the raw material to commit their assassinations and other crimes.

This is the birthplace of the sicarios—"the children who kill." The sicarios were first used to settle accounts in the drug Mafia's vendettas, killing people who didn't meet payments or who failed to come through with a delivery. But when the drug traffickers increased their terrorist attacks on the state, the sicarios ended up killing judges, police, cabinet ministers, four presidential candidates, leftist leaders, unionists, and journalists. The sicarios started using violence to defend themselves with knives and switchblades against people who were more dangerous than they; now they are professional assassins, skilled in handling sophisticated arms. Many of them were trained by Israeli mercenaries from whom they learned to detonate car bombs and pressurized devices for airplanes.

There are slums in many cities; Medellín is not unique. Slums have grown and proliferated in concert with the disorganized development of Latin America's cities. They have various names, *favelas* in Rio de Janeiro and *pueblos jovenes* in Lima, but they are all the same. The slums of Medellín are not even the worst. On the contrary, for those with money and legal property titles, Medellín has one of the highest coverage rates for public services in Latin America and one of the highest rates of students obtaining a university education. The contrast between the landed and the slum dwellers is profound.

Furthermore, the problems of slums (or ghettos) and homelessness are also growing in the United States and other industrialized countries where the per capita income is much higher than in Colombia. No wonder. The same problems of drugs and violence are at the core of social inequality wherever there is poverty.

The sicarios of Medellín are the most recent product of the tremendous impact of drug trafficking in a society dominated by social inequality. They have "the opportunity to find in the violence and in the drug trafficking their dreams, to be protagonists in a society which has closed them out," said Alfonso Salazar, a writer based in Medellín.

From the time they are children, the sicarios use violence to show they have guts. The money and power they receive are a symbol of prestige. But few of them really make money. Just like the drug dealers who hang out on street corners in New York City, they'll never accumulate much wealth. They want to become legends, to be tough, to bring home money and presents for their girlfriends. . . .

Many foreigners first heard of Medellín and its cartel in the early 1980s. Their image of the city was that of some sort of untamed jungle outpost from which fiendish drug cartels processed and exported their wares. The hyperpopular television show "Miami Vice" played no small role in spreading the frightening image of the Colombian drug dealers throughout the world; although the show's characters were accurate for that small group, the program did wide and reckless damage to the reputation of the whole country.

Medellín is, in fact, the second largest city in the country, and was the first industrial center of Colombia long before the arrival of the drug traffickers. Far from being some backwater campground, it is a city of five million people. The proposal by then mayor of New York Ed Koch to bomb Medellín was like suggesting that in the 1920s everyone in Chicago was a bootlegger and that U.S. authorities could enforce Prohibition (and get Al Capone) by dropping bombs on the city.

In the barrios where the sicarios lived, a new generation of young leaders started working to improve conditions and to fight the image: "In the United States, they believe that just because you live in Medellín, you have to be a drug dealer. And in Colombia, when you say you live in La Comuna Nororiental, everybody thinks you have to be a sicario," one such leader told me. . . .

My sister, Sylvia, was always my best source on La Comuna Nororiental. The Colombian justice system had issued arrest warrants against the first band of sicarios, the Priscos, for the assassinations of Justice Minister Rodrigo Lara Bonilla, [Justice] Guillermo Cano, and Magistrate

Vaquero Borda, among others. As Sylvia had discovered, the Priscos were already a legend in La Comuna. On Children's Day, October 28—a celebration little known elsewhere in the world—they always held a party. Along with them came everyone else in the barrio, even the police. "For the best disguise, there was a tricycle for first prize; they handed out dollar bills as well. . . . People liked them, but they also feared them. They were generous, but always for the purpose of exercising control," Father Tobón, a priest who was responsible for forty-four parishes in La Comuna Nororiental, told my sister in an interview.

"They say that one of them committed suicide, but the truth is that one of his brothers killed him," Father Tobón said. The Priscos held a big fiesta when the attorney general was killed, complete with roast pig for all. People contended that they had nothing to do with the assassination of [popular Liberal party presidential cantidate] Galán because they were supposed to be Liberals themselves," Father Tobón added.

While I was immersed in investigating the first paramilitary militia groups financed by the drug traffickers (who found their raw material in these outcast neighborhoods), Sylvia, with a much more sociological bent, was reading everything she could about the psychology of gangs. She had gotten to know a couple of gangs in Bogotá and had managed to get into some areas where few other journalists had succeeded in penetrating. While I tried to find out when and how the foreign mercenaries were training the hit squads formed by the drug traffickers, she was finding out about how they dressed, what they talked about; which heavy-metal rock bands they liked; and how, to her surprise, they were fervent believers in God and the Virgin. Seeking funding for more research, she accepted an offer to work on a British documentary. It was this job that eventually led to her death. . . .

Among her notes, I found an interview that Sylvia had conducted with Alberto, the chief of one of the many bands of sicarios in La Comuna Nororiental of Medellín. What follows is, in effect, our last collaborative effort, published four years after her murder.

The Magníficos of Medellín

The video stores in La Comuna Nororiental are heavily stocked with episodes of "The A-Team." The sicarios rent them and watch them intently, over and over again. They point out and analyze the mistakes that are made and applaud the way Fass, Murdock and Barakus, under the command of Hannibal Smith, all living underground because of a crime they didn't commit, always manage to evade capture. For Alberto, they are perfect heroes. His gang has often been in tough straits on the verge of being caught by the law or by their enemies. They got the name the Magníficos from two girls who hang out with the gang. "We're going to find a name for you," they told the boys one day. "They came back and said they were going to call us the Magníficos and it stuck—from then on we were the Magníficos."

In Alberto's world, where the link between fiction and reality doesn't mean much, they forget that the violence of American movies is clean: bombs go off, but you don't see the dead people; guns are fired, but no one ever dies.

The Magníficos under Alberto began living off death by taking away the lives of other human beings.

He's always wearing expensive Reeboks. He loves to go trailbiking on expensive 500-cc motorcycles. Life is a succession of sudden instants, like a gunshot, a [soccer] goal. All that matters is the present. Live for the day. Alberto has no time to reflect; he just listens to Hector Laboe, a popular Puerto Rican salsa singer. He loves tango; he cheers with every goal scored on Sunday by his favorite soccer team, Atlético Nacional. In his world, death is the only sure thing there is. He is completely centered on what he's doing, even when he's about to kill somebody. "In this work, it's me number one and number two. After that, who the fuck cares?"

He is in good physical condition and plays soccer as much as he can. He doesn't take drugs; the only person he trusts is his mother, nobody else, especially not the members of his gang. "Your best friend is the one who ends up selling you out."

He's also a man of experience and has much success with women: A poll taken at San Javier School showed that many high school seniors would like nothing better than to have a boyfriend who is a sicario just like Alberto.

The toughness on his face and words he uses reflect the despair of someone condemned, of those who "were born to be pushing up daisies," of those who could never start over again even if they wanted to. Alberto is cold-blooded. Everybody knows it. He's tough, and he's an old-timer. Alberto is nineteen years old.

If he lives to be twenty-five, he can feel like he accomplished some-thing. It means that he's earned the right to a "career" as a professional assassin in one of the more famous gangs, like the Priscos, the Nachos, or the Tesos—these are the gangs who win the all-important contracts with the drug Mafia. And, if they are very lucky, they can get to be bodyguards of one of the big shots like Pinina, Pablo Escobar's military chief until March 1990, when he was killed in a police ambush in Medellín. He was already old by gang standards. He had made it to thirty.

Most of the sicarios kill each other off; the ones who don't, die like Pinina or get killed, set up and knocked off by the Mafia bosses them-selves. "The Mafia is hard-core, you know," Alberto says. "Suppose that I got the contract from a mafioso to kill somebody. 'Yeah, know what? I need you to kill this guy,' he says to you; 'go and kill him.' But you know that down the road, the same dude that gives you the contract can turn around and do you. The thing is that you get sent to take out one of his enemies, get it? And the guy that was the enemy probably has some friends and the dude that hired you thinks that someday those friends will catch you and make you sing. Your life is always screwed . . . always fucked up."

But being in the Mafia for these boys is a way to climb up the ladder, to move up, "to be somebody." It is not only a way to come up with million-dollar contracts, but it's the best school for learning to be a professional in the art of killing. Many of the sicarios hired by the Mafia receive arms training in the techniques of using explosives, in new methods of kidnapping. They also use these skills on their own chores. When one of the bosses "goes down" and there's no work, common crime increases in Medellín. After the surrender of the Ochoa family and Pablo Escobar, car theft and kidnapping tripled in the city and in Bogotá.

Alberto has profound respect for Catholic law. He goes to mass without fail, and every time he commits a murder he prays to the Virgin de Carmen. "If they kill me, she will receive me in purgatory." He goes to confession after every homicide to eliminate any lingering pangs of conscience. He wears a medallion blessed by *Nuestra Señora del Perpetuo Socorro* (Our Lady of Perpetual Help)—"she watches over me"—and Saint Judas. Like many other sicarios, Alberto places them on his ankles. In his wallet he has pieces of paper reading: "Halt, the sacred heart of Jesus is with you."

They say that when a sicario is buried, the rest of the gang races all around La Comuna Nororiental on their 500-cc motorcycles in tribute. There are no tears. They fire guns in the air. Sometimes they take the body out of the coffin and give their departed friend one more ride around town.

"Do you believe in God?"

"Yes. When I'm on my way out to pull something off, I always pray. I believe in God and the Virgin."

"Isn't it a contradiction?"

"I believe in God, man! I always pray for Him to protect me, all right? Nothing bad's gonna happen to me. But no way . . . sure, the law of God is Do Not Kill! But you always kill! If one guy doesn't do it, somebody else will."

Judging by the number of people who go to mass, the church finds its most ardent parishioners here. Families become more religious still when they have sons who are sicarios . . . nothing is left for them except to pray.

Priests like Father Tobón are treated with a certain respect for being the representatives of God on Earth. It is he who will forgive them, because he represents "the forgiveness of God." This divine status does not stop him from receiving threatening phone calls every now and then, though up to this point, there has been no case in these parts of a priest being killed by sicarios.

The religious devotion of the sicarios is seasonal. They believe firmly in the sacrament of penitence but go to confession only during Holy Week; on those days, of course, the crime rate decreases considerably in La Comuna. So Father Tobón takes advantage of Holy Week to preach from the pulpit about reconciliation, to talk about the meaning of life and Christian values. In his sermons he emphasizes the value of human life and even came to the point of uttering the word sicario.

Their devotion to the Virgin is ambiguous. They pray to her but feel guilty. They feel that they are damned when they get past ten murders yet still maintain the hope that the Virgin is so good in her grace that she will pardon them. This fixation on finding forgiveness was evident when Pablo Escobar decided to choose a priest, the Reverend Rafael García Herreros, as the intermediary when he surrendered to Colombian authorities in June 1991. "Pablo deserves God's forgiveness. . . . In the eyes of God, all men are created equal," the priest said on the day that he arrived with Pablo Escobar at the Envigado prison. . . .

Alberto is a professional driver and an auto mechanic, but he doesn't have a job. When he has to fill out an employment form, he lists his profession as "student making the rounds, looking for work."

"What does it mean to be a sicario?"

"For me, it's a guy who likes what he's doing. You know what I mean? He likes to do it. And he does it because he wants to and not because anyone makes him do it."

"A sicario is a professional killer, isn't he?"

"Not always. For me, a professional killer means that he has always been doing that and that he knows how to do things."

They talk about death and killing as if they were part of a normal job that you do like any other. "When you make a contract with someone to kill a certain person, that guy that you hired is a sicario. Or a beginner if you want to put it that way. Can you dig it?"

Sicarios also do robberies and other underworld business. But they feel like amateurs because they really know one thing, one way of killing. For them a professional assassin is someone who knows the business well, who studies it over and over again from different angles, so that he doesn't get caught. "The sicario is different. The sicario only kills. And he makes a living from taking other lives. It's not like thieves who spend thirty or forty months in jail for stealing a watch. I'd never do that. I mean, I'd never steal a watch."

None of them wants to be a doctor, teacher or fireman. Their only other career aspirations: to be soccer players. They're obsessed with soccer but only root for Atlético Nacional because "many kids playing for them have come from here." So, scoring a goal becomes part of their special vocabulary. "Hey," they say, "I scored a goal that time, I scored."

Sicarios weren't born this way. They became murderers because of "what was in the air," because of bad influence. "Before they brought me to Medellín, I was completely sane." Many began using violence to defend themselves from others who were more violent than they were. In the barrio where Alberto lived, his house was across from a *jibaradiero*—a place where they sell basuco [cocaine paste for smoking]. The barrio bad guys showed up there and started hassling them all the time. That was the first time he got into a fight. Alberto remembers it very well because he was only seven years old. "When the bad guys saw that we were really going to fight, that we weren't going to get pushed around or anything, they backed off. The gang came together from that bunch of guys." They would only fight over a dispute in the local soccer game. "But we only used our fists . . . we fought in self-defense." They switched quickly from knives to guns. Now Alberto is always armed. "Yeah, because I have lots of enemies. People from other areas, you understand what I mean?" He has a 9-mm pistol because it's easy to carry.

He got his first "job" because he was flat broke. "A biker showed up at my house. He had a 500-cc bike. So, I'm on the corner, get it? I don't know this guy, but I did know the guy riding with him on the back of the bike. So the guy driving gets off and says, "You know what . . . I have a job for you. " So I say, what is it?

"Now, I have a *compa* [short for *compadre* or "pal"]. We were always together since we were little, him and me, messing around. I told them that I'd do it, whatever it is, but only if he comes with me."

They didn't tell him to bring a gun, but they did say to bring a knife. They took him to a bar. "There was a lady there, right? All fancy and everything. So it was to kill a woman, right? We were going to bump her off, right? So I killed her when she was getting off a bus on her way home. I stabbed her like three times."

Alberto got the pay that he asked for: two motorcycles, two guns and 200,000 pesos ($500). "We did it on a Friday, and they paid us the day after."

"Were you afraid?"

"You know what I did? While we were waiting to kill her, we bought a pint of *aguardiente* [Colombian anisette-flavored sugarcane liquor], but we didn't drink the whole thing, like, because we couldn't get drunk. It was only enough, like, to calm me down."

He said that the first time he killed he did feel something. "I don't know, killing someone, like, who hasn't done anything to you, like, killing 'em in cold blood . . . but no way, you like didn't think about anything but the money, because I was like broke. The day after I did the thing, was like Valentine's Day—we have money and the bikes—everything."

When the sicarios kill for hire they do it without even knowing who it is they're killing. And the people paying them don't tell them if the person they're killing is a union leader, a journalist, a politician, or a mafioso. "Sometimes you go and take a look before it goes down," Alberto admits. "You watch the person. And if the person is real cool you say: I won't do it and pass it off on another member of the gang. It's happened. Killing somebody that's too cool is no good."

"Would you handle a contract to kill a mafioso?"

"I'd think it over. You can kill him real quick. But the problems come later with your family."

"And when the Mafia hires you to hit union leaders and journalists?"

"That's a much bigger problem. That's really heavy killing."

"So you don't do that kind of job?"

"You take a chance if the deal looks easy. If it doesn't, you don't try. If you say to yourself, I can make it through this one, you do it. But you have to think it over pretty much."

"Do you ever have doubts about whether you should kill somebody or not?"

"No! As far as that goes, if there's money in it, that's cool. That's all I need."

After the first time, death and the act of killing become part of a routine. But frequently, in the solitude of his own room at night the sicario is attacked by remorse. "When you get into bed at night, you think of the person; it gives you trouble to get to sleep thinking about him. But he's already dead, so what are you going to do?" he tells me. "You know that sometimes you want to bring this person back somehow, but what's done is done. You have to think before you act. Before I do something I think about it first. Because after a hit, you get real exhausted, and the only thing you know is you don't want to go back to jail."

Strangely enough, sicarios like Alberto don't use drugs, not even when they're about to kill somebody. "I've always liked to drink but not a lot. But no drugs. Marijuana's the only thing that people do around here. The friend who tries to get you to smoke basuco is not my friend. I've never been into that."

They know that if a sicario is getting stoned, he can't be doing a good job. There are, of course, sicarios who smoke basuco, but they are a small minority. "The big bosses don't want to be hiring drug addicts who do bad work," I was told. Nevertheless, statistics in Medellín showed that more and more sicarios were becoming street dealers and that many of them were using as well.

Alberto's love of guns began when he started watching American westerns on television. "You know what I mean? Cowboy movies." The first gun he remembers was a friend's single-action shotgun. The first gun that he owned was one that he stole from a neighbor. "I wanted a gun, so even though this guy was a neighbor and all, I ripped it off. And I learned how to use it by myself."

On the slopes of the mountains you can hear the sicarios doing target practice. They buy their guns on the black market, often from the police themselves. And they go out to start shooting. They practice over and over again until they can just snap their wrists and fire. At the beginning Alberto was afraid to shoot because he couldn't stop his hand from moving. "The first time that you're gonna shoot—like a .38 . . . the bullet doesn't get there. You don't hit the target because you haven't had the practice. When the powder discharges, it moves your hand, you know what I mean? And you always, like, tell a new guy, that he has to hold it with two hands." Today Alberto brags about his sure one-handed shot.

As chief of the Magníficos, Alberto laid down his own rules and recruited people "who got put out front." The money from all the hits gets divided up equally. The rules of the gang are clear and precise: "Anybody who is a snitch gets killed. He goes down."

The solidarity among members of a gang is as fragile as their lives. The sicarios trust no one but themselves. And they know that even their best friends can end up being the people who kill them: "In our gang, for example, the guys here now are all friends, sure," says Alberto. "But the day you least suspect it is the day they're laying down money to knock you off, any one of them . . . the truth is that none of them has gotten to the point of trying to fuck me over. But you have to think that it's always a possibility, that money sucks."

"What's the money for?"

"To eat. We don't live off the air, you dig? And to buy bullets and guns, you know what I mean? The more guns we have, the stronger we get. Oh yeah, like we also need bread to buy sneakers."

"Do you save any money?"

"You make money, you spend money. When the money comes in, you have to pay for shit. You need more bullets, your shoes wear out. So then you have to go out and buy bullets and you have to buy shoes. And if there's anything left . . . you go out for a shot of aguardiente."

"So you kill for the money?"

"Yeah, sure, like, no clue."

But the truth is the sicarios don't kill only for money. Killing also means status in the eyes of their friends. Alberto brags that he's a big shot, known, "famous." He's already proved "he's got what it takes," that he has guts. "When you get to be known, you're the one that's hired for the hits, you know what I mean? People come looking for you," he says with a degree of arrogance. The sicarios use their power in the barrio in their own twisted way of looking for respect. Each gang has its own territory, its own barrio, its own block. On their turf, they are the law; the only justice applied is that which is imposed by them. The rules depend on the mood. "A guy that's really tough can get ticked off real easy . . . if you're a trained killer, like, you're gonna kill for no reason, when somebody makes you mad."

They kill for any reason at all. Because something bothered them, because they woke up that day in a bad mood, or because they just felt like killing somebody. Sometimes they could kill somebody because they didn't show up for an appointment. "We have a friend who plays by the rules. So if he lends you a gun and says to bring it back at 4:00 and at 4:00 you don't bring it back . . . at 4:30 he kills you. That's the way he is: do it right or die. It's by the rules."

The first time that Alberto shot somebody, it all happened in a flash, in a chance encounter. "I'm with a buddy one night. We're hanging around, doing nothing. We're on some steps and on this side of me there's this drunk, you know what I mean? We're going up the stairs. So I stop here, next to him, you know? And while I'm pissing, he pushes me, you know? He thinks we're gonna rob him or whatever, I don't know. So he pushes me again and I get pissed off, you understand? I pull out the gun and I shoot him twice. That was it."

Like many gangs, Alberto's A-Team started out doing small-scale "jobs" in the barrio. But they soon branched out. "You wanted to improve, to get better, to get out of the barrio and do work in El Poblado," says Alberto. El Poblado is the residential neighborhood where the big, wealthy families live and where more recently, drug dealers and successful sicarios have set themselves up.

"We wanted to get out on our own and pull off bigger deals. We wanted to get into those places where the big Mafia guys live, where they have everything—Betamax, television, cars, everything. We wanted all that stuff."

"What do you call crime?"

"Breaking the law."

"Have you committed any crimes?"

"Yeah, I was in jail for a while. See, laws were made to be broken, you know. But let me tell you something, lady, not everybody in that jail is a criminal. There are innocent people in there! I'm telling you, the law—doesn't work at all."

Even though he knows what it means to break the law, the sicario doesn't have any problem crossing over the line. The strong arm of the police come into their houses on a bust, breaking things and mistreating innocent family members. After . . . war measures were adopted following the death of [the Liberal presidential candidate] Galán, the roundups and the raids increased in these barrios. "They went into a house without warning, busting up everything, asking about our boys," said one mother in the barrio known as Manrique. "Many times they took them away without leaving word of their whereabouts, saying that it was because they were sicarios."

It got to the point where many young people who went looking for work in Medellín would be turned away for the simple reason that they live in La Comuna. "How do they want to put an end to sicarios, if when somebody tries to get a job he has to say that he lives somewhere else?" asked one of the many youth leaders who have cropped up in La Comuna.

Police harassment is just one problem. In La Comuna, dealing with the law is shorthand for corruption: It has nothing to do with justice. "I like to work in Medellín more than any place else because here you can have cop friends on the inside," said Alberto. Corrupt cops work with the gangs. They sell them guns and ammunition, and they take advantage of the situation by shaking down a piece of action for themselves.

"In this world where law has always been a synonym for abuse, persecution, and mistreatment, killing a policeman sometimes becomes an affirmation of justice rather than a crime," said Victor Gaviria, a film director who has studied the sicario phenomenon in Medellín for some time.

Sicarios like Alberto usually talk about killing policemen as if it were an act of triumph. They go fishing for an unsuspecting cop, then trap him in the labyrinths of the steep barrio roads of La Comuna. "My buddy on the street corner picks up on this cop passing by and cons him into chasing after him; they get to where I am and wham! All of a sudden, he's chasing me, too. So I set the cop in a trap since I know where everybody is. I go running onto a dead-end street with him behind me and bang! we get him," says Alberto proudly, as if cop killing were an act of virtue.

For them robbing is "taking" and killing is "finishing off." And robbing a bank isn't a crime at all because "the bank isn't owned by anyone."

"What happens when you do a hit and there are innocent people who get caught in the middle and get killed?"

"Let's say there's a bank robbery. First you analyze the setup. But you know there's always somebody who gets in the middle of it all, trying to protect something that isn't his. A bank doesn't belong to anybody, you know what I mean? So, sometimes innocent people get killed. But that's not your fault; it's fate. If you don't kill somebody who's making a lot of noise, the cops catch you and they kill you instead. You come first; as for the innocent guy, that's the way it goes."

"What about the guards that get in the way?"

"It's not like you're a fucking killing machine. But for instance, if a guard is going to take a gun or something, then you kill him. And if the guy is quiet and doing nothing, why are you going to take his life, just like that? No way, man!"

The victims of the violence have no redress here; the justice system just doesn't work. There is no confidence in government institutions. The sicarios are controlling a state unto itself. In La Comuna, violence creates more violence. The only way for victims to respond to the law imposed on them by the sicarios is to fight back with the same methods. That's how vigilantism starts to appear in the barrios of the Medellín slums. Youth groups dedicated to wiping out the sicario bands are formed. They say their goal is to eradicate the crime and terror that exists in their barrios. But the militias build up just as much power as the sicarios and become just as terrifying for the rest of La Comuna. Here you respond to violence with violence.

They don't think about getting married or having a family—only about leaving some money to their mothers when they get killed: "I want them to remember me for having left my mother with a refrigerator," said one sicario who wasn't even twenty years old. The sicarios all pay supreme homage to their mothers. Fathers are, for the most part, symbolic; few are there at all. "You only have one mother, but any son of a bitch can be a father," goes the saying in La Comuna.

This is a crisis of family disintegration. If the father is even present, he exercises control by means of violence—there are many stories of fathers who beat and sexually abuse their children and their wives. But the sicarios bring their money from murder contracts to their mothers, and the money opens doors, more than they ever could dream of before. The sicario becomes the provider, the surrogate father . . . the mother looks to the son as the dominant figure in her world. She accepts his life as a sicario and, with a certain banality, she talks matter-of-factly about the violence. "That boy was killed by a very nice-looking kid," they would tell you.

When mothers in La Comuna ask questions, there is always an easy explanation. "What did we do to have this kind of children? Why do they grow up twisted?"

The answer is always somewhere else; it's somebody else's fault. "It comes from outside; it's the neighborhood that makes them be like that; it's that bad friend of his that is a bad influence; well, you have to eat."

"Are you a man of your word?"

"Yes. I'm straight. If you give your word, you have to keep it. Like when I promised I would come to see you. How could I leave you waiting after having told you that I was going to come? I would have said to myself: I didn't keep my word! And even worse than that, I did it to a woman; . . . I didn't keep my word to a woman and that's worse than death!"

"Why?"

"Because I respect women a lot. I would say that I respect them too much, you know what I mean? I would say that a woman is the most beautiful thing that exists in life. It's because of a woman that you are here; your mother is a woman. So breaking a promise to a woman is a serious thing, you know what I mean?"

"So what do you do for your mother?"

"If it were for my father I wouldn't do anything. But I love my mother a lot, you get what I mean? And let me tell you something. The day my mother dies, she'd better die a natural death. It better not be from somebody doing something to her . . . because the day somebody hurts my mom, I'll kill whoever killed her with my own hands. If you don't love your own mother, who else are you gonna love?"

Even though he admits his first killing was a woman, Alberto says he has changed the rules, and insists that the drug Mafia knows that he won't kill women. He doesn't recognize the contradiction. He says that if somebody's ripping off a woman in his barrio, he's the first to go help her out.

"They offered me good bread to knock off women and I've turned it down. It's like an abuse. Women are more defenseless, more fragile. I don't know."

The truth is that the sicarios kill women all the time; the proof is that women are frequently found among the innumerable victims of hit teams. Among them are judges, journalists, and leaders of the Patriotic Union, not to mention countless others killed in domestic quarrels.

Father Tobón is concerned about the disintegration of the role of young women in the barrios. According to him, the woman's role has become the same as that of Manuelita Saenz, the companion of the Great Liberator, Simón Bolívar: Keeping an eye on their men's weapons, serving as connections and for sexual satisfaction. He contends that the jealousy factor does seem to be a motive for murder. "You love your girlfriend and give her a lot of presents. If she betrays you, you kill her. They say that the worst cases of harassment and battering are against women.

"The sicario hates himself; he knows he is the lowest of the low. He's always trying to enhance his ability to destroy, his capacity for pure evil. He ends up being exactly what he expects himself to be. He hates everything, the outside world, the upper class, the rich. He just rejects the values of society."

Sicarios like Alberto are no recent novelty but have existed since the times of the Roman emperors. The word *sicario* comes from the Latin sicarius—hired killer. In Rome the *sicarios* murdered emperors and were part of the underpinnings of major conspiracies. In the Middle Ages they became known as *condotieris*. They were paid by the great feudal lords to murder their enemies. They are also related to today's most sophisticated version of mercenaries, like the Israelis hired by the drug bosses to train teenagers like Alberto in the art of killing, or as in the case of the British mercenaries who murder the members of the Medellín cartel.

They all live from the spoils of death, and they all deny their status in life.

The sicario doesn't think of himself as a murderer. He likes to be what he is but being called a sicario is considered an insult. He doesn't use that name; the society around brands him with it. The same thing happens to mercenaries or to arms traffickers who hide their activities under the flashy name of security companies. . . .

There is little difference between Alberto, boss of the Magníficos, and the top leader of the gangs of South Central Los Angeles where it is said

25 out of every 100 young black men are likely to be killed by gunfire before they reach the age of twenty. And how different are they from the Chicago gangs, or from the "Palestinians," the assassins who protect the Colombian Mafia in the poor outskirts of New York? Or from the "Loubards" who live in the "HLMS," the slums on the outskirts of Paris? They all live in the same desperate reality: They are the marginalized, the unemployed members of society. They live where there is no social security, only crack and basuco and death. They are the damned in a society that condemns them to purgatory, hidden away in the ghettos.

"We are winning the war against drugs," William Bennett, the former U.S. drug czar, often pronounced. He said it one last time as he announced his departure from office in 1990, as he held up graphs and surveys showing a decrease in cocaine consumption. The statistics were based on questions posed to white middle-class youths in white American middle-class cities.

In Los Angeles or in Medellín, the only war that has been won is the war over who kills whom. "If I don't do it, somebody else will," Alberto told Sylvia.

DISCUSSION:
The Vice Lords

The Conservative Vice Lords were the subject of two ethnographies done in 1969. They were the focus of attention because they had apparently changed from a violent gang to a community action group (Dawley, 1972, 1992; Keiser, 1969). It was believed that the Vice Lord Nation originated in 1958 in "Charlie Town," the Illinois State Training School for Boys at St. Charles, Illinois. They were known in the Lawndale area of Chicago as a fighting gang and were a source of conflict and violence until the late 1960s, when the group gained media attention in a public bid for peace. Later, they sponsored self-help programs such as "Teen Town." They had reportedly received more than $200,000 in federal grants by 1969. There was no formal evaluation of the success of their community work, but to one observer, the results were obvious: less crime, grass where there was glass, and storefront programs that served the community. Residents walked freely, business owners appreciated safer streets, and young men dared to dream (Dawley, 1992, p. xvi). Yet rather than changing the nature of the group, the Vice Lords remained violent. According to Knox (1994), ill-conceived gang programs and policies increased rather than decreased the problem. Well-intentioned social services programs made their resources available for gangs' manipulation and found out later that something had gone wrong.

One basis for violence came from the gangster belief that if you do not attack, you will be attacked. Others will prey on you. Such a world-view implies attacking while the competitor is most vulnerable. The level of violence increases as the level of fear in specific situations increases. Gangsters will not admit being afraid. They believe that the best defense against attack is to represent themselves as fearless. Extremes of violence are the result of experiences of threat from other gangs that leave the gangsters feeling vulnerable. The intensity of violence increases in situations in which members believe that they are acting with the approval of the entire organization. Rationalizations such as "They told me to do it" or "It was an order, I had to follow orders" function to neutralize feelings of guilt and remorse and ultimately restraint. Violence increases when a competitor commits an act that the gang thinks is inappropriate, such as a drive-by shooting. The level of violence inevitably increases in situations justified on retaliatory grounds. The level of violence also increases with the level of sophisticated weapons available to the gang (Jankowski, 1991). The actual root causes of violence are fear, ambition, testing, and frustration, but situations affect the intensity and extent of gang violence.

The persistence of violence in Chicago's inner city is illustrative of differential access to resources. Despite the promise of change in the late 1960s and early 1970s, the Lawndale area, where the Vice Lords thrive, remains marginalized and outside the mainstream. It is one of the results of disparities in political influence and power. The history of the Vice Lords supports an economic inequality interpretation of lethal violence (Martinez, 1996). Patrick (1973) found that gangs are related to appalling housing conditions where inhabitants have grown accustomed both to cramped, verminous houses and to brutal, barbarous violence. The combination of inner-city squalor and violent gangs was found in Hong Kong, Glasgow, Scotland, and Kingston, Jamaica, as well as in Medellín, Colombia, and Chicago, to name only a few radically different cultures and societies. A deteriorating urban community provides a fertile field for gang growth because it is a safe haven where the gang can be protected from law enforcement and other gangs. If gangs were not able to establish a mutually beneficial social contract with their communities, ultimately they would cease to operate. Gangs recruit new members from their community. Within decaying city neighborhoods, there are many frustrated and rebellious young men who are likely to adapt well to gang life. The gang is also dependent on the community for information and transport. Inner-city communities provide gang members with identification and a sense of belonging. In the process of realizing both functional and psychological interests, a social bond is formed between the gang and the community. It is this bond with the community that makes it possible for gangs, like the Vice Lords, to persist for generations.

There is an analogy between the violence of the U.S. frontier of the 19th century and the violence on the streets of Chicago in the 20th century. A Vice Lord was quoted by Keiser (1979):

> As long as they don't mess with us, we don't mess with them. Yeah, just like Wyatt Earp, see? Wyatt Earp was supposed to be a law abiding man. If anybody messed up, they seen Wyatt Earp. But if you didn't mess up, you didn't see Wyatt. The same way with us. (p. 78)

As Courtwright (1996) explained, young, single men account for the largest share of violence. Groups of young, single men who are ethnocentric and defensive, are willing to use violent means to overcome obstacles, and have a high degree of alcohol consumption are the most likely to be called on to use violence in OC situations. These young men frequent gambling places, saloons, or street corners where violence is prevalent. The criminal conditions that once clustered about frontier towns can now be found in decaying cities.

6

Excerpt From
There Are No Children Here

Alex Kotlowitz

Chapters 4 and 5 (pp. 33-51) of *There Are No Children Here: The Story of Two Boys Growing up in the Other America,* by Alex Kotlowitz (New York: Doubleday, 1991)

Four

On a warm day in mid-July, a caravan of three cars pulled up to the sidewalk at the [Henry Horner housing projects in Chicago]. Two young bodyguards stepped out of the first and last sedans. Then from the middle emerged Jimmie Lee, a barrel-chested, square-jawed man who was no more than five-feet-seven. A bulletproof vest sometimes made him look even bulkier. He held his cellular telephone at his side as a band of worshiping teenagers mobbed him.

A commotion caught Lee's attention. In the entranceway of one of the buildings, a drunken man berated his young daughter. "You bitch. What did I tell you?" the father screamed at the cowering girl. Lee walked toward the building and, with a suddenness that left the father defenseless, slugged him in the jaw, knocking him to the ground. Lee stared at the crumpled drunk.

"You don't give no kid disrespect," he told the man.

"But that's my daughter," the fallen man explained.

"I don't care if she is your daughter. She's thirteen years old and you're calling her a bitch. Don't do it again," Lee walked into the building, where he had a meeting with some of his workers.

Lafayette, Pharaoh, and the other children knew to keep their distance from Jimmie Lee. But they also knew that he and no one else—not the mayor, the police, or the housing authority—ruled Henry Horner. The boys never had reason to speak to Lee or to meet him, but his very presence and activities ruled their lives.

When he pulled up in his caravan, they knew enough to go inside. When nighttime fell and Lee's business swung into action, they knew enough to stay away. And when something happened to Lee or one of his workers, they knew enough not to talk about it. Jimmie Lee, it was said, was everywhere. He knew who was talking about him, who was finking, who was flipping to the other side. And when he knew, someone would pay.

Jimmie Lee headed a drug gang called the Conservative Vice Lords. Its name had nothing to do with its political affiliation. The members controlled Henry Horner. No one could sell drugs without their approval. Their arsenal included pistols, Uzis, and even grenades. Some of its members were well schooled in torture techniques, and once allegedly threatened to shove a hot nail up an opposing gang member's penis. Lee even had an "enforcer," according to the police, a young man whose job it was to maim and kill and who kept a two-shot derringer for such a purpose.

Residents so feared and respected the gang's control that they refused to call 911. In Chicago, the caller's address automatically flashes at police headquarters, and police will sometimes then appear at the caller's home, seeking more information. Snitching could get you killed. The police installed a hot-line number and promised confidentiality, but in all of 1986, public housing residents called the number twenty-one times. One woman so feared the long tentacles of the gang that after she drew a rough diagram of a recent gun battle for a friend, she ripped it into small shreds for fear that the Vice Lords would find it.

By 1987, Lee's notoriety had grown to such an extent that his photo, taken with five other high-ranking Vice Lords, hung on the walls of every police station on the city's west side.

Next to the others, all of whom glared menacingly at the camera, Lee looked calm, even pensive. He sported a full beard and aviator glasses.

His red sweatshirt had BULLS emblazoned on the front; he also wore blue jogging pants and high-tops and a thick gold necklace. Lee worked out with weights, and that showed even in his baggy jogging suit. His upper torso and neck were thick and wide; his closely cropped hair made him look that much heavier. The information under the photo identified him as weighing 210 pounds.

The rest of the text warned: "They are known to be involved in drug traffic, home invasions of dope flats, extortion (especially of narcotics operations), and other crimes. They have been known to employ fully automatic weapons, travel in car caravans, usually with tail cars for protection."

But Lee ruled by more than fear. To neighborhood residents, he could sometimes be a positive force. He reportedly didn't take drugs himself and, if he drank, did so in moderation. He occasionally bought food for families who needed it. Because of his love for children, he refused to let "peewees," those around thirteen or fourteen, gangbang for the Conservative Vice Lords. In fact, young boys periodically received lectures from Lee to stay away from drugs and the gangs. On occasion, Lee gave children dollar bills or, if their shoes were torn, bought them new ones.

Lee's efforts paid off. To the residents of Horner, he became a figure of contradictions. To some, he was a model. In a neighborhood of runaway fathers, Lee had been married to the same woman for nearly twenty years. And adults and children alike pointed to his generosity.

"The thing I liked about him was that he gave kids and women respect. He really wasn't a bad person," said one resident. "I have a lot of respect for Jimmie Lee," said another.

Even Charlie Toussas, a plainclothes officer known for his tough manner, conceded, "He was a real gentleman."

Jimmie Lee might be considered by some the hero of a Horatio Alger story. As a child, he didn't have much going for him. He grew up in Horner. His father was a construction worker, his mother an assembler at a plating company. He had a child by the time he was eighteen; he dropped out of school in the eleventh grade with only a sixth-grade reading level. Later, while in prison, he received his high school equivalency.

The police speculate that Lee had been associated with the Vice Lords, which has over twenty factions, for possibly as long as twenty years. One of his first tussles with the authorities was when he was seventeen, charged with killing a fourteen-year-old boy who was found in the gangway of a building, shot through the heart. A jury found Lee not guilty. Two years later, Lee and some buddies robbed three men at gunpoint. A letter to the court from Lee's counselor at the American Institute of Engineering and Technology, where he had received drafting instruction, noted: "While he was with us, Mr. Lee was quiet, and passive. He lacked self-confidence and disparaged himself. He handled his conflicts by retreating." But Lee went on to serve a little over four years in one of the Illinois prisons, which are notorious for their large and strong gang populations and where most gang leaders earn their rank.

After his release, in July 1974, Lee was in and out of trouble with the law, including a conviction of unlawful use of a weapon. The preceding November, in 1986, the police caught Lee with fifty-six grams of heroin. He met the $50,000 bond and continued about his business. To the residents of Henry Horner, he seemed to operate with impunity.

A taciturn man, Lee, who was sometimes known as General Lee or by his middle name, Oswald, came from a long Chicago tradition of smart, sophisticated gang leaders. He was no youngster; he was thirty-eight years old.

The city's black street gangs, of which there are three main ones—the Vice Lords, the Disciples, and the El Rukns (formerly known as the Blackstone Rangers)—originated in the early 1960s mostly as young kids duking it out over turf rights. At Henry Horner, the Vice Lords and the Black Souls, a faction of the Disciples, fought fist to fist with white gangs whose turf lay just north of the complex. As the whites moved out the Vice Lords and Black Souls fought among themselves. Eventually, the city's gangs split into two main groupings known as the Nation and Folks. The Vice Lords and El Rukns belonged to the Nation; the Disciples to the Folks.

By the late 1960s, the gangs had won some standing among the establishment, particularly with liberals who felt that these young hoodlums, given proper guidance, might turn their energies and enviable organizing and leadership abilities to bettering their neighborhoods. The gang leader who served as a prototype for others, Jeff Fort, the El Rukns' head, managed to pull in over $300,000 in funds from federal agencies for ostensible job-training programs. During the riots following the death of Martin Luther King, Jr., the El Rukns took to the streets to calm the neighborhoods. Businessmen whose windows had DO NOT TOUCH posters signed by the El Rukns' leadership later held a press conference to commend the El Rukns for helping people protect their property. The gang had won such legitimacy that Fort was invited, at the behest of a United States senator, to President Nixon's inauguration.

At Henry Horner, the Vice Lords gained a similar standing when a local hospital bequeathed a former Catholic boys' school it owned, coupled with a grant of over $20,000, to local gang leaders in the hope that they would open a neighborhood center. The three-story, nine-year-old structure had oak floors, oriental rugs, chandeliers, and silver place settings.

Efforts, though, to convert the bad to the good failed miserably, some quicker than others. Within months, the gangs had gutted the Catholic school. The chandeliers and place settings were gone. The gang used much of the grant money to buy an old fire-engine-red ambulance, which they used to transport friends around the neighborhood, as well as new clothes, mostly army fatigues and jump boots.

The El Rukns' good intentions unraveled, too, though not as quickly. In the early 1970s, a judge sentenced Jeff Fort to five years in Leavenworth for conspiring to misapply federal funds. He was released in 1976, but went back to prison again in 1983 for drug trafficking. And then, while in prison, he was sentenced to an additional eighty years as the first United States citizen to be convicted for conspiring to commit terrorist acts on behalf of a foreign government. Prosecutors contended that Fort had made a deal with Moamar Ghadhafi in which the El Rukns were to receive $2.5 million to bomb buildings and airplanes in the United States for the Libyan leader.

By the late 1970s the city's gangs, once organizations of neighborhood pride and turf rights, had turned into big business: the marketing and selling of narcotics. Ironically, the well-intentioned efforts of the late 1960s left the gangs with strong organizational structures, which they needed to have in place when applying for federal and local funding.

The gangs became so powerful in Chicago that they . . . managed to do what no big city police force has done: they kept crack out of the city. Not until 1988, long after the crack scourge had devoured entire neighborhoods in cities like New York and Washington, D.C., were there any crack-related arrests in Chicago. Even then, crack made up only one part of an extensive operation, which they swiftly closed down. If crack found its way to Chicago, the inexpensive, highly addictive drug would open the market to small entrepreneurs, and possibly break the gangs' oligopoly over the drug trade.

The gangs also became an institutional force in many of the city's neighborhoods, so that even in recent years they have been used for seemingly legitimate political purposes. In 1983, a state representative, Larry Bullock, allegedly paid the El Rukns $10,000 to campaign for Jane Byrne in her quest for the mayoralty. Police say they pocketed the money and never worked for Byrne.

At Henry Horner, a young local politician recruited gang members from playgrounds to pass out leaflets and accompany campaign workers in his successful 1987 bid for Democratic ward committeeman. He paid each gang member $20 a day. Because of two threats on his life and because his campaign van had been riddled with bullets, he needed the protection.

Residents and police tell the story of one former west side alderman who announced that he would move into a public housing project for a few nights. . . . He wanted to draw attention to the awful conditions there. The housing authority found him a vacant apartment in a high rise, but it happened to be controlled by the Vice Lords. The gang eagerly awaited his arrival. The alderman, it seems, had previously aligned himself with the rival Disciples. He never moved in.

The city's top gang leaders and drug lords have such standing in the community that every summer they throw a huge bash for friends at the Dan Ryan Woods on the south side. One summer, residents of many of the city's poor black neighborhoods received mimeographed invitations to the "Players' Picnic." Fliers promised free food and drink, softball for the children, and a car show and wet T-shirt contest for the adults. The flier brazenly identified some of the sponsors of the party by their nicknames: Highsmith, Fat Cat, Bub, and Disco. About two thousand Chicagoans attended the get-together, dancing to the funk rock of a live band and grilling hot dogs and ribs. Cars were so backed up going into the park that the police had to assign extra traffic details. The kingpins showed off their glistening new Mercedes-Benzes, Rolls-Royces, and Jaguars. They danced and drank until ten p.m., when the police broke up the festivities.

At the age of ten, Lafayette had his first encounter with death; he saw someone killed. It was the beginning of Henry Horner's brutal drug wars, when Jimmie Lee and the Conservative Vice Lords made their move to take control of Henry Horner. By 1985, drugs had swept through Chicago's west side. Big money was involved. And Lee began his efforts to establish his part of the trade.

The Vice Lords, with the aid of another gang, pushed to oust the Disciples from the east end of Horner, the more populated section of the complex and thus the more lucrative. They even brought in thugs from other parts of the city. The first victim was a young Disciple named Baby Al, who was shot with a .357 Magnum not far from [Lafayette's] building. Wounded, he ran into the high-rise, where, while trying to climb the stairs, he fell backward and lost consciousness. Lafeyette came running out of his apartment to see what all the commotion was about. He watched as Baby Al bled to death. Two years later, his blood still stained the stairwell.

A couple of weeks later, as Lafeyette and Pharaoh played on the jungle gym in midafternoon, shooting broke out. A young girl jumping rope crumpled to the ground. Lafeyette ran into his building, dragging [another kid] behind him. Pharaoh, then seven, panicked. He ran blindly until he bumped into one of the huge green trash containers that dot the landscape. He pulled himself up and over, landing in a foot of garbage. Porkchop followed. For half an hour, the two huddled in the foul-smelling meat scraps and empty pizza boxes, waiting for the shooting to stop, arguing about when they should make a break for their respective homes. Finally, the shooting subsided and they climbed out, smelling like dirty dishes. They watched as paramedics attended to the girl, who luckily had been shot only in the leg. Her frightened mother, who had fainted, was being revived. It was at that point that Pharaoh first told his mother, "I didn't wanna know what was happening."

By late 1986, the Conservative Vice Lords occupied two of Horner's high-rises just across the street from [Lafayette's apartment]. Lee's soldiers used the building's four stairwells to escape from the police. They found refuge in several of the vacant apartments, some of which were connected by large holes knocked in the cinder-block walls, through which they could make their getaways. The gang also controlled three apartments. The tenants were young single women who in exchange for money or drugs rented out the entire unit or just a bedroom to Vice Lords. In these so-called safe houses, the gang's lieutenants stored their drugs, guns, and money. In the underbelly of a refrigerator in one of the apartments, they hid a disassembled machine gun. The gang had also outfitted an eighth-floor vacant apartment with a sofa, lounge chair, and a television set; it was a sanctuary for members who needed a place to stay. No guns or drugs were allowed. Jimmie Lee lived farther west, outside of Horner, with his wife and three children.

The Vice Lords added to the natural defenses—most notably the stairwells and the vacant apartments—the buildings provided. They knocked out all the lights in the open breezeways so that even during the day it was difficult if not impossible to see in. Wandering sentries warned of approaching unmarked squad cars, which even young children could identify on sight. They communicated through walkie-talkies, the kind used by football coaches. Their code word for police was "boppers."

Most wore baseball caps with the bill turned to the left, an indication that they were Vice Lords. Many wore earrings in the left ear, and some hung such heavy gold jewelry from their necks that it seemed a wonder they could hold their heads upright. Also, the Playboy bunny had become a Vice Lord symbol, so a member might sport a gold one around his neck. The five-pointed star, the gang's insignia, decorated the entrances to the two buildings, as did other items identifying the area as belonging to the Vice Lords. The top hat signified shelter, the cane stood for strength, the glove meant purity, and the champagne glass symbolized conservatism or propriety. Members often learned the meaning of these symbols while in prison, where the gangs did much of their recruiting.

Much of the business was with people in the neighborhood, but the bulk of it was with outsiders, who drove their cars up Wolcott Avenue and parked in front of the Vice Lords' two buildings. Usually they didn't have to get out of their cars; the young runners took their orders. The "soldiers" sold the cocaine and heroin and then returned a certain percentage of the proceeds to the bosses and kept the rest. Both the police and former gang members estimated that Lee's business grossed $50,000 to $100,000 a week.

On December 13, 1986, there began a frenzy that would last through the summer. Four top Vice Lords chose to show their force against a rival drug gang, the Gangster Stones, that was encroaching on their turf. They had already successfully moved the Disciples farther west.

The four waited until after midnight to launch their attack. They knew that was when the tough plainclothes cops of the city's gang crimes and public housing units went off duty. They had no third shift. The Vice Lords strolled into the breezeway of a nearby building, carrying with them an Uzi, two sawed-off shotguns, and a .25 caliber automatic handgun.

The first rival gang member they came on in the dark lobby was Larry Wallace or Wild Child, a thirty-one-year-old heavy drinker who had recently moved from Horner but was back visiting friends. People in the neighborhood continue to dispute whether he was an active gang member at the time. The gunfire lasted maybe thirty seconds. Wallace was shot five times. One bullet pierced his chest and exited from the back, and another entered through the upper back and lodged in his left cheek. Buckshot pellets littered his buttocks. The Vice Lords had fired at him from just about every conceivable angle. Even at Horner, the viciousness of this slaying unnerved people. By summer's end, as the Vice Lords established their dominance, the war had touched the lives of almost everyone living in Henry Horner. Lafeyette and Pharaoh, as well as the adults, began talking of the "death train" that drove smack through their community.

Five

Bird Leg loved dogs. And for that reason, Lafeyette loved Bird Leg. His real name was Calvin Robinson, and though he was three years older than Lafeyette, he let the younger boy tag along with him, in part because he had few friends. The older boys made fun of his obsession with dogs; the younger ones seemed to understand it.

Bird Leg and Lafeyette hunted for German shepherds, mutts, and even pit bulls in the small, fenced-in back yards of the Hispanic and white neighborhoods just north of the housing project. Ordinarily, the dogs growled and fought with Lafeyette and other strangers, but Bird Leg could communicate with them in ways the other children found uncanny. As he climbed into the back yards, he talked to them, consoled them, cajoled them, lured them, until they sidled up to him, drooling on their newfound friend. Then he unchained them, lifted them over the yard fence, and brought them home.

"The dogs would always come with him," recalls one boy, with a combination of amazement and respect. "He had more dogs than he did friends."

With Lafeyette's assistance, Bird Leg kept his assortment of canines—some stolen, some strays, some raised from birth—in an abandoned garage catty-corner from Lafeyette's building. Bird Leg often got down on his hands and knees to speak to his companions. Sometimes he kissed them on their sloppy chops, a practice the other children shook their heads at in disbelief. A few nights a week, Bird Leg scrounged through the trash bins behind the nearby Kentucky Fried Chicken, and collected half-finished meals to feed his pets. Lafeyette often helped. Bird Leg occasionally spent the night with his animals in the worn, leaning garage, huddling among them for warmth. On one unusually cold fall night, Bird Leg, only twelve at the time, built a fire by the garage door, fueling it with cardboard and rags. The heat, he hoped would warm his shivering friends. Instead, the old wooden building, without much coaxing, quickly caught fire and burned to the ground. The police brought Bird Leg to his mother, who, though angry, couldn't help laughing at her son's misguided intentions. It was the first of what were to be many brushes with the law.

As Bird Leg got older, he became involved with the Vice Lords, and he and Lafeyette grew apart. Lafeyette was too young and too wary to join the gangs, but he cherished all that Bird Leg had taught him about dogs. And he missed him.

Bird Leg, his mother suspects, sought protection from the gang in the same way he sought love from his dogs. Jimmie Lee, said his mother, had become like a big brother, though Bird Leg didn't run drugs, for him. In fact, many of Lee's older workers didn't even know Bird Leg. Also, a close relative was a Vice Lord, which meant that Bird Leg, who lived on the western edge of Horner, Disciples' territory, frequently had to withstand a beating just to enter his building. Uncles' and cousins' associations with a particular gang can mark children too young to have chosen their own affiliation.

As a teenager, Bird Leg became increasingly reckless and hardheaded. By the age of fourteen, he had for all intents and purposes dropped out of school. Friends say he would sometimes borrow a shotgun from a friend and randomly shoot at Disciples, a practice not uncommon among the very young gang members. He also started raising pit bulls to fight. His favorite was a light brown muscular terrier named Red. . . . The police eventually confiscated the starving and scarred terrier; Bird Leg had used it to threaten an officer.

Bird Leg had always lived on the edge and, indeed, earned his nickname when at the age of four he chased a tennis ball into a busy street and was struck by a speeding, drunk driver. The doctors had to insert pins in one knee and ankle. When the chest-high cast came off after many weeks, his leg was so thin and fragile-looking that his grandmother started calling him Bird Leg.

In the summer of 1986, while shooting dice with some friends, he was approached by a man with a shotgun, demanding his money, and Bird Leg, in his youthful defiance, ran. The man emptied a cartridge of buckshot into Bird Leg's shoulder. That caused his mother to move her family into an apartment on the city's far north side. But, as is often the case when families move, Bird Leg and his brothers kept returning to Horner to visit friends.

Sometimes at Henry Horner you can almost smell the arrival of death. It is the odor of foot-deep pools of water that, formed from draining fire hydrants, become fetid in the summer sun. It is the stink of urine puddles in the stairwell corners and of soiled diapers dumped in the grass. It is the stench of a maggot-infested cat carcass lying in a vacant apartment and the rotting food in the overturned trash bins. It is, in short, the collected scents of summer.

In mid-August of the summer of 1987, the Vice Lords and their rivals reached a temporary truce. Because of the season's violence, the police had increased their presence at Horner. The gangs knew that more police would only disrupt their drug transactions, so they agreed among themselves to stop, in their own words, "clowning." But for young members like Bird Leg, such business acumen seemed at odds with what had become almost instinctual for young members: Vice Lords got along with neither Gangster Stones nor Disciples. Truce or no truce.

On a Thursday night late in August, a rival gang member shot Bird Leg in the arm with buckshot. After being treated at the hospital, he joked with his older brother and cousin that if he were to die he wanted to be buried in his white jogging suit. They laughed and told him they would oblige him.

The next evening, August 21, Bird Leg, despite his mother's protestations, left his north side apartment to visit friends at Horner. As he sat in the late day's heat and watched two friends play basketball, a group of young Disciples started taunting him, tossing bricks and bottles at his feet. His thirteen-year-old sister, who also was at Horner visiting friends, pleaded with Bird Leg to come inside the building to their cousin's apartment. "Get your ass upstairs," Bird Leg ordered her. "I'm gonna kill some of these punks today or they're going to kill me." It was tough talk for a fifteen-year-old; his sister ran inside, crying. By the time she climbed the six floors to her cousin's apartment, a single pistol shot had echoed from below.

Twenty-four-year-old Willie Elliott had stepped from between two parked cars and aimed a pistol at Bird Leg. Only two feet away, the boy froze like a deer caught in the glare of a car's headlights. The bullet tore through Bird Leg's chest; He clutched his wound and ran through the breezeway of one high-rise. "Man, I've been shot!" he hollered in disbelief. He appeared to be heading for the safety of a busy street. He didn't make it. The bullet, which had hit him at point-blank range, entered his chest and spiraled through his body like an out-of-control drill, lacerating his heart, lungs, spleen, and stomach. Bird Leg, struggling to breathe, collapsed beneath an old cottonwood, where, cooled by its shade, he died.

Word of death spreads fast in Henry Horner. Sometimes the killing happens late at night when most people are asleep. Then, since few witnesses are around, the incident can take on mythic proportions. A stabbing becomes a butchering. A shooting becomes an execution. Sometimes it can take days for the correct name of the victim to surface. But a daytime killing here draws a crowd, and as Bird Leg lay against the tree, a young boy mounted his bike to deliver the news.

From a friend's second-floor window, Lafeyette heard the boy's breathless rendering of the fight, but he decided not to join the other children who ran across Damen Avenue to the crime scene. "I just didn't want to go," he said later. He had already seen enough.

PART
IV

OPPORTUNITY

*An explanation of gang membership has to be based
on the overwhelming impact of racism, sexism,
poverty and limited opportunity structures.*

Chesney-Lind and Shelden
(1998, p. 50)

Throughout history, in studies of OC, the idea of opportunity has appeared as an important explanatory factor. As with other kinds of careers, opportunities to be a gangster are not equally distributed. Some individuals have many opportunities to get involved; others have few or none. It is significant to examine situations that provide more or fewer opportunities and to study the ways that OC opportunities are structured. Previous sections discussed ways in which opportunities in OC are structured by ethnicity and community. In this section, two other important aspects of opportunity are considered: the ways in which opportunities are structured by gender and sex (Chapter 7) and the influence of larger economic structures.

Opportunities for Women

Looking at the differences between male and female experiences lets us better understand not only OC but also the structure of opportunities in general. Being female is a characteristic that has kept many out of OC. For those girls and women who have gotten involved, OC has had patterns of domination and exploitation that parallel the patterns of other organizations considered legal. In the study of enterprise, it is noteworthy that women are very seldom active in the highest levels of corporate crime. Their roles are more likely to fit into a clerical or administrative pattern rather than decision making or control. Just as traditional institutions often exclude women from top positions, so do criminal organizations. Some writers see increasingly more participation by women in upper world crime. They assume that women are acknowledged and respected in the highly lucrative world of illicit enterprise (Taylor, 1993, p. 198). But in fact, OC opportunities for women seldom afford them respect, and women's importance to crimes of enterprise is almost never acknowledged.

It is likely that women's roles in OC have diminished with the contemporary trend toward rationality and internationality. Historical analysis provides more examples of female ringleaders and gangsters than contemporary studies. In moonshining organizations, women's roles were more diversified because the operation was usually located at or near the home, and the entire family was likely to be involved in production and marketing. Block (1980, 1981) studied the role of women in big-city OC at the turn of the century and found women in control of brothels, saloons, and other OC enterprises. These women were members of crime families and had opportunities in OC because of their connections.

Women in positions of power in Chinese triads are almost unheard of. One woman known as "Big Sister Ping" was said to be the queen of "Snakeheads," or smugglers of Chinese immigrants (Kerry, 1997). But in the international drugs and arms trade and other sectors of OC, women have not been known to have a leadership role. In the Japanese Yakuza, there was no known woman ringleader or crime boss. The same was true for the Medellín cartel. Steffensmeier (1983) pointed out that crime in its more organized and lucrative dimensions is virtually a male phenomenon. OC usually operates in ways that emphasize secrecy, trust, reliability, sophistication, and muscle. Compared to their male counterparts, potential female offenders are at a disadvantage in selection and recruitment into criminal groups. They are less likely to have access to crime skills and relationships of tutelage. OC as a career path is closed to most females, and the huge profits from illicit enterprise do not usually go to women. Where the stakes are high and the risk is great, OC is highly sexually segregated. The greater the profit, planning, monopoly, and stability of a criminal organization, the less likely are women to be in positions of power within it (p. 1026).

In street gangs, there is another pattern for women members that has been studied for more than a decade in the United States. Up to one third of the people involved in street gangs are likely to be female (Moore, 1991). Yet although the gender realities of street gangs are complicated, the media stereotype is clear and intensely male. Every so often, the media discover that there are girls in gangs and that girls can also be violent. Currently, the media are focusing on girls' commission of violent crimes in youth gangs. The idea is, "Girls are meaner now than girls in earlier generations." But generally speaking, the public's image of gangs is all male. Perhaps if it included girls as well as boys, it would be too humanized.

Women, like men, can find that gangs fill a void that grows daily due to the continued presence of homelessness and unemployment. In many inner-city neighborhoods, 80% of the African American families living below the poverty level are headed by single women. The dismantling of social service programs devastated some urban-dwelling families. Because so many mothers with children have been reduced to moving in and out of shelters, more and more women have formed alliances to survive. According to Taylor (1993), "The difference between females and males is their method of survival. Women are more involved in the less dangerous crime; they tend to try and trick people out of their money" (p. 195).

Girls in gangs challenge the conservative view of women as "wife and mother" that is promoted in other OC groups. They are viewed as having moved outside the realm of traditional values.

Being marginal, girl gangsters may substitute strong ties to other outlaws for weak ties to their conventional families. Toughness, meanness, and aggression are highly valued for all gang members. Respect means a lot to boys and girls. The streets may be dominated by young men, but girls and young women do not necessarily avoid the streets. They are involved in "hanging out," "partying," and the occasional fight. During the 1990s, research on girls' gangs moved beyond simple, stereotypical notions about these groups as auxiliaries of male gangs to a more careful assessment of girls' lives (Chesney-Lind & Shelden, 1998).

According to Campbell's (1984) examination of the roles for females in street gangs, there are some essential patterns in girls' gang membership. The girls' heterosexuality is crucial to their membership because it perpetuates male control. "Dykes" are scorned and abused. The separate nature of men and women is an explicit part of gang philosophy. The men control the women's sexuality by labeling women as "cheap" and abusing them if they dispense sexual favors too freely. Reproductive functions also are a matter of male decision but are women's responsibility. An important female role is that of mother figure, offering advice and counsel on personal matters. The mother figure plays the role of social and emotional leader. A woman is afforded respect as a maternal figure. There are also aggressive girls in gangs who try to succeed on male terms. They are accepted with the same indulgence accorded to junior males. "The tomboy will grow out of it and have children, and a decent male will provide for her, keep her at home, and save her from the streets," according to the fundamentally conservative philosophy of gangs (p. 246).

Males control gangs and continue to live out the male roles with which they grew up, casting girls in all-too-recognizable complementary positions to themselves. In street gangs, girls find, not a new sense of self or a new set of values, but the old values and roles disguised in a new way (Campbell, 1984, p. 257). For girl gangsters, as for their mothers, the most enduring bond in their lives is with their children. Children represent an escape from the abiding sense of isolation, the possibility of continuity and loyalty and unconditional acceptance. Campbell (1984) provided the "new" woman's dream, the "new" agenda that she found among the gang girls she studied:

No more suffering or poverty. No more lonely, forced "independence," living alone on welfare in a shabby apartment. First, a good husband, strong but not violent, faithful but manly. Second, well-dressed children. Third, a beautiful suburban apartment. Later for the revolution. (p. 267)

DISCUSSION:
Outlaw Motorcycle Gangs

Several studies of outlaw bikers have examined the participation of women in them. In 1966, Hunter S. Thompson studied the Hell's Angels. Although Thompson did not take the views of the women involved into account, his description of degradation and sexual perversion was intensely personal. He carefully described one scene that he labeled as "somewhere between a friendly sex orgy and an all-out gang rape" (p. 247). Thompson explained the contradiction when he wrote: "So the Hell's Angels are working rapists . . . and in this downhill half of our 20th century, they are not so different from the rest of us as they sometimes seem. They are only more obvious" (p. 249). Thus, he saw a relationship between OC patterns and roles and the patterns and roles in legitimate society.

The role of women in outlaw biker gangs is illustrative of the role of women in other OC enterprises. Though women have a more or less active role in the various organizations, sexuality is a factor that separates and defines women's membership. The sex trade itself is often run by OC groups, including bikers. Because women may be commodities on the sex market, their care and control is important to the group's income. Control is a major factor if people are to be sold and used as objects. The most effective form of control is voluntary. Outlaw bikers are able to control women, to some extent, on the basis of a philosophy about appropriate male dominance and female submission. To some extent, the control exerted on female gang participants is also based on fear. The threat of punishment and the arbitrary nature of rules to which punishments are attached leave women who are involved with outlaw bikers feeling insecure and powerless.

Many women who are participating in the outlaw biker gang lifestyle had a history of involvement in prostitution and other sex-related services before they became part of the group (Quinn, 1987). For them, affiliation with outlaw bikers offers social status and a sense of physical security from abuse by customers and pimps. Many veteran biker women see their male companions as somewhat interchangeable agents of status and protection.

Hedonistic activities for outlaw bikers involve sexual excesses as well as substance abuse. The public image of bikers as "adventure-seeking dropouts" was replicated in a study of gang members. Jackson and Wilson (1993) found that motorcycle gang members in Great Britain were tough, aggressive, dogmatic, sensation seeking, impulsive, risk taking, irresponsible, and lacking in self-esteem and ambition. They were also significantly anxious and depressed. Despite these self-destructive tendencies, it appeared from other sources that outlaw bikers were taking increasing control of importation, distribution, and sales of illicit drugs, contraband alcohol, and the black-market tobacco trade throughout North America. The British Columbia Hell's Angels were regarded as one of the wealthiest outlaw motorcycle gangs in the world in 1996 (CISC, 1996).

The outlaw biker gangs' public image contrasts with their private OC role. Their nature as hedonistic and thrill seeking on the one hand and rationally profit motivated on the other puts women at a double disadvantage in these gangs. Females' roles as obedient followers and their status as objects make outlaw biker gangs extremely gender segregated and lead women into roles increasingly defined by sexuality. With opportunities for females structured by value as a sexual commodity, the status of women in OC is necessarily controlled by men, who run the market and who are the buyers.

7

Women and
the Outlaws

Daniel R. Wolf

Chapter 6 (pp. 131-162) of *The Rebels: A Brotherhood
of Outlaw Bikers,* by Daniel R. Wolf (Toronto: University
of Toronto Press, 1991)

The newest and fastest-growing phenomenon on the asphalt highways
of contemporary North America is the solo female rider. Every year more
and more women are turning to motorcycles and motorcycling, *on their
own.* For the purpose of mutual companionship and support these sisters
of the highway have begun to organize themselves in groups that are
independent of males. The following is an excerpt from a letter to the
editorial section of *V-Twin* magazine in September 1989: "Our name is
Against All Odds MC and our patches will consist of the Queen of Hearts
playing cards in the background. In front will be two dice showing three
and four circles representing the number seven. . . . We will hopefully
show that women can ride motorcycles and still be ladies and that we
actually have brains in our heads, not mashed potatoes" (p. 9). . . .

Little has changed, however, in the world of outlaw bikerdom. The
frontier of the outlaw biker "riding for freedom in the wind" *remains an*

ostensibly male domain. The women's liberation movement that emerged in the sixties and crystallized in the seventies and eighties has not yet made any impression on the outlaw subculture. The very chauvinistic attitudes that have traditionally dominated biker ideology remain intact. Formal membership in an outlaw motorcycle club is restricted to males; women do not become members. Women do not participate in official decision making regarding club activities or policy formation, and they do not attend the weekly business meetings. The regular female associates of members do not wear club emblems, nor are they allowed to appear at the clubhouse without escorts. The pervasiveness of chauvinism in the outlaw-motorcycle-club subculture is explained in this chapter by relating it to the need to (1) ensure the overall psychological appeal of the group to men as an elite organization; (2) minimize the potentially disruptive effects of the male-female bond on the ties of brotherhood; and (3) reduce the occurrence of confrontations with outsiders by maintaining the stereotype of the feared biker.

A man's relationship to the outlaw subculture is a direct one, achieved by owning a hog (Harley-Davidson motorcycle) and earning his colours (club membership). A woman gains entry into the outlaw subculture in an indirect manner, by virtue of her having established social-sexual ties with one or more members. The reason women do not ride their own motorcycles or become club members in the outlaw subculture does not relate to lack of interest, ability, or desire. Rather it is because the fabrication of male and female gender identity and roles within the subculture requires female participation only in a marginal and supportive manner. A man's image of "machismo" (dominance and aggression) is achieved in part by contrasting it with a woman's image of "femininity" (subservience and passivity). From a comparative perspective, gender relations defined by outlaw motorcycle clubs are not a radical subcultural departure from but, rather, an exaggerated statement of the traditional values that have dominated North American society for several centuries.

The exclusion of women from formal participation and the pervasive attitude of chauvinism do not negate the importance of the female presence, nor do they result in the complete absence of a female influence. Women who participate in the outlaw subculture fall into one of three major categories: "broads," "mamas," and "ol' ladies." These categories are fundamentally distinct statuses and represent different ways that women relate to the club and to its members. "Broads" is a general term used to refer to the wide range of women who drift in and out of the subculture. It is an introductory stage of social interaction with one or more members on a casual and usually temporary basis. "Mamas" are women who maintain an informal affiliation with the club as a whole. This informal affiliation includes social-sexual interactions with the members and, in some clubs, an economic arrangement. "Ol' ladies" are women who have established a long-standing personal relationship with an individual member. An ol' lady may be the member's girlfriend, covivant, or wife. . . .

The psychological appeal of membership in an outlaw motorcycle club rests heavily on the club's ability to provide its male participants with a distinct sense of personal identity. As the membership requirements of an organization become more exclusive, so also does the identity; and the more specific the identity provided, the more compelling membership becomes. The outlaw subculture supplies a rich repertoire of symbols and rituals—values and behaviors—that allow an individual patch holder to both locate and define himself as a valid social entity within a distinct group. A critical part of the outlaw image is the male mystique, a quality of being proudly and unabashedly masculine.

All societies take the biological fact of sex differences and construct sexual identities: status positions, role expectations, and personality traits that are ascribed on the basis of gender. The specific nature of the values and behavior assigned to an individual by virtue of his or her sexual identity will vary from society to society. However, the social reality of the male/female dichotomy rests on a universal process of differentiation wherein masculinity becomes the antithesis of femininity. Anthropologists Spradley and Mann (1975) conclude their study of sexual identity and social interactions with the statement that "masculinity can only acquire its meaning in contrast to femininity." In order for the outlaw-motorcycle-club subculture to establish itself as a bastion of masculinity, its male participants must distinguish themselves from anything that resembles a female influence or femininity. Furthermore, this extraordinary emphasis on masculinity results in bikers being more chauvinistic than males in larger society. That is, the achievement of a masculine biker identity is ensured in part by restricting women to a highly "feminine" presence: "Femininity pleases men because it makes them appear more masculine by contrast" (Brownmiller, 1984). While women are integral components of the outlaw subculture as a whole, to allow female participation as club members would necessarily dilute the psychological pay-off for the male members. Female membership and competition would break down the gender contrast and result in a blurring of roles, power, and identity. In effect, the presence of women as club members would change the very idea of what a biker is. It would detract from the authenticity of the outlaw biker identity by robbing it of one of its major reference points: masculine prowess. This has not happened. Within the outlaw-motorcycle-club subculture, the activity of motorcycling and the role of patch holder remain exclusively male enclaves.

In the social philosophy of the outlaw-biker culture, being male means being tough. Outlaw patch holders have to be strong and power-ful enough to maintain the freedom and independence that they believe underlie the integrity of one's being. The "freedom ethic" of an outlaw biker is continually tested in terms of persevering in his commitment to the club despite the social censure and moral condemnation that the biker lifestyle receives from mainstream society. For Blues, being an outlaw is synonymous with having the independence to exercise free-dom of choice: "We're an outlaw club because we do what we want to do, and not what the average citizen expects us to do. . . . In the club's eyes, an outlaw biker means doing what we believe in, not what every-body expects us to be like. After you've stood up for your patch [club emblem] then it's an outlaw patch." To earn his colours a striker has to go out of his way to demonstrate a commitment to the Rebels Motorcycle Club and the brotherhood under adverse conditions. . . .

In the outlaw-motorcycle-club subculture a striker establishes his identity by emotionally and symbolically breaking dependency relations with the host society. Because of their dependency needs and the cultural restrictions on their behavior, women are less likely to make such a radical departure from social conventions. A woman may view her entry into the biker subculture as an act of rebellion in the name of personal freedom; but she is not the rebel, only the companion. She becomes an important part of the outlaw scene, but she never actively defines or shapes it. "For me it was like a rebellion, mainly against my father and my lifestyle, all the boring superficial people. It was a way to break away from all the rules and more of an opportunity to be myself. I relate to this [biker] lifestyle because you don't really care what other people think about you. I don't feel like I have to do anything anymore that I don't want to. . . . No, I have no desire to ride my own bike. That would take away from it. I'm perfectly happy on the back. My trip is to be John's woman riding on the back of his Harley" (Marilyn). Marilyn's rebellion is vicarious. Her independence and power are a reflection of her man's and, as a consequence, her freedom is limited by her man. "John usually decides what we're going to do and when we're going to do it. . . . Yeah, in a lot of ways I have to be very careful about who I talk to. . . . I used to be single and very outspoken. That was hard to change. We had lots of arguments about that. But now people who knew me a year ago wouldn't recognize me. I had to become a lot more passive. . . . The hardest thing to get used to was being told what to do" (Marilyn).

An outlaw patch holder achieves a sense of personal satisfaction and authenticity by being able to stand up resolutely for club values, remaining true to these ideals under adversity. The fact that a woman could do the same would by itself devalue this sense of accomplishment. In effect, female membership in an outlaw club would blunt a man's experience of being set apart by virtue of his having achieved a special goal. In the outlaw-biker community, rebellion as a road to independence remains a male venture. It is highly unlikely that women will ever gain equality in the social philosophy of the outlaw-motorcycle-club subculture; females as equals would shatter the image of a biker as a rare breed of male independence and courage.

In addition to promoting a positive male image and precluding the participation of women in the club on an equal basis, the machismo ideal extends its influence, not surprisingly, into the arena of male-female relations. Women play a role in members' self-definition in that interaction with women becomes part of the process of defining maleness. Male chauvinism is cultivated as part of the machismo ideal: male dominance and aggressiveness are complemented by female passivity and subservience, especially in the area of sexual gratification. The asymmetrical quality of sexual relations reflects the nature and distribution of power in the outlaw subculture. Certain club events in particular feature sex-oriented role performances that express the machismo theme of male power. These ritual performances both define and communicate what is considered appropriately masculine and feminine; participation confirms that identity. "Women are here to serve, so we make them serve. . . . The first thing we do when a visitor comes to town is get him a woman to get his balls off, and give him lots of head. At this one party we had, splashing [passing females around in a group orgy] got to be a little boring; so we started pouring wine up their pussy, and we used cunt for wine glasses" (O.J., Coffin Cheaters MC, Sudbury, Ontario). The above example is both exceptional and extreme; most events of this nature are more restrained, such as wet-T-shirt or no-T-shirt contests for women at inter-club parties. The portrayal of these masculine (dominance) and feminine (submissive) traits is not as deviant as may first appear to outsiders. From a comparative perspective, these dramatizations of the machismo ethic are extreme statements of traditional values in the larger society. It is noteworthy that when these intermittent instances of extreme machismo do occur, they are limited to "loose broads" and mamas; they do not as a rule involve ol' ladies, the long-standing personal companions of members. The presence of these distinct categories of females allows members to separate dramatizations of the machismo ethic from displays of emotional togetherness and companionship that are reserved for their ol' ladies. . . .

Surprisingly, the major threat to the social cohesion of the outlaw motorcycle club is an internal one: members' personal ties with women. Unless a member's female companion (ol' lady) is effectively integrated within the outlaw subculture, the strong male-to-female bond will compete with the club as an alternative social commitment. Caveman, a road captain with the Rebels, pointed out that the club doesn't always win these competitions: "I've seen a lot of members fall because of ol' ladies." Club members work on the assumption that their brothers will not compromise the priority each gives to club participation: "The club comes first and that's the way it is! It has to be that way" (Blues). When members were faced with a possible one-or-the-other choice in a conflict situation, the club always received priority over outside commitments such as the member's job, other organizations, parents and siblings (family of orientation), immediate relatives, or outside friends. Members did not hesitate in giving precedence to their club commitment, as is exemplified by Steve's response: "If it came down to a choice between the two? The job would definitely go by the boards. I'd say: 'Shove it up your ass!' I'll be a Rebel" (Steve, Rebels MC).

However, when the issue becomes one of the club taking precedence over a member's wife and children (family of procreation), some very significant differences in members' collective expectations become evident. Representing one extreme are patch holders such as Blues and Caveman who believe that club members should not be married while active in the club. For Caveman it was a matter of membership and marriage being incompatible by virtue of the tremendous time and effort that both required: "Marriage and biking don't mix. If the time ever comes that I want to get married and settle down, I'll quit the club, because I know that I won't be able to put the proper amount of time into both. Like I'd have to be devoted to one or the other, but not both." As far as Blues was concerned, the idyllic biker existence was one that was not bound by the obligations of marriage: "There are no biker weddings, only ex-biker weddings."

There are a number of Rebels who don't agree with this position in either theory or practice. Larry and Steve, for example, are both active members; and the fact that they have been elected to executive positions—Larry as treasurer, Steve as sergeant at arms—indicates that their performance as club members has been "righteous" in the eyes of their brothers. Yet both Larry and Steve have ol' ladies to whom they are married and with whom they are raising children. Larry furthermore claimed that he would choose his ol' lady and family over the club if the situation arose: "Yeah, my ol' lady is ahead of the club. She and my family are number one to me." Steve differs with Larry on this point, and for him the question isn't an academic one: "It's already come up several times now. She [ol' lady] threatens to leave me because of the club; but in the end, she never does." For other members, who fall somewhere between these two polar perspectives, the choice is neither an obvious nor an easy one: "Well, what kind of question [one-or-the-other choice situation] is that, Coyote? Cut off your balls or cut out your heart? I don't really know. I love 'em both. I think it would depend on who pushed me first" (Ken).

The subcultural value of not compromising club participation for the sake of outside commitments is reinforced by the way it is merged with the outlaw biker freedom ethic. Ideally, having no social entanglements— such as a marriage that entraps—allows a biker to revel in "the magic-carpet freedom of being able to take off any time, for anywhere, on any whim . . . [to be an individual who] doesn't fear the wildness of life, but instead is a part of it and free" (Via, 1980, p. 30). According to Wee Albert, a Rebel patch holder who is married: "It's a single man's club with a single man's freedoms. They [vested members] look down on marriage.

They like the members to be in a position where if the chick crosses him up at all, he can say: 'The hell with you!' and end it all right there; and then move on to someone else."

These ideals have far-reaching ramifications for the type of personal relationship that members can establish with women. Striker Loud moved in with a woman who was an "ex" ol' lady of a member of the Warlords MC. It was an affair that eventually led to his expulsion. "We didn't approve of his ol' lady. We asked that he just drop her at first. Then we saw that he was reasonably serious about the girl, so we just asked that he spend more time with the club. . . . He was going overboard on this chick and finally he was asked to leave and his striker patch was picked up. We could see that this chick was no good and taking up too much time. We warned Striker about this chick" (Snake, Rebels MC).

If a striker is already married his wife will be casually interrogated and their interaction will be closely scrutinized to ensure that there is no conflict of interest regarding the striker's impending commitment to the club. "Basically, the members want to find out whether the striker can get his own way when they want him to" (Dianne, Wee Albert's ol' lady). Dianne recalls one afternoon when several Rebels rode their bikes over to down a few brews with her ol' man while he was striking for the club: "Before they'd consider Albert [as a potential member], they put me through the third degree. They'd come over and sort of harass me to see how much I'd take, and to see if Albert got his way when he wanted it. Finally, I just said: 'Look, as long as the club doesn't step on my toes, I'll be the last person to step on theirs.' They want the women to be around to pour the coffee, make the meals, keep the house clean, and fuck them when they decide to be around. They look on marriage as something perverse." Dianne referred to her informal interrogation session as "my very own striking period."

In addition to looking for reassurances that she will not be an interfering element, the members will converse with the ol' lady with the expressed purpose of deriving information about the striker's character that otherwise might not surface until a later date. "A man's old lady is a mirror of himself. They've grown accustomed to each other and they think alike. Although a guy may be very interested in becoming a member, he sometimes camouflages his true personality. He may cover up some trait that he might feel isn't good for the club. His old lady will let something like that slip" (Wee Albert). . . .

The Roles of Women:
Broads, Mamas, and Ol' Ladies

Broads

The term "broad" is often used in reference to unattached single women who are engaging in initial or casual contact with the club. This category of women represents a transitional stage of association that will either terminate after one or several social encounters or, alternatively, result in a woman establishing ties with the club either as a club mama or as a member's ol' lady. The somewhat uncomplimentary label "broad" is not restricted to this subcultural context, but is commonly used for women in general. Nor is the term universally used by bikers. Depending on their mood or what their intentions are, members might use terms such as chick, fox, pussy, bitch, honey, sweetheart, or lady to refer to the wide variety of would-be "scooter starlets" who drift in and out of the outlaw-club subculture. The number of broads present at any given time will vary according to the situation, from several women who like to sit with the Rebels at the club bar to any number that members might encounter at a private or clubhouse party.

These women appear to be similar to the bikers in that many of them are young, restless, and bored. One woman who was being "hustled" by a Rebel patch holder in the club bar offered the following commentary: "When it comes right down to it, most of these guys are really nice. Some, like Caveman, are pretty awesome; I guess you could say scary. But then that's a big part of it [the attraction]. These guys are action. I get a lot of stares [while riding on the motorcycle] from straight chicks stuck in boring cars; and I just know what their fantasy is. Just being around, being part of the [outlaw club] scene, brings an excitement all its own" (Deborah).

The Rebels present an intriguing alternative, practicing their night moves within the shadows of the outlaw mystique. The women themselves are initially attracted to the heavy macho image that the bikers embody, the intrigue of association with an outlaw, the thrill of flouting social norms, and the partying and excitement of the hedonistic lifestyle.

The majority of broads are transient visitors in the subculture. The full extent of the interaction is usually limited to socializing over drinks at the club bar, "getting it on" at a club party, and a possible one-night sexual stand. Accepting an invitation to "go for a ride on my bike" may be extended to a visit to the clubhouse. Providing that the member "gets lucky," the visit converts into an overnight stay. As is the case with most outlaw clubs, the Rebels' clubhouse features a "turnout room" where members who "get lucky" can complete the sexual liaison in relative privacy. Turnout rooms are generally not very elaborate; typically the contents will include one or two mattresses on the floor, a chair, a nightstand, and possibly carpeting. The Rebels have two such rooms on the second floor of their clubhouse. For a nominal fee members are able to rent one of these rooms as a temporary residence if they so require.

If the girl consents to having sex with the member who brought her, there is the possibility that she—with or without a little "friendly persuasion" in the form of booze, dope, or covert intimidation—will be shared sexually among several members, a practice known as "pulling the train." On one occasion the girl's pink panties were removed and nailed to a ceiling rafter to announce the "free lunch." It should immediately be pointed out that, as far as the Rebels were concerned, "friendly persuasion" was never to include physical coercion. . . . Despite the questionable chauvinistic treatment that they sometimes receive, there never appears to be any shortage of young girls who are willing to risk "taking a walk on the wild side." . . .

Social interactions with broads are usually temporary in nature. They involve the compartmentalization of feelings of emotional warmth in favour of satisfying purely sexual desires. The naivety of some girls—"Do you think that he'll respect me after this?"—is returned with scorn: "Baby, if you want to be wild, you've got a lot to learn!" There are, however, those patch holders who yearn and search for that "special lady" who will provide them with the pleasure and security of constant female companionship. A patch holder who is attracted to a particular woman to the extent that he would like to try to establish a steady relationship within the context of sentiments such as caring, affection, and love certainly won't "turn her out" (share her sexually with his brothers). If the two are successful in this emotional venture and the relationship stabilizes over time, then the woman will be protected and respected by the club as the member's ol' lady. If a woman does not establish herself as an ol' lady, but continues to have social and sexual interactions with a number of club members, there is the possibility that she might be incorporated within the outlaw subculture as a club mama.

Mamas

Mamas are women who have established an informal association with the club as a whole. At the outset it should be stated that the majority of outlaw clubs do not have mamas per se. Among those clubs that do, mamas are the numerically least significant—from one to several—of the three categories of females (broads, mamas, and ol' ladies). The Rebels had one woman, Athena, who could be classified as a mama, over a period of four years. The actual significance of the role that mamas play in the outlaw subculture will vary substantially from club to club.

A mama's interactions with a club are usually limited to those of a social-sexual nature. As distinguished from an ol' lady, who maintains an exclusive relationship with, and "belongs to" a particular patch holder, a mama has inclusive ties—including sexual availability—with the club as a whole. For example, while the Rebels were partying at the clubhouse of the Bounty Hunters MC in Victoria, two young women visited the clubhouse on an almost daily basis. Brenda, a cocktail waitress, and Helene, a secretarial student, maintained an easygoing relationship with the Bounty Hunters. The two women would clean the clubhouse premises, cook an occasional meal, party, ride, and have "a good time" with the members. It is part of the outlaw code that the host club will share these females with a visiting club. Brenda and Helene engaged in sexual liaisons with a couple of Rebels whom they found attractive and "got off on" during the course of our visit.

For a small number of outlaw clubs, the mama role will take on an added economic dimension. The club may require that the mama bring in living expenses. For instance, a mama may donate part of her wage earnings as a waitress, secretary, or dancer to the club coffers. Under certain circumstances the mama may work for the club itself in some money-making venture. For example, several of the twenty-seven chapters of the Outlaw MC that are located primarily in the eastern United States—Chicago, Tennessee, North Carolina, and Florida—operate massage parlours that employ club mamas. A variation on this theme is for any number of members to use mamas to obtain money from the sale of sexual favours. Two members of the Grim Reapers MC in Calgary, Alberta, were recently charged with living off the avails of prostitution (1984). A number of the Hell's Angels MC chapters reportedly utilize mamas to sell narcotics such as methedrine and cocaine. As a rule, however, clubs or members involved in trafficking operations will employ ol' ladies who, by virtue of their close personal ties with members, pose less security risk. In return for her various contributions, the club provides the mama with access to drugs, alcohol, and physical protection if required. The element of social support in this arrangement may enable the mama to achieve a sense of belonging in a social community, albeit as a marginal participant.

Once these relations terminate, so too does the mama's affiliation with the club. A woman's role as club mama, especially the aspect of sexual promiscuity, precludes the possibility that a member will consider her as an ol' lady.

Ol' Ladies . . .

Ol' ladies are the dominant female force in the outlaw-club subculture, in terms of both the role that they play and their overall numerical presence. An ol' lady is a woman who has established a personal relationship with a particular member. When a member states that "this is my ol' lady," he tells his brothers that the relationship is "solid" (stable), and that it is to be respected and not to be jeopardized by "making a run on" (advances towards) the woman. Provided that the relationship is of a permanent nature—or intended to be so—the term "ol' lady" is used irrespective of whether the woman is the member's girlfriend, covivant, or wife. A woman might be introduced as "Lorraine, Blue's ol' lady," or "Donna, Clayton's ol' lady." Sixteen of the twenty-four Rebels have ol' ladies: fourteen of these arrangements involve cohabitation, five members are married, and three members have children as part of a nuclear-family situation. The use of the term ol' lady rather than more socially conventional labels, such as wife or girlfriend, has significance other than just creating a convenient linguistic border marker between the club and host society. Within the ethos of the outlaw-biker culture, ol' lady comes to mean much more than a wife and implies some very definite personal values and behavioural orientations.

It is somewhat ironic that while the ol' lady is the most important female element in the outlaw-motorcycle-club subculture, she is also the principal threat to the solidarity of the brotherhood because of the competition she offers. Conversely, the reality that an ol' lady has to face is that her greatest rivals for her ol' man's time and attention are an iron mistress—the motorcycle—and the brotherhood. This rivalry is rarely subtle, and at least once a week it is expressed within the context of formal club activity. Every Thursday night is Boys' Night Out. On this evening the presence of ol' ladies at the club bar or clubhouse is forbidden. The express purpose of Boys' Night Out is to provide an opportunity for members to get together privately—without their ol' ladies—to discuss personal matters and intensify the ties of brotherhood while having a good time partying. During these evenings and similar events such as a stag run, an ol' lady will have to reconcile herself to the fact that her ol' man is out riding, partying, and "getting it on" without her. During a moment of reflection, Denise, Larry's ol' lady, conveyed the following sentiments to Sandra, my ol' lady: "Oh, there'll be nights when you'll be lying alone in a big empty bed, and you'll be either swearing sweet somethings at the ceiling or worrying about whether he's dead or alive. But it'll sure feel good when he's home beside you."

The reactions of ol' ladies to their ol' man's subcultural affiliation will vary along a continuum ranging from resistance and challenge to support and personal identification as a biker's woman. If an ol' lady chooses to resist her ol' man's involvement with the outlaw-biker lifestyle, her own participation in club events such as runs and parties will be minimal. Furthermore, if this resistance becomes too overt and intense—to the point of noticeably interfering with the member fulfilling his obligations—the member will eventually be faced with a one-or-the-other choice between his ol' lady and the club. Alternatively, an ol' lady can accept her ol' man's club affiliation, respect the bond between him and his machine, and become involved in the outlaw-motorcycle-club subculture in the role of supportive companion. This supportive-role position will involve the ol' lady in formal and informal club events and result in her going through changes in personal identity (value and behavioural orientations) that are consistent with those of her ol' man and the collective self-image of the club.

Ideally, the primary concern of an ol' lady is her ol' man. She is expected to accept him as the major decision maker. As a result, ol' ladies assume a secondary position within the extended social network of the club. Within the context of the outlaw-motorcycle-club subculture, women do not act either as initiators or as mediators in social liaisons; all social activities, projects, and ideas are first screened by the man. Most ol' ladies will respond to these restrictions on their social initiative and manoeuvrability within the subculture by maintaining independent (non-club) social ties. In sharp contrast with the members, the more significant personal ties of ol' ladies—measured in terms of whom they would contact for work or leisure activities—tended to fall outside the outlaw subculture. This difference in social network orientation, in particular in the degree to which members become totally encapsulated within the club, can lead to situations of interpersonal discord. The resultant disagreements between a member and his ol' lady are particularly pronounced if the woman feels that the club is becoming involved in what she would like to consider as their personal or family life together. "We've [member and ol' lady] lived together about five years or more. Call us in love or whatever, but she's definitely the woman for me. But when it comes to the club we clash, we clash very bad. Whenever something [requiring assistance] happens she says: 'Oh, I'll go get my dad, I'll go get my brother, I'll go get my aunt.' Meanwhile I'll be saying: 'I'll go get two or three guys from the club and this'll be all cleared up.' Then she'll say: 'Why? The club has nothing to do with this!' And I'll say: 'What do you mean? The club has everything to do with this!' " (Ken, Rebels MC)

An ol' lady's loyalty to her ol' man extends through him to his brothers. Her home and hospitality are always open to other club patch holders; she may be asked to provide a meal or a "place to crash" (stay the night), without notice and without question. For example, one Rebel striker, Yesnowski, was provided with room and board by Larry and his ol' lady Denise until the striker was able to find a job and get established in a place of his own. The Rebels will reciprocate the ol' lady's accommodating hospitality with feelings of friendship and respect. They will assist the ol' lady in any way possible and be there as a unit if anything should happen to her ol' man.

The role of a biker's ol' lady will influence her style of dress. The wardrobe is pragmatically selected to suit riding on the back of a Harley-Davidson. The female dress code is very similar to that of a male biker, and includes articles such as blue jeans, T-shirt or tank top, shades, riding boots, jean jacket and/or leather jacket, and gloves as its basic components. A skirt or dress may be worn occasionally, but an ol' lady must keep in mind that many of her social soirees may still revolve around the club and its "scooter tramp" members. Choosing such an evening to reveal the latest in vogue fashions would appear somewhat ostentatious. While an ol' lady will never wear club colours, official emblems, or club T-shirt, she will accumulate various other articles of biker paraphernalia. Over time her fundamental biker attire might be supplemented with items such as Harley pins attached to her leathers, a Harley-Davidson eagle wings patch sewn on the back of her jean jacket, biker T-shirts with Harley insignia or sayings such as "Bikers Have More Fun Than People" or "Genuine Harley Parts" inscribed across the breast, biker pendants, wrist chains, and earrings. There are a number of clubs that do allow the ol' ladies of members to wear a "property badge" on their jean jackets or leathers. An ol' lady wears a property badge as a matter of choice and prestige. It will usually consist of the club's colour emblem, for example, an Angel's death head, with "Property of Rogue" (member's club name) written beneath the emblem. Like many members who have their club colours tattooed on their shoulders, an exceptional ol' lady may go so far as to have the property badge tattooed on her shoulder or some other area of her anatomy.

An ol' lady must be prepared to adopt the motorcycle as a top priority. This may mean backing up her ol' man's passion for biking in terms of time, sweat, and money. She will have to make certain accommodations; such as when the winter snows silence the Harley engines and her ol' man decides to "tear down" (disassemble) his "sled" (motorcycle) and make those repairs and modifications that he has imagined, planned, talked about, and anticipated all summer long. An ol' lady must accept the fact that the motorcycle-maintenance role of the male takes precedence over the domestic female role of keeping the house tidy. She should not start to wonder aloud when overly expensive motorcycle parts, greasy tools, and nausea-inducing chemicals leave a trail from the garage, up to the porch, and through the entry hall and end somewhere in the basement (if she's lucky). Raunch was one of three members who solved the problem of spreading his tools around by constructing a ramp over the porch stairway, and then rolling his chopper directly into the living-room: "It relaxes me if I can work on my tranny [transmission] with the television on. Hah! I guess I do my best work while watching Gunsmoke." Snake's ol' lady, Melody, who rents the top floor of the house, was none too pleased with Raunch's technical innovation. Melody did admit, however, that Raunch had been considerate enough to place a protective tarp over the hardwood floors. My lady made the following comment on this aspect of learning to live with a biker: "From talking with some of the members' ol' ladies, I get the impression that one of the first things you have to do is forget about being the best housekeeper on the block. That's not a big deal; and I don't mind you bringing parts of 'Harley' to bed and spending some of our time together polishing them. But I don't want to see the decor of our living room changing from early American to late-model Harley-Davidson" (Sandra, Coyote's ol' lady). . . .

In the outlaw-biker subculture women lack both the solidarity and the power to exercise direct influence as a well-defined integral unit. As a result, relationships among ol' ladies are both derivative and dependent upon the men's club/brotherhood status. The woman becomes dependent on the man for social contact in the subculture; and while most of his friends become hers, her old friends are gradually dropped. "Most of my old friends are gone," Marilyn related, "and all of my new friends that we hang around with I met through John." In the Rebel community ties between ol' ladies are not independent of club politics. For example, the friendship of Dianne and Gail was close enough that Dianne was the principal architect and organizing agent behind Gail's wedding. Nevertheless, when Dianne's ol' man quit the club, her friendship and interaction with Gail stopped.

There is tension between ol' ladies wanting to protect their steady relationships with members on the one hand, and mamas, whom the ol' ladies "affectionately" refer to as "sleaze bags," on the other. The ol' ladies maintain an informal communications network among themselves that provides them with information regarding their ol' man's activities and monitors the behaviour of potential female rivals. If the situation demands action, ol' ladies will make things very uncomfortable for any broads or mamas with indiscreet designs. . . .

The way that a group reacts to internal conflict will reflect the relative sociopolitical power of the parties involved. While conflicts between male patch holders were considered serious business, conflicts among ol' ladies were treated lightly—at least in public. . . .

The outlaw-biker ethos attaches no stigma to members who have extramarital sexual relations or sexual liaisons with females other than their ol' ladies. Such relationships are expected and often joked about. This joking is a vehicle for legitimizing behaviour that is marginally acceptable in the club, but not sanctioned in wider society. It should be noted, however, that not all the Rebel members engaged in promiscuity. "I've been living with Gail for nine years now. We've got two kids and a great thing going between us. I've never really picked up on any of the offers or come-ons that I get here in the bar. Hey, I've got one sweet honey waiting for me at home" (Jim).

Engaging in promiscuous affairs is strictly a matter of personal discretion; some members participate, some don't, but it certainly isn't discouraged. The male perspective on sexual indiscretions reflects a traditional double standard of the wider society. When a brother tells you that sexual variety is the spice of life, he means for himself and not his ol' lady. If an ol' lady is found out to be "making it on the sly," the member would be expected to "drop the chick." Conversely, an ol' man is afforded the luxury of being able to compartmentalize his feelings of warmth and affection, which are usually reserved for his ol' lady, from the impetus of sexual gratification, which may extend beyond his ol' lady to include other interested parties: "Bikers like to party—particularly if the party is female."

The men of the outlaw-motorcycle-club subculture are in part defined by how their women act. An ol' lady must always be aware of the machismo ideal and her own man's image, especially when interacting in a group context. While a woman will almost certainly be more outspoken and independent when interacting with her man in private, when in public her guiding principle must be one of compliance. An ol' lady who attends a club function must consider that her actions reflect on her ol' man and his "honour." The woman must not assert herself to the social detriment of her man; open disagreements that question his authority are to be avoided at all costs. As a rule members will not subject their ol' ladies to extremes of machismo behaviour—aggression, domination, or blatant sexual exploitation—that may befall an occasional broad or mama. The one vehement outburst between a member and his ol' lady that I witnessed at the clubhouse over a three-year period was settled by the member abruptly and with brute force. But a member who uses force on his ol' lady puts himself in a no-win situation. The aggressive assault or beating of a woman—especially one's ol' lady—was not promoted in the club and such behaviour was not a source of prestige. Rather, the use of force by an ol' man suggests that he is not in control of the situation. It is essential to the biker's self-image that he have total control over his bike and his woman: "A man who has no control over his woman loses status very quickly," commented an ol' lady named Marilyn, "almost as fast as a man who can't keep his bike running."

Ideally, a Rebel can maintain the integrity of his position as a man and club patch holder on the basis of a mutual understanding with his woman. Conflict should not be necessary and is considered an indicator of weakness. Both the man and woman are expected to share a definition of masculinity as a positive force that results in personal resolve and a capacity for action that leads to control; but that control is never to be divorced from compassion and mutual respect. . . .

If the situation demands it, an ol' lady may find herself transporting, concealing, or registering weapons for her ol' man in her name. Nearly all the Rebels (twenty of twenty-four) possess firearms. For the most part these weapons are not of the concealable variety, such as handguns, but rather high-powered rifles and shotguns. These weapons are kept for security reasons and because many of the brothers enjoy hunting together in the fall. To display hardware that they are proud of and to ensure ease of accessibility, members often mount these weapons on a gun rack on either their living-room or bedroom wall. Those Rebels who do own guns have also obtained the necessary firearm acquisition certificates, in compliance with Canadian federal statutes. If, however, a member of an outlaw club is unable to procure a firearm certificate, for reason of having a criminal record or being on probation, it is not uncommon for his ol' lady to secure the certificate and legally possess the firearm. Having an ol' lady assume proprietorship over the weapon is a particularly effective strategy in the United States where, under federal jurisdiction, it is illegal for an ex-felon, or anyone under federal indictment, to possess any firearm.

An ol' lady has to learn to balance the good, the bad, and the ugly of motorcycling. The good times are sharing a summertime dream with her ol' man, waking with the sun, riding with the wind, chasing down lonesome stretches of grey after a sun descending behind the blue Rockies, setting up the tent, "smoking rolled ones" and "drinking cool ones" around a campfire, and watching the stars come stealing in. Bad times are having to face a flat tire a hundred miles from another sign of life except for ominous black storm clouds that are no longer off in the distance, or the pain and numbness of getting caught in a late spring snowstorm. The ugly times are those when bikers have to deal with incidents that reflect the fact that 50.8 percent of all motorcycle accidents result from violations of the motorcyclist's right-of-way ([according to the] U.S. Department of Transportation, National Center for Statistics and Analysis, [in] 1980). . . .

References

Brownmiller, S. (1984). *Femininity.* New York: Random House.
Spradley, J. P., & Mann, B. (1975). *The cocktail waitress: Women's work in a man's world.* New York: John Wiley.
Via, J. (1980, December). The last frontier. *Easyriders*, p. 30.

DISCUSSION:
The Russian Organizatsiya

Since the fall of the Berlin Wall in 1989, increases in crime in Eastern Europe have been seen as a direct result of the introduction of capitalist principles (Shelley, Saberschinski, & Sinuraja, 1995). The collapse of law and order has contributed to the growth of an octopuslike organized crime group that specialized in political corruption; common market fraud; illegal trade in drugs, sex, and armaments, even nuclear materials; and trafficking in the international market for art, antiques, and human organs. The vast profits gained from these illicit enterprises have not even been threatened by the fragmented and ill-conceived countermeasures of crime control mounted in the former Soviet Union (Freemantle, 1995).

Kerry (1997) wrote that the Russian Mafiya is a perfect illustration of contemporary OC because it corrupts any specific financial and business system in which it operates. That corruption inevitably taints other systems in the society, including the executive, the courts, the legislature, business sectors, and even the media. In contemporary organizations, the corruption is not confined to its country of origin. The impact on economic and political life is more important than the individual crimes committed by members and hangers-on of the syndicate. Wherever economic development and exchange of money are rapid and regulation does not keep pace, criminal opportunities are increased (Rhodes, 1984, p. 11).

In some ways, the expanding opportunities for OC in Eastern Europe in general and Russia in particular are unique and unparalleled in modern times. But in other ways, the patterns are ages old. Varese (1994) pointed out common elements between Sicily in transition 100 years ago and Russia of the 1990s. For example, in both states, there was distrust in the state's ability, along with a lack of codes and enforcement, to deal with opportunities for deceit. Also common to the two states was the presence of a group of unemployed men trained in the use of violence who were formerly military and police officers and, in Russia, former members of the KGB. Russian OC was particularly menacing due to its connection to key sections of government bureaucracy, its impressive history, and the large networks of corruption already in place before the breakup of the Soviet Union. Smuggling profits was the basis for wealth in the new society. Policymakers believed that corruption and crime were inevitable. OC paralyzed Russian politics, leaving the threat that Russian citizens might turn away from free-market corruption and OC and toward more tyrannical types of politics (Handelman, 1994).

The Russian Federal Agency on Counterintelligence Sources reported that, due to a lack of loyalty and confidence in the new legal authorities in Eastern Europe, one half of all Russian enterprise was controlled by OC gangs to a certain extent (Wessell, 1995). Reports from the U.S. Department of Justice, the New York State OC Task Force, and the Criminal Intelligence Service of Canada agreed that Russian OC was spreading and becoming more of a threat to the Americas. All reports mentioned fraud and financial manipulation as a specialization of Russian OC. Political upheaval and monetary system changes provided an open field of opportunity for gangsters in Eastern Europe.

Volobuev (1990) drew a model of Russian OC that paralleled the organizational arrangements of many international crime groups. According to his model, OC is a pyramid. The base of the pyramid is the operative block of dealers, professional criminals, and swindlers. In the middle are two more groups with higher status, acting as agents of supply and security for the larger group as a whole. At the top is the small elite group of "shadow leaders" who meet the gangsters' needs for organization, administration, and a value system. The elite are the intellectual center of the entire system.

This same pyramid model has been used extensively to describe other OC groups. At the same time, international OC groups with the most effective organization for multinational markets and smuggling are made up of "task forces," or groups that come together to reach a certain goal, then disperse into other arrangements as other goals arise. The fluid and flexible organization of task forces can more easily meet the changing demands arising in the world market. It is this image of international OC that leads enforcement authorities to refer to it as an octopus or a hydra.

The task force model can be combined with the pyramid model for a more dynamic illustration of OC. Members at all levels work toward specific goals in small flexible groups with others having different skills. This is not a democratic arrangement of work groups with equal votes about organizational policy. The pyramid arrangement is maintained by members' shared understanding about status. Members may move up in the pyramid as a reward for loyalty, for some special skill that is needed, or for seniority. In addition to status, members at the middle of the pyramid have access to communication with the upper level but also work in groups with some members on one job and with others to meet other goals. Only at the level of the elite at the top is the arrangement more fixed. At this level, the few real leaders may each have an individual area of special responsibility, but decisions are usually left to them as a group.

With the international opportunities arising in the world monetary system, more complex and sophisticated models of OC develop to meet changing demands. As gangs become better able to establish flexibility on the one side and definite lines of authority on the other, they become increasingly more effective in multinational markets. The linear, hierarchical, bureaucratic arrangement found in most governments and state efforts against OC is at a disadvantage. The streamlined and open arrangement that has evolved with the multibillions of dollars of profits gained for international OC is difficult to infiltrate and almost impossible to destroy.

8

The Organizatsiya

William Kleinknecht

Chapter 11 (pp. 271-286) of *The New Ethnic Mobs,*
by William Kleinknecht (New York: Free Press, 1996)

On Saturday morning, May 4, 1985, Evsei Agron, a middle-aged Soviet emigré, was preparing to leave his apartment at 100 Ocean Parkway in Brooklyn for his weekly trip to the Russian and Turkish Baths on Manhattan's Lower East Side. He said goodbye to his common-law wife, a platinum-blonde cabaret singer, and stepped out into the hallway outside his sixth-floor apartment at 8:35 a.m. With his ill-fitting blue striped suit and balding pate, Agron could have been mistaken for a retired merchant going on a Saturday-morning errand. But any illusions that the tenants of 100 Ocean Parkway may have had about their neighbor were dispelled on this Saturday morning. As Agron stood in the hallway waiting for the elevator, two gunmen stepped from behind a corner and cut him down with small-caliber bullets.

Few tears were shed for the slain Russian among the tens of thousands of law-abiding Jewish emigrés in Brooklyn's Brighton Beach section. Agron was a diminutive man weighing less than 140 pounds, but despite his mild appearance he was a ruthless gang leader who had survived 10 years in harsh Soviet prisons and had come to these shores a dangerous criminal. He had been extorting money from Brighton

Beach businessmen since the early 1970s, making his rounds with a cattle prod that he used on recalcitrant victims. Agron was said to have extorted $15,000 from one emigré by threatening to kill his daughter on her wedding day. Not suprisingly, his slaying was only the last of several attempts on his life. After one gunman's attempt, outside Agron's apartment in 1984, the surgeons operating on him found several bullets in his body left over from previous shootings.[1]

Agron was a pioneer of a new organized-crime threat that has sprung up in the last 15 years in several major American cities—a loose-knit assortment of thieves, extortionists, confidence men and white-collar swindlers that has been dubbed the "Russian Mafia." These cunning and extremely sophisticated criminals—they call themselves the *Organizatsiya*, or organization—are the newest cast of gangsters to gain a foothold in the United States, and they are proving to be among the most insidious. Most were veteran gangsters in the former Soviet Union, where survival in the criminal underworld meant evading the dreaded KGB and carrying out their activities within the tight confines of a totalitarian system. The Soviet police did not need search warrants to sweep through a gang's headquarters, and beatings and torture were the favored interrogation techniques. By comparison, Russian gangsters have found police in this country to be pushovers. "I had one guy in here for questioning whose leg looked like a pretzel," a Brooklyn detective said a few years ago. "It was broken in a dozen places in a Soviet prison. He showed it off and said, 'You're going to do worse to me?' "[2]

Criminal life in the Soviet Union equipped many Russian gangsters with skills perfectly suited to white-collar crime in the United States. Soviet citizens were forced to negotiate their way through the vast communist bureaucracy with a never-ending flow of documents: papers were needed to work, to travel, to buy certain consumer goods, to get medical care, to buy a car. In order to survive, criminals had to master the bureaucracy and learn the fine arts of forgery and counterfeiting. In America, those skills have brought Russian gangsters fortunes from white-collar crimes so sophisticated that they confound all but the most highly trained federal agents.

The most ingenious of these crimes are the so-called "daisy chains" of bogus-fuel wholesalers that beat the federal government out of hundreds of millions of dollars in gasoline and diesel fuel excise taxes. The scam is not all that complex. Since 1982, federal law had required that fuel wholesalers collect the taxes on all their sales and then turn the tax money over to the Internal Revenue Service. Russian crime groups made enormous amounts of money by passing the wholesale fuel through a string of companies and then dissolving the company that sold to the retailers and collected the tax. When the IRS came looking for the hundreds of thousands or even millions of dollars it was owed, the company no longer existed and its officers turned out to have been fictitious. The scam has been used with the sale of both gasoline and No. 2 oil, which can be used as either diesel fuel or home-heating oil. Since no tax is levied on home-heating oil, mobsters would pose as home-heating companies when purchasing No. 2 oil and then turn around and sell the product as diesel fuel, pocketing the taxes they collected from retailers. Among the first Mafia figures to see the potential in the fuel-tax scams was Sonny Franzese, the Colombo family underboss. In the early 1980s, he formed a partnership with several Russian mobsters in a gas scam that was broken up by a federal task force on Long Island.[3] After that, the Russians became the masterminds of most large-scale fuel scams, but they have been required to give the Italian Mafia a cut of every gallon they sell. And still there is enough money to keep everyone happy.[4] . . .

. . . The amount that the fuel-tax-evasion schemes were costing the public only became known for certain after federal authorities clamped down on the daisy chains. On January 1, 1994, a law went into effect requiring taxes to be paid when the wholesaler draws the fuel from the terminal. The new law also requires that No. 2 oil be dyed red if it is to be used as home-heating oil. That means that any clear oil that police now find in a home heating truck can be assumed to be part of a fuel-tax-evasion scam. The savings to the taxpayers produced by these reforms have been stupendous. The Federal Highway Trust Fund, which is the recipient of fuel excise taxes, projected that its revenue would increase by $1.3 billion in 1995 because of the clampdown. The largest share of that savings is believed to have come out of the pockets of Russian crime groups.

But that does not mean that fuel-tax evasion is over. Russian mobsters in the New York area are pushing another scam: they buy gasoline and diesel fuel at New Jersey terminals and sell it in New York without paying the Empire State's steeper sales tax. Robert Shepherd, the top enforcement official in the New York State Department of Taxation and Finance, estimated in June 1995 that Russian crooks were netting up to $1 million a week in the scam.[5] The Russian mob is also believed to be evading fuel taxes by mixing gasoline or diesel fuel with cheap waste oil and selling the concoctions to retailers. That scam is known as "cocktailing." "They have some involvement in almost every aspect of gasoline and diesel fuel distribution," said Robert Buccino, an organized crime investigator with the New Jersey Attorney General's Office.[6]

Russian gangsters are fanning out across the United States. The headquarters of the Russian Mafia is southern Brooklyn, which is home to about a quarter of the 200,000 emigrés who have come to the United States in the last two decades. But the FBI says Russian gangsters also operate in Los Angeles, Boston, Philadelphia, Miami, Detroit, Seattle and other cities. FBI Director Louis Freeh told a congressional committee in May 1994 that the bureau had elevated the Russian Mafia to its highest investigative priority after an internal survey of field offices in April 1992 counted 81 investigations involving Eastern European criminals. Thirteen of those investigations involved organized crime, a number that had nearly tripled by early 1994.[7]

The Russian Mafia is particularly brazen in New York and Los Angeles. Brighton Beach and nearby neighborhoods have been the scene of nearly two dozen gangland slayings involving Russians since 1982. Everyone in the tight-knit Russian neighborhood, often called "Little Odessa," knows who the gangsters are—and indeed they are not hard to spot. Their Cadillacs and BMWs can be seen double-parked at night spots like Rasputin on Coney Island Avenue, where portly mobsters and their fur-clad women reserve the best tables for views of the ostentatious floor shows.

The emergence of Russian organized crime in this country is rooted in the Cold War. In the early 1970s, as the Nixon administration's policy of detente began thawing the deep freeze in East-West relations, the United States pressured the Soviets to prove their good intentions on the world stage by allowing the emigration of Soviet Jews. While anti-Semitism was officially proscribed in the Soviet Union, the centuries-old patterns of repression still ran deep. Jews were effectively barred from the highest echelons of the Communist Party, the military, and other important circles. And anti-Semitic tracts were common in the press. So when President Gerald Ford signed into the law the Jackson-Vanik Amendment, which required the Soviet Union to grant exit visas to increasing numbers of Jews in order to receive the benefits of trade with the United States, there was no shortage of people waiting to emigrate. Between

1975 and 1980, some 90,000 Soviet Jews immigrated to the United States. The number leaving the Soviet Union climbed every year after the amendment, peaking at 51,000 in 1979. And though emigration dropped off after a new freeze in U.S.-Soviet relations in the 1980s, it has resumed its growth since the fall of the old Soviet Union in 1989. In 1990 alone, 185,000 Jews left the Soviet Union.

Estimates put the number of Russian emigrés in the United States at 200,000, the majority of whom have settled in southern Brooklyn. Brighton Beach, a dingy working-class Brooklyn neighborhood just east of Coney Island, has become the city's center of Russian emigré life. Russian restaurants, bakeries and meat shops line Brighton Beach Avenue, and the rough cadences of Russian can be heard among the groups of people strolling the wooden boardwalk on summer nights. In more recent years, thousands of Russian Jews have moved into Bensonhurst, Brooklyn, a traditionally Italian neighborhood. Additional neighborhoods of Soviet Jews have also sprung up in Los Angeles, Chicago, Philadelphia and other cities. For the most part, Russian Jews are honest and hard-working people who open small businesses and strive to send their children to good colleges. Rita Simon, a University of Illinois researcher, surveyed 100 families of Russian Jews in 1983 and found that virtually all of the fathers and most of the mothers had the educational equivalent of four years of college. Among the respondents she found doctors, engineers and others with advanced and highly technical skills.[8]

But among those law-abiding and industrious emigrés, an organized criminal element was present from the very beginning. The Russian *Organizatsiya* is distinct from some other ethnic crime groups in not having grown out of its members' immigrant experiences. Russian mobsters were not groomed in adolescence in overcrowded immigrant neighborhoods where the only place to find a sense of belonging was in a street gang. Russian emigrés face many of the same pressures as other immigrants—the same feelings of cultural alienation, the sense that they are not welcome in this country and have to work harder than others to get a fair shake in the job market. But for the most part, Russian Jews came to this country with far more education and technical skills than most other immigrant groups. And their integration into the American economy has been fairly swift. The Russian criminal class is not a product of economic disadvantage. And that's what makes the Russian Mafia unique: most of its mobsters were already hardened criminals when they arrived here. They came here looking for economic opportunity, just like every other emigré. To them, says Lieutenant John Gallo, a Philadelphia police investigator, "the U.S. is like a big candy store with no one minding the store."[9]

The white-collar background of Russian criminals meant that they did not have to follow the pattern of other ethnic-crime groups and huddle within their own neighborhoods for a generation, forming crude street gangs and sucking the blood out of immigrants like themselves. Though they had no qualms about preying on other emigrés, they arrived here almost immediately ready to prey on the community at large. The victims of the earliest swindles were major credit-card companies, banks, the Internal Revenue Service, and even major department stores, which they looted of millions of dollars with their sophisticated shoplifting and burglary rings.

Federal law enforcement is more accustomed to letting new ethnic crime groups go through their crude street-gang phase before cracking down on them. In the case of the Russians, there was no such phase. They were playing in the big leagues from the day they arrived. But because they did not fit the usual model of an organized-crime group, many federal agencies ignored them. The U.S. Secret Service investigated specific counterfeiting and credit-card schemes. The IRS set up task forces to crack down on gasoline-tax scams. But no one looked at Russian organized crime in its totality. The FBI did not set up a Russian squad until 1994, and as late as 1995 its top officials were admitting that they still knew little about the Russian crime groups in the United States.

The first Russian gangsters in Brighton Beach formed organized bands of swindlers who preyed on other emigrés in the 1970s with an array of confidence schemes. One early Russian crime group was known as the Potato Bag Gang because of a ruse it repeatedly used to steal from emigrés. A member of the gang would tell an emigré that he had just arrived from the Soviet Union with all his money in antique gold rubles. The victim would be shown one of the gold rubles and told he could have a whole bag for a sum of cash. After paying the money and bidding farewell to the new immigrant, the victim would open the bag and find that it was filled with potatoes.[10]

Russian hoods became involved in a mind-numbing array of scams. They pulled off jewelry-store robberies and fur robberies. They pawned off fake diamonds and other jewelry. One group of Russians posed as representatives of Volvo International interested in doing a luggage promotion. They managed to walk away with tens of thousands of dollars in luggage from a Suffolk County distributor without putting down a cent.

One particularly harrowing crime occurred in October 1981. A Russian woman named Larisa Schulman arrived in Philadelphia to invest in a condominium for a friend. After she had chosen the apartment in Northeast Philadelphia, her friend, an Austrian businessman named Richard Egit, was to wire $50,000 in cash to New York. Gary Esterman, a Russian business associate of Egit's who was living in Philadelphia, offered to drive Schulman to New York to pick up the money. Esterman's little nephew accompanied them on the trip.

Inexplicably, Esterman drove around New York for several hours after they picked up the money in the bank. At one point, he left the woman and the small boy in the car for three hours while he was supposedly attending an antique auction. The real reason for the delay became apparent when the three pulled up in front of a home in Northeast Philadelphia later that evening. Three men descended on the car. One of the men maced the woman and the boy and another grabbed the purse with the $50,000. Police believe the heist was set up by a Russian gang in New York. Schulman originally identified two of the robbers but, scared to death, she later fled the country and the charges were dropped. Police later discovered that she had hidden out by signing herself into a mental institution in Switzerland.[11]

Out of this rabble of con men and swindlers, Evsei Agron emerged as something of a kingpin in the early 1980s. The Leningrad-born gangster had been a killer and black marketeer in the Soviet Union and had spent years in prison. He was obviously feared on the streets of Brighton Beach, but police learned only so much about him. "He was a grandfatherly type guy," said Joel Campanella, a U.S. Customs investigator who was then a detective in the New York City Police Department's intelligence unit. "He wasn't a big person. But he was tough. We talked to him in the hospital the first time he was shot, and he said, 'Don't worry. I'll take care of it.' "[12]

Agron was a rogue who even at his advanced age liked to pick fights in the nightclubs of Little Odessa. He left the deep thinking to his chief financial adviser, Marat Balagula, a Russian-born criminal who came to the United States in 1977. Balagula had picked up degrees in business and economics back in the old Soviet Union and had spent years making money in that country's black market. He had a much greater knack than his boss for the kind of white-collar swindles that would propel the

Russian Mafia into big-time crime. And the biggest swindle of them all, the one that would give the Russians their alliance with La Cosa Nostra, was the gasoline-tax scam.

Balagula was reportedly making millions on the gas scam by the mid-1980s. He lived lavishly, driving expensive automobiles and spreading money around Brighton Beach nightclubs. Freelance writer Robert Friedman quoted an underworld source as saying that Balagula would cruise around New York Harbor in luxury yachts and drive around in a white stretch limo. "Marat throws around diamonds the way we throw around dollar bills," a Genovese family soldier was overheard saying on a wiretap.[13]

The FBI was not investigating Russian organized crime in the early 1980s, and the police department had only a skeleton crew with no wiretaps or informants.[14] So it is not known how Agron reacted to his underling's success in the gas scam. But Balagula is not likely to have wanted to take orders from a ruffian like Agron when he was making millions of dollars in white-collar crime on his own. What is known is this: Agron was murdered with his own bodyguard, Boris Nayfeld, standing in the street below. Nayfeld then became Balagula's bodyguard. What is more, Balagula took over ownership of El Caribe, Agron's Brooklyn health club. "Balagula moved into Agron's shoes in all respects," said Campanella, the Customs investigator. "This is the classic type of thing you see when a traditional organized-crime boss dies."[15]

It would not be the last time investigators would suspect Balagula of playing a role in a murder. In 1986, Boris Nayfeld and his brother Benjamin—both loyal employees of Balagula—became embroiled in a dispute with a Russian mobster to whom they had just sold a gasoline dealership, the MVB Energy Company in Linden, New Jersey. The purchaser of the company, Michael Vax, accused the Nayfelds of trying to swindle him by selling a dealership that owed gasoline taxes to the federal government. On February 3, 1986, Vax went to the Platenum Energy Company in Sheepshead Bay, Brooklyn, a gasoline dealership owned by the Nayfelds. Vax confronted them about the back taxes. While they were arguing, two men opened up with automatic weapons through Platenum's side door. Alex Zeltser, the Nayfelds' partner, was killed and Boris Nayfeld was wounded in the thumb. Vax disappeared during the gun battle but later that day showed up at Coney Island Hospital with bullet wounds in his chest.

No one would talk to police about the shootings and the authorities never made a case against Vax. But it was well known in the Russian underworld that Vladimir Reznikov was one of the gunmen. Reznikov had a reputation as a renegade gun for hire in the *Organizatsiya*, a man whose name had surfaced in more than a few Brooklyn murder investigations. "Everybody was afraid of him," said Campanella. "He didn't align himself with anyone. He was a complete cowboy." In this case, a few friends might have helped. On June 13, 1986, he walked out of the Odessa Restaurant on Brighton Beach Avenue and got into a brown Nissan parked at the curb. As he pulled the car out of the parking space, a man approached the driver's-side windows with a .380-caliber handgun and shot him dead. Campanella later found out that Balagula had warned a friend to stay away from the Odessa that night, showing that he had advance knowledge of the rub-out.[16]

Balagula was not on the streets of Brighton Beach for long after Reznikov's murder. Along with the Nayfelds and several others, he was convicted in Philadelphia on charges of heading a scheme in which the credit-card numbers of Merrill Lynch customers were stolen and used to buy more than $300,000 in furs and furniture at Brooklyn stores. Rather than face prison, Balagula fled the country. There were sightings of him in Atlantic City, California, Paraguay, South Africa, and Hong Kong before he was arrested and extradited to the United States in 1989. He is now in federal prison.

Until the early 1990s, the *Organizatsiya* was composed of about 2,000 members nationwide who operated in small criminal cliques. The structure and memberships of these gangs constantly shifted, and police were unable to identify a single person who acted as the boss of a large criminal organization. The FBI did not even include the Russians on its list of ethnic-crime groups in need of close scrutiny.

But the picture changed drastically around 1992. The crumbling of the old Soviet Union in 1989 set off a tidal wave of organized crime that flooded Moscow, St. Petersburg, and other Russian cities. Gangsters placed a stranglehold on many of the private enterprises struggling to emerge in Russia's new market economy. Their power in Russia's new capitalistic society has been compared to that of criminal syndicates in the United States during Prohibition, but that is far too modest a comparison. Russia's new criminal syndicates far exceed in reach and power even the old Capone-Torrio mob. As it makes the difficult transition from state-controlled industry to a private economy, Russia is wide open for plundering by the 5,600 organized-crime groups said to be operating in the country. Russian officials have erected none of the safeguards that the United States employs to prevent criminality. Russia's banks and securities, for instance, are completely unregulated. In this tumultuous period, as millions of new entrepreneurs fuel the growth of Russia's newly liberated economy, organized crime has turned commerce into a bloody free-for-all. Gangs openly extort money from many of the new industries that have sprung up in the country. Even some American companies operating in Russia have had to hire armed guards to fend off extortion attempts.[17] Russian President Boris Yeltsin has called organized crime the biggest threat to Russian society in the 1990s. Nearly 40 percent of the country's new businesses and two-thirds of its corporations, Yeltsin has said, have ties to organized crime. "Organized crime is trying to take the country by the throat," he said in one speech.[18]

Bombings and assassinations linked to organized crime have become commonplace, even in the middle of bustling neighborhoods. Five people were slain by gangsters in downtown Moscow in one week in February 1994. One was Sergei Dubov, publisher of the weekly magazine *New Times*. Dubov, who was shot in the head while walking to his car one morning, had been getting extortion demands from gangsters. Another victim, the manager of a luxury food store's foreign-currency department, was shot down outside his apartment. His briefcase was untouched, so authorities ruled out robbery. In some cases, the assassinations have been of major crime figures whose funerals were of the lavish variety once favored by Chicago gangsters.

Some of the gangs are commanded by *vory v zakone*, or "thieves-in-law," who made up an elite group of criminals in the old Soviet Union. In the harsh Soviet prison system, the thieves-in-law were the thugs most feared and respected by their fellow inmates. One could only be named a thief-in-law by the recommendation of another, and there was usually an elaborate coronation ceremony. Thieves-in-law are paid homage by other criminals when they are back on the street. They were naturals to take the helm of the new gangster state emerging in Russia, but they have not gone unchallenged. Some of the toughest new mobs in Russia are ethnic gangs that have their roots in other former Soviet republics, such as Chechnya and Azerbaijan.[19]

As Russian crime groups have grown in sophistication, they have begun dispatching emissaries to Western Europe and the United States to conquer new territory. Russian gangsters are now responsible for much of the organized crime in Poland, Germany and other European counties. And a new generation of gangsters has been appearing in New York, Los Angeles and other U.S. cities. Part of the reason is the new influx of Russians coming to the United States on tourist visas. In 1992, for instance, there were more than 129,000 nonimmigrant U.S. visas issued to residents of Russia, the Ukraine and Belarus, compared with some 3,000 in 1988. Between 10 and 20 percent of the visa holders do not return to Russia before the documents expire, and authorities say many of these overstaying their welcome are gangsters.[20] Indeed, police have seen dozens of cases where Russian hit men or swindlers are brought into the country to commit specific crimes and then shuttled out of the country.[21]

U.S. authorities have watched with alarm as gangsters well known to the Russian authorities as top crime bosses have started showing up in Brooklyn, Los Angeles and other cities. The authorities fear that these newcomers will forge crime groups that are far more dangerous and organized than their predecessors in the Russian-American community. "Before we had the second stringers," said James Moody, chief of the FBI's organized crime program in Washington. "Now we're getting the first team."[22]

The most closely watched of these new arrivals was Vyacheslav Ivankov, who goes by the nickname Yaponchik, or "Little Japanese." Ivankov, known to Russian police as one of the most respected *vory v zakone*, slipped into Brooklyn in January 1993 after a long criminal career in Russia. Ivankov is a short, compact man with thick brown hair and an elfin beard. He has eight-pointed stars tattooed on the front of either shoulder, which reflect his status as a *vory v zakone*. In 1980, he founded Moscow's Solontsevskaya gang, which specialized in posing as police officers and robbing the homes of wealthy Russians, according to authorities. Ivankov was convicted of one of those robberies in 1981 and sentenced to 14 years in a Soviet prison. But he allegedly bribed a judge and was released from Tulun prison in Siberia in 1991.[23] He fled the country two years later as Russian officials were seeking his arrest for a parole violation. Russia's Ministry of Internal Affairs immediately tipped off the FBI that he was headed for New York, and he could have been deported for lying about his criminal past on his visa application. But federal agents decided to let him stay and watch his movements.

Federal officials say Ivankov planned to use his reputation to tie together the nation's loosely organized Russian gangs into a criminal syndicate. "We believe that he has been sent here to take control of North America for a Russian crime group," said a high-ranking federal law enforcement official. FBI agents watched Ivankov meeting with other Russian mobsters in New York, Miami, Los Angeles, Boston and Toronto. He kept his base in Brighton Beach but also had an apartment in Denver. By early 1995, the FBI had intelligence that Ivankov's New York branch of the Solontsevskaya gang had about 100 members and was recognized on the street as the premier Russian crime group in Brooklyn. "Among the Russian organized crime groups in this country, his is the strongest," said Raymond Kerr, who heads the Russian organized crime squad in the New York FBI office.[24]

But his meteoric rise in the Russian rackets would not last. In June 1995, Ivankov was charged with attempting to extort $3.5 million from two Russian-born owners of Summit International Corporation, a Manhattan investment firm. The Russian mobsters who carried out the extortion were recorded on wiretaps getting instructions from Ivankov on a cellular phone. In one conversation, the mobsters informed Ivankov that the father of one of the victims had been beaten to death on a Moscow subway platform. On May 25, 1995, the mobsters kidnapped the victims, Alexander Volkov and Vladimir Voloshin, from the lounge of the New York Hilton and brought them to the upstairs of the Troika Restaurant, described in court papers as a hangout for Russian gangsters in Fairview, New Jersey. There the two were forced to sign an agreement to come up with $3.5 million in a series of payments.[25] Federal authorities pulled in the net a month later, charging Ivankov and eight others in the extortion scheme. Little Japanese was arrested at his girlfriend's home in Brooklyn, where he cursed at federal agents. He was in no better a mood the next day. As he was led in handcuffs across Federal Plaza in Manhattan, he kicked and spat at several reporters and photographers.

Notes

1. Author's interview with Joel Campanella, U.S. Customs Service agent, March 19, 1993; Robert I. Friedman, "Brighton Beach Goodfellas" *Vanity Fair,* Jan. 1993, p. 26; *Washington Post,* June 24, 1990.

2. Daniel Burstein, "The Russian Mafia: A New Crime Menace Grows in Brooklyn," *New York,* Nov. 24, 1986, p. 40.

3. Campanella interview.

4. Friedman, "Brighton Beach Goodfellas," p. 36.

5. Author's interview with Robert Shepherd, June 22, 1995.

6. Author's interview with Robert Buccino, June 21, 1995.

7. *International Organized Crime and Its Impact on the United States*, witness list and prepared statements for hearing on May 25, 1994, before the Permanent Subcommittee on Investigations, U.S. Senate, Louis Freeh's prepared statement, p. 7.

8. Rita J. Simon, "Refugee Families' Adjustment and Aspirations: A Comparison of Soviet Jewish and Vietnamese Immigrants," *Ethnic and Racial Studies*, October 1983, pp. 492-504.

9. Mike Mallowe, "From Russia With Guns," *Philadelphia*, May 1983, p. 143.

10. Campanella interview; *New York Times*, June 4, 1989.

11. Mallowe, "From Russia With Guns," p. 142.

12. Campanella interview.

13. Friedman, "Brighton Beach Goodfellas," p. 32.

14. Campanella interview.

15. Ibid.

16. Ibid.

17. *New York Times*, July 8, 1994.

18. *International Organized Crime and Its Impact on the United States*, witness list and prepared statements, Louis Freeh's prepared statement, p. 1.

19. Author's interview with James Moody, head of the FBI's organized crime division in Washington, Jan. 18, 1995.

20. Louis Freeh's prepared statement, p. 6.

21. *New York Times*, April 11, 1992.

22. Moody interview.

23. Arrest complaint in *U.S. v. Vyacheslav Ivankov*, Complaint No. 950899M, U.S. District Court, Eastern District of New York.

24. Author's interview with Raymond Kerr, June 20, 1995.

25. Arrest complaint in *U.S. v. Vyacheslav Ivankov*.

PART
V

CRIMINAL JUSTICE POLICY

Crime is a political phenomenon.
Chambliss (1995, p. 9)

This final section examines what Chambliss (1995) referred to as "state organized crime" (p. 183). The most important type of criminality organized by the state consists of acts defined by law as criminal and committed by state officials in the pursuit of their jobs as representatives of the state. It involves the institutionalized policies of the state. Law is a two-edged sword; it creates one set of conflicts while it attempts to resolve another. Today, states organize smuggling, assassinations, covert operations, and conspiracies to criminally assault citizens, political activists, and those perceived as a threat. These acts are criminal in the laws of the nations perpetrating them, yet examples persist throughout history.

It is essential to examine the role of the state in the development of OC in the Americas. Two well-known examples have been used here to illustrate the ways in which OC and the legal authorities are inextricably linked throughout history and into the future.

DISCUSSION:
Chicano Prison Gangs

Chicano gangs are a reflection of legal authorities in a society in which institutionalized racism operates in education, the job market, the housing market, and the criminal justice system (Moore, 1994). Gangs resulted from economic restructuring. The unemployability of young males is a common denominator in gangs that develop where there are gaps in the existing institutional structure. Cultural barriers in the classroom and high levels of dropouts lead to a serious educational gap (Vigil, 1997). Youth gangs develop among socially marginal adolescents for whom school and family do not work. Street socialization takes on increased importance (Moore, 1991). This may be even more true for females than for males. Moore found that girls who were involved with gangs were much more likely than boys to have come from a family of origin that had been involved with gangs too. Gang girls found themselves confined by their past and their membership in the gang to a street-oriented lifestyle. The gang was a support group and refuge but also a milieu within which they were doubly stigmatized by others in the community and by members of society at large. Traditional values "protected" most of the young women in the community, but they increased risk of a street life for gang girls because they were the basis for labeling (Moore, 1994).

Girls in Chicano gangs often reproduce a pattern of several generations that they feel powerless to avoid.

Urban youth gangs develop in a climate of "multiple marginality" (Vigil, 1997, p. 172). The predisposing factors for development of gangs found in Los Angeles, for example, include friction between residents and law enforcement, diversity of language, deep family stress, lack of control over social institutions, and high unemployment, along with a lack of leisure-time activities (Vigil, 1997). Chicano neighborhoods in Los Angeles, known as *barrios*, provide a sense of identity and an environment for maintaining the customs and values that Mexican immigrants brought with them. Los Angeles has been known as the Mexican capital of the United States. But the barrios there have been strongly affected by urban growth and technology (Romo, 1983).

Prison is an omnipresent reality in Chicano neighborhoods. Contact with prison has been continuous and drastic and has affected nearly everybody in the barrio (Moore, 1978). Many youths in the Chicano barrio followed a lifelong journey to prison. Overrepresentation of Hispanics in prisons has been documented for more than 100 years in the United States. The most common offenses for which Chicanos have been incarcerated are narcotics related. In 1929, they were marijuana related; in later years, they were heroin related. Because drug-related offenses carry long mandatory minimum sentences, Chicanos spend longer prison terms than other ethnic groups. Reliance on peer and primary groups in prison tends to increase with the length of the sentence. Chicano gangsters in California prisons have grown more strongly identified with their gangs as they have done increasingly longer sentences.

Prison is the climax in a series of dealings with progressively more punitive institutional agencies: health, welfare, education, economy, law. Chicanos both in the barrio and in prison operate within various social structures: They are dependent on people-processing bureaucracies, involved in a complex web of bartering in contraband, and self-identified as a racial minority, relegated to the secondary labor market and working at the margins of the system (Moore, 1991). The Chicano prison gangs in California developed in an environment in which money was scarce yet necessary and where there were corruptible authorities and willing participants. The continuities between street socialization and prison socialization are striking. There is the cycle of poverty without end. There is low status in the legal hierarchy. There is lack of education and training. And there is also the involvement with narcotics and the familiar support network of friends and family members. Gangs grow strong in this fertile environment among men imprisoned most of their lives. Their motives are pecuniary: domination of the prison economy and ultimately control of the illegal economy of the streets.

The California Department of Corrections has a long, extensive, and intensive experience with prison gangs. California gangs have demonstrated more violence and gained more attention than in other states. Prison gangs there originated in state prisons and moved to the street. At the same time, gangs began on the streets and moved into the prison, where they met up with prison gangs with strong organizations and particular criminal goals. Sometimes, the result was conflict; in other instances, combinations resulted. California prison authorities first noticed, in 1957, that groups inside prison had given up their street gang identities for prison gang identities with the collective purposes of mutual protection, power, and control over illicit business. The gangs recruited the most violent inmates. When the administration became aware of these tough Chicanos banding together, they reacted by dispersing them to other state prisons. In retrospect, it was claimed that this move gave the gangs new recruiting grounds (Camp & Camp, 1985).

Assuming that the issue was mainly a racial one, prison officials separated the groups into facilities by race. Rather than suppressing the gangs, this measure enabled the violence to continue to grow into the early 1970s. The department responded by locking all leaders and known gangsters in special control units, and the violence stabilized. Yet at the same time, even stronger core groups of gangsters were created who identified deeply with gang life. Police saw that as gang members were released, they carried orders to the streets. As more gang members were rearrested, problems came back to prison. By the late 1970s, the corrections department had developed a standard policy of isolating gang members and cooperating with law enforcement to monitor gang activity (Camp & Camp, 1985). This policy virtually ensured that gangs would be perpetuated. It intensified the commitment of the core leadership group and lengthened the amount of time that Chicanos remained incarcerated.

During the 1980s, a stereotypical image of violent prison "supergangs" arose with general increased repression in the barrio. By the early 1990s, the gangs were more entrenched, more institutionalized, more important to the lives of the members, and more deviant than they had been in the 1950s, when they were first observed. The differences are not dramatic. What is surprising is the continuity over generations (Moore, 1991, p. 132).

Moore (1991) wrote an extensive history of Chicano gangs. The earliest years were the 1930s and 1940s, when the gangs started out as friendship groups of adolescents, committed to defending one another, the *barrio*, and their gangs. The introduction of heroin in the late 1940s was a major turning point in the history of Chicano gangs. California state laws became more punitive, and more and more gang members were sent to prison. Los Angeles gangs began to incorporate traditions about prison survival (p. 25). Prisons became regular repositories for most active gang members (Vigil, 1988, p. 175).

Chicano gangs are one example of the type of gangs that formed in response to prison life. Prison gangs are often found in old, large, overcrowded prison facilities (Camp & Camp, 1985). They are close-knit groups whose organization varies from loosely to tightly structured and whose direction ranges from informal word-of-mouth slogans and rules to formal and written creeds and regulations. Their purposes range from mutual caretaking of members to large profit-making enterprises. Membership is based on race and ideas of racial superiority. Gangs are likely to be linked to neighborhoods outside the prison. Members have strong beliefs and share a lifestyle that makes the gang likely to be extremely influential to them (Kenney & Finckenauer, 1995).

In most prison gangs, membership is considered a lifetime commitment. The phrase "Blood in, blood out" was a code of honor meaning that blood was shed in initiating the gangster and blood would be shed if the gangster ever left the gang. Yet the reality is that gang affiliation after release varies widely (Camp & Camp, 1985). One can move up in the ranks by passing tests of loyalty, daring, and cunning. Or one can lose interest, eventually drop out of the organization, and move on to another lifestyle. If the gangster returns to prison, however, there is little likelihood of getting out of the gang alive.

Most studies have noted that gang activities are often exacerbated or facilitated by prison authorities. In some cases, the gang's influence over authorities is extreme. In many more cases, extremes are applied by corrections authorities against the gangs. In the history that remains from their day-to-day interaction, it appears that extremes of violence and illegal actions on both sides are essential characteristics of the relationship between prison gangs and legitimate authority structures.

The study by Davidson that follows provides one of the most graphic descriptions of Chicano prison gangs ever published, but it was criticized for glamorizing the prison gangsters. Davidson misinterpreted the gang as being both benevolent and effective. He also had a limited perspective. Since he saw the gang as confined to the prison, he missed the social structures in the neighborhoods outside (Moore, 1978).

9

Baby Mafia
or Family

R. Theodore Davidson

Chapter 5 (pp. 80-100) of *Chicano Prisoners: The Key to
San Quentin,* by R. Theodore Davidson (Prospect Heights,
IL: Waveland, 1974)

Outsiders are inclined to think that the longer a prisoner stays in prison
the better he understands the prisoner culture. This is not true. Most
prisoners spend years inside without ever fully understanding their own
culture. Views of this culture vary according to the depth to which a
prisoner knows his culture. . . . In order to gain a full comprehension of
what really takes place inside San Quentin—as well as in most other
California prisons—an understanding of the deeper, third level of the
prisoner culture is necessary.

This third level—the Family level—is relatively unknown to most
prisoners, because the activities at this level are extremely secret and
controlled by a group of Chicano prisoners. Only by comprehending this
particular group and its activities can one get a complete picture of the

prisoner culture. This group is the real key to a full understanding of the prisoner culture, for its activities and influence intrude into most of the major aspects of the prisoner culture. Without this key, one would have to guess how the culture works.

One of the first public acknowledgments of this Chicano group was made by Warden Louis S. Nelson in September 1968. He spoke on television, noting that a Mexican-American inmate had been killed by the "Mexican Mafia." He discussed the group, noting that it was composed of Mexican-American gunsels. He concluded by claiming that his staff had "eliminated the Mexican-Mafia." The members of the group were amused by Nelson's statements, for they are not gunsels, they are not the "Mexican Mafia," and they are far from being eliminated.

This Chicano group initially called itself the Baby Mafia. Later they changed the name to Family. Since Baby Mafia is no longer used, I normally will use only the term Family henceforth. Baby Mafia was intentionally included in the title of this chapter to avoid confusion with that basic kinship institution called the family. Family is not family, as will soon be seen. Let us now look into the history of the group—why it was necessary to form the group; why it is valid to insiders.

History

Even though most Family members are literate, one must look at the group as one would look at a group in a nonliterate culture. Because of the seriousness of the group's activities and the resulting secrecy, no member has ever written down Family's history, goals, ethics, and bylaws. To be in possession of such material would be extremely dangerous and potentially self-incriminating. Therefore, the members know these well; and they are able to tell them to new members, as they have told me. However, as with oral literature, each version may differ slightly from others, being colored by the perception of the teller. Nevertheless, members generally agree on the important points.

A major factor that ultimately led to the formation of Family is the Chicanos' feeling that they (as well as other prisoners) are being subjected to physical and mental abuse and manipulation by staff. It should be noted that this factor has been keenly felt by most prisoners—regardless of ethnic background—for many years. . . . Because of their personal experience and knowledge, Chicano prisoners seriously question the morality of many staff members and administrators. The Chicanos see gross hypocrisy in the system, and their *macho* reaction against it is strong. However, the reaction cannot be overt and still effective.

In 1964, a Chicano convict was sitting in the "hole" of a California prison. He had time to pose many questions about the powerlessness of prisoners. Why are prisoners so powerless in the face of manipulation by staff? Why are individuals, cliques, and even larger groups always kept off balance, being vulnerable at all times? How can the staff get away with breaking or avoiding the very rules which supposedly govern their actions? Isn't there some way to stop these abuses? How can the staff "rehabilitate" and punish at the same time? Couldn't the prison system be changed so as to eliminate the hypocrisy and abuses of the system? How can the prisoners protect themselves? How can they counter these abuses and give some stability to their lives, avoiding manipulation by staff? How could there be some sort of counteractive force to protect the prisoners? How could a large, acephalous group protect itself when there are so many interest groups that put their own good above the welfare of any larger group?

This Chicano convict reasoned that a counter force of prisoners would be necessary. In order to avoid being picked off as groups or cliques, the prisoners would have to show a strong, united front. Being aware that the entire prison population would be too great a group to unite, he thought it might prove successful if this counter force was started among the Chicano prisoners. Since most Chicano prisoners are either convicts or very convict like, and since they have an additional strong unity on occasion or in opposition to another group, they would have a distinct advantage from the beginning. Later, in another California prison, he discussed his ideas with two other Chicano convicts. Plans and decisions were made. The Baby Mafia was born. It started as a very small group and experienced many growing pains; however, it soon came to be a very tight counter force which protects its members and the deserving prisoners among the Chicano and convict populations. For many, Family is a force that effectively counters much staff manipulation. Family has had to fight for its survival, but its strong unity has enabled Family to win, to grow, and to prosper.

Goals and Ethics

The founding members of Family recognized that the subcultural background of the Chicanos normally places them at the bottom of the totem pole in California prisons. They felt that the "typical" Chicano is very undereducated. Also, he is either unskilled or poorly prepared to make a decent living. While on the streets, Anglos and authorities often treat him with contempt, failing to accord him a reasonable amount of human dignity. In prison, the same actions are intensified through maltreatment by many staff members. Chicano prisoners feel that this is a non-*macho* situation for them, that they are not able to live with the pride and dignity deserving of adult males. Therefore, the primary Family goal is to preserve the right of Chicano prisoners to live as human beings, in a *macho* manner. . . .

Family ethics pervade all Family activities and are a principal factor in the attainment of Family goals. To act in an unethical or immoral manner, or to break the convict code, would be hypocritical and non-*macho;* it would be counter to the goals of Family, especially since Family ethics are based on the ideals of *machismo.* . . . Family members take great pride in their daily dealings with each other and with other prisoners. They feel that their morality and ideals are above reproach, especially when compared with the immorality or lack of ethics of some staff members and most inmates. Members are fair and trustworthy. If a member says he will do something, there is no questioning by others; for it is done. Group decisions are carefully considered and adjudged moral. Family goes to great effort to be sure that its actions are right; if mistakes are made, they are honest ones. Consequently, when something is "ordered" by Family, there are carefully considered reasons behind the "order" that are understood by members and others who are aware of what Family is trying to do. Family actions accord with the highest ideals of *machismo;* they are honest and moral when viewed from within the prisoner culture.

An example of Family concern for the morality of their behavior can be seen in the pattern of Family violence. . . . If someone who is subject to the convict code (that is, all who are allowed to knowingly deal with Family) should be so foolish as to cheat or threaten Family in some way, there is little doubt about the potential consequences. With Family, the pattern of violence is even more extreme than among Chicano prisoners.

It only occurs for carefully considered ethical (to them) reasons. However, when it does occur, Family violence does not stop half-way—with knifing of an opponent; it goes all the way—to the death of the non-Family individual. Those who knowingly deal with Family members are well aware of this reputation and treat members with appropriate respect.

An additional example of the manner in which Family ethics pervade Family activities is evident in the member's extreme emphasis of *machismo* in sexual practices. . . . Since Family is considered the epitome of *machismo*, there are no broads in Family. As a Family member said, "There is a certain weakness in punks." (One can detect that the claim of other Chicanos, that Chicano broads are respected, might be exaggerated; for there do seem to be some subtle, negative feelings about broads, regardless of their . . . acting like convicts.) There was a "punk" in Family in the past who was observed in a compromising position (in another institution) by a non-Family convict. The "punk" had even been so stupid as to pick a non-Chicano for point man during the act. The point man (lookout) became the accuser. It should be noted that it took a great deal of nerve to approach Family and accuse one of its members; if it had been an unjust accusation, it might have brought about the accuser's untimely death. The convict accuser and the Family member were brought together for a face-to-face accusation. From the accused's reaction, which was observed by several Family members, it was apparent that the accuser was right. Since this was a direct challenge involving the two individuals, Family did nothing. Later the non-*macho* Family member (one of only two "strays" in Family's history) was killed. There had been tacit agreement to allow the accuser to do this, so Family did not retaliate against him.

Members are proud that Family has been able to attain its goals. The conditions of many Chicanos and convicts has been significantly improved. Many Chicanos claim that they are in a better position than any other group inside prison. Family has been able to perfect the natural sense of unity among Chicanos to an extreme degree—and to their immense advantage. Only through such unity can prisoners effectively ameliorate their condition to the degree that Family has. Also, the means to their goals are actually a part of the goal itself, since they have taken great care to reach those ends through highly ethical means. Their activities have furnished additional outlets for their *machismo*. They are able to move through the prisoner culture with pride and dignity, knowing that their actions are *macho*—honest, honorable, and manly. There may be those among the staff who do not accord Family members the human dignity and respect that they deserve as human beings. Members realize that those who treat them in such a manner are ignorant of the reality of much that takes place inside—in the depths of the prisoner culture that are known by relatively few prisoners. However, members can readily draw personal support and security from Family accomplishments.

Four Types of Family

At this point, the term Family should be discussed. Actually, Family may denote any of four types of Family. Members find no need for additional terms; for regardless of the particular type of Family being discussed, the meaning is obvious to an insider from the context of the conversation. One use of Family refers to the overall organization, which includes nearly 300 members throughout the state: on the streets, in jails, and in California prisons. This has been the way the term has been used to this point in the text. However, in order for outsiders to see and understand the distinctions between the four types of Family, further explanation is necessary.

In context, Family may also refer to the Leadership Group. The Leadership Group is the ultimate ruling body in Family affairs. Currently there are 25 members in the Leadership Group; at one time it had 31 members. Its members usually are the most influential and outgoing of the larger group. It is felt that they normally are the sharpest individuals, possessing a great deal of common sense. Additional details about the Leadership Group will be presented later, when treating the power structure of Family.

A third usage of Family can be distinguished when one hears a Family member refer to "my Family," "his Family," "our Family," or "your Family." When used in this manner, a member is referring to one of the smaller units of Family which collectively comprise the larger, nearly 300 member group. Members do not have nor need a term to distinguish these smaller units. However, to facilitate discussion by outsiders, I have taken the liberty of calling these units "sub-Families." Each sub-Family is a type of cell; and the members of these cells have developed very close relations with each other. However, when a sub-Family grows to about twenty members, it splits into two such groups.

A fourth usage of Family is apparent when a member refers to his "Third Family." Members of a Third Family are actually related in the traditional kinship manner. At least 40 percent of Family members have Third Family in Family too. However, Third Family members do not necessarily belong to the same sub-Family. It should be noted that about 10 percent of Third Family members are exceptions—they are *not* related; but, they are individuals who have been so very close to each other in the past that they feel and act like brothers. Regardless of these exceptions, one can see how Third Family, by drawing on the strong bonds of actual kinship, adds a strong personal element to the feelings of unity held for the larger group.

In normal conversation among Family members, a numerical designation is used only in reference to Third Family. There are First and Second Families too; however, the normal context of a conversation usually makes the use of First and Second unnecessary for insiders. When used, First Family refers to the Leadership Group, and Second Family refers to the larger, nearly 300 member group. The sub-Family unit has no numerical designation.

. . . Henceforth, when referring to the four types of Family discussed above, the following terms will be used: Leadership Group (First Family), Family (Second Family), Third Family, and sub-Family. . . .

Membership

Membership has been steadily growing since Family began in 1964. Family secures its necessary protective unity and assures its success through its extremely rigid selection of new members from convicts who have been tested through prior association with members. Either individuals or small groups may be admitted as members, with small groups possibly becoming a sub-Family. Potential members must be unquestionably *macho*. Also, as a Family member expressed,

> We are interested in Chicanos who are sharper than the average—convicts who are acutely conwise. These individuals need not be freewise or worldwise; they might even appear to be dull to freemen or outsiders;

but they must really be aware of the prison world, even if they can effectively function *only* in prison.

Family is aware that some of these individuals may be unable to function in an acceptable, conventional manner on the streets. Their enculturation into the larger society of the outside world often has been incomplete and unsuccessful. Since some of these individuals need financial support when they are released to the streets, Family often sends money from inside to help them. In prison though, these individuals are strikingly different, for they excel in their knowledge of and ability to use the prisoner culture. And since most Family activities take place inside, these individuals are quite useful as members.

Many more Chicano convicts would like to become Family members than are granted the honor. Most who are selected to be members have had a long, close association with Family members, either prior to, or in prison. For example, there are many Chicanos who have never been in prison, yet who have helped Family. These individuals may be friends, relatives, friends of relatives, or relatives of friends. Some may come very close to becoming Family on the streets, but no one does so without coming to prison. However, if they should come to prison, they officially become a Family member. Some Chicano convicts—who have worked closely with Family inside, who feel that they have been tested, and who would like to become a Family member—have difficulty understanding why some Chicano newly arrived from the streets is admitted to Family, while they are not. Obviously, when this happens, the Chicano from the streets has already earned himself a place in Family.

There is an additional prerequisite that must be met in order to become a Family member. It may seem extreme, but it probably has been a key factor in Family's ability to succeed and preserve the tight unity among its members. It also assures that *all* members are truly *macho*—even when it involves "gut level action." The prospective member must have killed someone! A kill, or hit, does not have to be made inside prison in order to qualify one for membership. However, just because a man has killed is not automatic qualification. If the man has pled guilty to murder, thereby cooperating with and aiding the authorities, the hit does not count. Also, if the man's hit is judged as being non-*macho*, he probably would never be able to become a Family member. Therefore, since all Family members have "made a kill," it is obvious that Family (as an organization) and

Family members are not taken lightly. To outsiders this extreme prerequisite may appear quite unreasonable, but to Family members it seems perfectly rational. They know the prisoner culture well enough to realize that severe means are necessary for the survival of Family.

In exceptional cases, an individual may become a member without having met this prerequisite. This could occur when a small group is admitted as members and one of the group had never had reason to make a kill. Or, it might be one of the Chicanos from the streets who is automatically admitted as a member on entry into prison for his past help although he may not have made a kill yet. In either case, the individual is able to prove himself fairly soon—with one of the next "ordered" Family kills.

Some additional details about Family membership should be noted. The majority of the roughly 300 members are quite young. About 90 percent are in their twenties, and there are only seven members older than forty. A mere eleven Anglos constitute the entire non-Chicano membership. There are no blacks in Family; for even though exceptions are recognized, Chicanos normally feel strongly that all blacks are potential snitches. In addition to Family members, there are convicts who are associated with Family and work closely with its members. These non-Family convicts quite effectively swell the number of individuals who are actively engaged in Family activities inside California prisons. Of the 300 members, not more than a third were on the streets in 1972—which was a very low figure. However, there are many people who work closely with Family members on the streets; and these individuals increase the number of persons who are actively involved in Family activities outside the prisons.

There has been little attrition in Family membership. Members feel a very definite sense of responsibility toward Family which is tied in with their own personal pride. If a member should want to change his way of life and retire from Family, he is not denied his request and forced to remain active. However, even though the member is allowed to live his own life, the feeling of responsibility seems to remain. He still is there if Family should ever need to call on him. A member of the Leadership Group commented about the individual who "retires":

I'm quite sure that he would even jeopardize his personal family or friends, or what have you, in responding to our call, if we requested it. I have never found one that wouldn't, and I don't think anyone else has. Of course, some of them have never been tested. But there's no such thing as you *can't* completely retire; you can if that's what you want to do.

Family would never fear their "retired" members in any way. It is almost beyond members' conception to think of some "retired" member hurting Family by testifying against it. Members are fully aware that such an act would be certain "suicide."

Power Structure

Because of the necessity of secrecy, Family's power structure is almost totally unknown to outsiders—even to those non-Family convicts who are active in Family economic activities. If Family did have a written set of bylaws, they might reveal some of Family's power structure. For example, one bylaw might state that the welfare and unity of Family, as a group, will always be more important than any individual member; therefore, all members are subordinate to the group. A second bylaw might state that all members are equals. And, a third bylaw might state that the Leadership Group is the ultimate authority; but its authority is to be exercised in a benevolent, advisory manner which keeps the goals and ideals of Family, as well as the egalitarian nature of its members utmost in mind. But, even if Family did have formal bylaws, they would be minimal in number and quite general in essence. Perhaps a Family member was right when he stated,

> When all members of an organization are sincerely devoted to its very highly regarded goals and ideals, then few specific rules are necessary. As long as members generally know how to get things done, then there is a great amount of potential flexibility. There is little need to spell out all actions in specific detail, because all members are devoted to those goals and ideals. They have no reason to quibble over relatively minor particulars as long as things get done.

Family members are not inclined to think of the interrelationship of the various parts of Family (from the individual member to the entire group) in terms of formal rules. Members often find it difficult to be specific regarding Family power structure, which apparently tends to be obscured by the following: the distinctive type of leaders who are very different from the typical leaders manifest among most Chicano groups; the absence of a chain of command; and the egalitarian nature of much Family activity—in which special status is not accorded the leaders, a wide range of potential decisions may be made by each member, and the contingencies of prison lead to flexibility and exceptions in the decision-making process.

The founding members of Family recognized the serious problems and pitfalls of typical leadership among most Chicano groups—both inside prison and on the streets. These problems of leadership have been, and continue to be, extensively discussed among Family members, enabling Family members to know what they want to avoid. They feel that many Chicanos have an aversion for most leaders—whether in prison or on the streets—stemming from the hypocrisy between the words and deeds of many Chicano leaders. Furthermore, they believe most leaders are involved in ego trips and put themselves above those that they would lead; consequently, they lose contact with the real grass roots. Most Chicanos react to this non-*macho* hypocrisy by quietly rejecting the leader. They will not allow the leader to "rule over" them, they refuse to follow the leader, and they usually avoid any further association with the leader.

Acting on their ideas about typical leadership among Chicanos, the founding members of Family set out to avoid the normal pitfalls. Keeping in mind the ideas expressed in the three possible bylaws that were earlier noted, they have been able to set up a successful power structure. The leaders of Family have averted hypocrisy between words and deeds, personal ego trips or personal gains, and loss of contact with the grass roots element of which they are a part. Consequently, Family members have not rejected their leaders. In fact, they have voluntarily and enthusiastically subordinated themselves to the group. Members have a great deal of respect for the astute, yet considerate guidance abilities of their leaders and have willingly accorded them permissive authority.

Leadership Group

The founding members of Family recognized that "someone was going to have to do some leading"—to make major decisions and coordinate the many Family activities. Therefore, the Leadership Group was established as the ultimate authority in Family. Those who came to fill these roles had their special abilities, too. One member of the Leadership Group described them as

> the sharpest, most outgoing individuals in Family. They had quietly demonstrated their leadership ability as effective leaders. It just seems that they floated to the top, as a normal thing to do. They know how to advise or ask, not tell. They *never* show their power by commanding people or telling them what to do. This is a *very* important thing, because our leaders are not the kind that most other groups have. The members of the Leadership Group have their special abilities; they can do the leadership kind of things best; but all Family members have their special abilities, too, all are on the same level, and all are equals. All members of the Leadership Group are *macho* on a very active, physical level, too.

The Leadership Group can be seen as being somewhat like a council of elders in a tribal group. Although age is not a factor, in their actions, members of the Leadership Group have proven that they epitomize the goals and ethics of Family. Members find it difficult to even imagine that these men would do something that would be detrimental to Family. Generally, members of the Leadership Group have a deep understanding and respect for others; they make a conscious effort to avoid hurting the feelings of others, to avoid putting individuals down. Their consideration and understanding have enabled them to subtly settle internal problems without hurting feelings. Through their benevolent, "suggesting" type of leadership, they are able to avoid the potential resentment and hostility that is a danger to the solidarity of most groups.

A further manifestation of the egalitarian nature of Family members is evident in the Leadership Group. All of its 25 members are equals, with no single member having more influence or power than any other; there are no special ranks or positions. Decisions are made by majority vote. However, the voting often is done in bits and pieces, for not all members of the Leadership Group are ever in any one place at the same time. This means that internal problems may take time to solve, because members are not able to gather for meetings at their will. In the past, this sometimes has led to the acceptance of a minority decision, when the majority failed to come to any agreement. However, communication does take place, and decisions are made. And, once a decision is reached, all Family members follow it without question.

With one out of every twelve Family members being a member of the Leadership Group, one can see that it is a highly representative group. It is far from being some remote governing body. When a major decision is made by that group, it is democratically made by equals. Consequently, Family actually is an acephalous group, because there is no single chief or leader on whose shoulders final responsibility or authority rests. The Leadership Group needs no coercive power behind it, because its decisions are a collective, democratic opinion (somewhat like a consensus) made by a relatively large group, of which each member has already demonstrated his effective, acceptable leadership ability. The decisions are carried out with almost a total absence of formal administration.

As noted earlier, there is open discussion of the problems of leadership and the ability of individuals to lead. A member of the Leadership Group noted that

> each sub-Family does not necessarily have a representative in the Leadership Group. If the sub-Family doesn't have a born leader among its members, obviously none will appear from that sub-Family.
>
> But nobody feels hurt; they're willing to admit among themselves that none of them have that particular special ability, and they see no reason why they should try to ease into something they can't quite handle.

By way of contrast, he noted a large, 17-member sub-Family, that has three of its members in the Leadership Group.

> None of the three is even a sub-Family head. They're just members of the sub-Family, yet all three of them are among the top.
>
> They're not only keen in a general sense; each has a little individual path that they follow that they're double-keen on. If we chose leaders, all three of them would undoubtedly be in the top positions. But you see, they themselves admit one thing. They lack the kind of ego thing involved with typical leaders—of getting up there and communicating in front of a lot of other people. If it was all left to them, without having to think of anyone but themselves, they would choose to be loners. They're really just the antithesis of the glib ego-trippers who have disappointed us too many times in the past. Ours are the only kind of leaders that can succeed and get around the Chicano's individualism and the strong feelings Chicanos have about typical leaders.

Major decisions—those that potentially will have an impact on Family in several prisons—are normally made by the Leadership Group. Most of these decisions are in the areas of recruitment, economic activities, internal problems, and security. In recruitment, for example, the Leadership Group determines whether or not a group is to be admitted to Family as a sub-Family. In economic activities, the Leadership Group makes decisions regarding whether or not to "turn" money (manipulate the value of prisoner money) in a particular prison. Or, the decision whether or not to "back another horse" (get involved with a guard who will become a "runner" and bring contraband goods into prison for Family) is made by the Leadership Group. . . . An instance of an internal problem involved two sub-Families, each of which (unknown to the other) was "pushing for the same horse" (trying to get a "runner" established who would do business just with them). Both sub-Families succeeded—but only to a degree. Their investment was not returning what they thought it should, and it became obvious to each that they were in competition with some other group of prisoners. Therefore, they consulted with the Leadership Group to draw upon its extensive, collective information. The Leadership Group decided that the situation should be openly discussed and settled so that hard feelings between the two sub-Families would be avoided. An additional result of this situation was that Family members came to better realize that such secrecy was not necessary or advisable among themselves.

An example of a major decision concerning Family security is the "ordering" of an execution by the Leadership Group. Most individuals who knowingly deal directly with Family are aware that they are subject to the convict code. If an individual should betray Family's confidence or break the convict code by threatening Family security or activities in some way (such as by snitching), the Leadership Group would judge the case. If determined guilty, the man would be "ordered" killed. The insiders' view should be stressed here. All who are subject to the convict code are aware that, in certain activities, they are virtually at war with staff. It is not unlike the United States being at war. If someone who is privy to secret information that is vital to the security of the United States should sell that information to the enemy, all parties involved are aware that he has committed treason. And, if he should be caught and convicted, all parties fully understand that the traitor will be executed as prescribed by the law. Those individuals who function within the convict code and are subject to it are also aware that if a prisoner sells information to the enemy (snitches to the staff), he, too, is guilty of a treasonous act. Therefore, all parties fully understand that the traitor, if found guilty, will be executed in accordance with the convict code—as prescribed by the convicts' law. Family activities to this date have necessitated 73 "ordered" executions. Most of those have been snitches. Two Family members have met their death in carrying out ordered kills—once this resulted in a second ordered kill; but ultimately all those ordered executed have been killed.

Actually, of all Family decisions, those made by the Leadership Group are relatively few. However, if a major decision is to be made, in most cases it is understood that all members of the Leadership Group should be in on the decision—especially in cases such as an ordered execution or the admission of a group to Family. However, due to circumstances such as time limitations, some major decisions may be made by a few members, or even a single member of the Leadership Group. There are no formal rules to guide members. It is understood that each member will reasonably exercise his decision-making ability in accord with the circumstances and his knowledge of the facts, such as information gained from the suggestions or advice of a Money Man (an economic expert advisor) if the decision deals with economic activities. For example, it is not uncommon that Family in a particular prison needs to have a major decision made almost immediately. Under those circumstances, the members of the Leadership Group in that prison will agree on a decision; and if they feel that most of the other members of the Leadership Group would approve of their decision, they will take immediate action on their decision. It is even possible, in exceptionally rare cases (such as in a small prison or camp), that a major decision has to be made immediately; and, because of the small number of Family members present, the decision may be made by a single member of the Leadership Group, or a single Money Man, or a single sub-Family head, or even a few of the nonleadership members of Family.

Most Family decisions, although usually important and serious in nature, are not considered major decisions that must be made by the Leadership Group. However, a member of the Leadership Group, a Money Man, or a sub-Family head will frequently be asked for his opinion or advice regarding some of these lesser decisions. Their advice or suggestions are usually followed. As one Family member noted, "After all, why ask their opinion if you just turn around and ignore it?" Family members have learned, often through negative experiences, that "it's not foolish to ask about something or mention that you think you have something going, but that you don't want to cut in on the wrong guy—can somebody help me here? It's not really asking permission to do something. It's just using the Leadership Group as a source of knowledge." This is a positive attitude that benefits Family. Members of the Leadership Group (and to lesser degrees the Money Men and the sub-Family heads) have the knowledge that a single individual can never have. What a single member doesn't know, somebody on the Leadership Group will know or be able to find out. Collectively the Leadership Group knows almost everything that is going on. This is a key function of the Leadership Group—the gathering and coordination of vast amounts of knowledge. Family members have learned that members of the Leadership Group, Money Men, and sub-Family heads are men they can consult to obtain informal advice and information regarding the larger Family position.

Money Men

The leadership role of Money Men differs from the other two Family leadership roles. Members of the Leadership Group and sub-Family heads seem to assume their roles naturally. However, the special abilities of potential Money Men are recognized by the Leadership Group, and they are assigned to their role. Therefore, in economic affairs, it can be seen that the Leadership Group voluntarily shifts to the Money Men some of the permissive authority granted to it by Family members. The Money Men have no formal authority as such, but are highly respected for their special abilities in economic affairs. Their advice and suggestions are followed. Family members would cease to heed a Money Man only if he should fail to lead them well in economic affairs. When not involved in leadership activities, Leadership Group members and sub-Family heads are just Family members. In contrast, because of their exceptional ability and the vast scope and importance of economic activities, Money Men are not allowed to engage in the same routine activities as all other members. Money Men are protected from the hazards of hustling to satisfy their own personal needs; they are kept from engaging in any activities that might "put the heat on them." All of their needs (consumer goods and services available in prison) are supplied by Family. However, this is not viewed as a special favor, because Money Men work very hard.

In 1972 there were 33 Money Men. A member of the Leadership Group said,

> That's much more than we usually have. We have between 9 and 11 more than we really need right now because of the circumstances—where men are placed in different prisons by CDC.
>
> There are too many in one place and not enough in another. We have three in one place right now, and there are only 19 members there all together, yet they make decisions that affect Folsom and San Quentin. I personally feel that we're overloaded in that spot right now. These men are specialists in money matters, who are capable of making financial decisions because they know the financial situation behind the scenes in all spots at all times. Money Men essentially are bookkeepers without books. They are super-sharp individuals who are able to keep a fantastic number of financial details in their heads.

From their position of specialized knowledge, Money Men are able to advise Family members—and most frequently members of the Leadership Group—in financial matters. Money Men are highly respected for their special ability—not only in financial matters, but in day-to-day activities inside. In economic activities the Money Men follow a pattern of leadership that is successful among Chicanos and deserving of respect—a pattern of asking, suggesting, or advising, not telling or commanding.

Sub-Family Heads

A sub-Family head might also be referred to as the leader of a sub-Family. Yet there can be a distinction. A sub-Family head, talking about his role, cautioned, "You have to qualify the term leader. We're really talking more about a drawing together ability than what some people would think of as leadership. There might be somebody in his sub-Family that is much sharper and really runs it by making the decisions on things." This latter individual would probably be a member of the Leadership Group. Later he referred to a sub-Family head as the "father" of the sub-Family, and noted that he would be "the one who brought the sub-Family together; he'd be the founder." Family members recognize that sub-Family heads have a charismatic quality that may be lacking in Leadership Group members. In some instances though, a member of the Leadership Group may also be the head of a sub-Family, having both charismatic qualities and leadership abilities. Sub-Family heads who are not members of the Leadership Group are drawn into considerable interaction with it. Consequently, sub-Family heads are much more knowledgeable of Family's overall situation than the general Family members are. Knowing this, and having strong personal feelings for their charismatic leader, sub-Family members frequently approach their sub-Family head for advice or suggestions regarding nonmajor decisions. Sub-Family heads have no binding authority; their power is only advisory. However, their advice is usually followed.

A member of the Leadership Group noted that Family members do not make the distinction between Family and sub-Family as often as it might seem from their activity. He admitted the difficulty of distinguishing between Family and sub-Family at all times, because Family members "may be talking about Family, but not really thinking about whether it's Family or sub-Family." He gave an example, using a small prison where only a few Family members are present.

> Regardless of whether a man is a Money Man, or a member of the Leadership Group, or happens to be the head of a sub-Family, it might be very likely that you would go to the guy for his suggestions. So we're not talking about a decision being made by a sub-Family; it really is a Family deal.

In a larger prison, where many members of a sub-Family are present, it is quite likely that a sub-Family

> will have something of its own going. Why not? We're all Family. It's just that they are very close to each other and do it together. We're not really talking about sub-Family activities though; we're talking about Family activities.

Distinctions between Family and sub-Family *can* be made, but they are not nearly as important as "who's around that has the ability to make a decision." Family members think of most of their activities as Family activities, without making the sub-Family distinction.

Family members find it difficult to distinguish precisely the power structure below the Leadership Group, because there is no certain point above which Families are prohibited to make decisions. When discussing this, the head of a sub-Family said,

> I could go pretty high without ever thinking that I should consult with somebody else. And some of the members in my own Family could go much higher without ever thinking that they would have to consult with me. We are all individuals when we stand alone, when the rest of us aren't there.

There may be times in a small prison or camp that a member of the Leadership Group, a Money Man, or a sub-Family head may not be present to consult regarding a serious decision. At that time, the few regular Family members who are present make a decision.

> They're men too, and they've got to make a decision when necessary. They can't just put their face to the wall and say they'll just ignore something and be walked over or miss out on a profitable business deal. They have their rights and responsibilities too. And it's this kind of flexibility that makes it difficult to decide how the power structure within Family works.

However Family members do not see this as a confusing situation. Sub-Family members have a close relationship with each other; and it is recognized that "all members have a head on their shoulders, they're sharp, they're intelligent." All members are involved in many nonmajor decisions. Even though they may frequently draw upon the knowledge of others (Leadership Group members, Money Men, and sub-Family heads), all members are personally and actively involved in the decision-making process. For example, admitting an individual to Family is a sub-Family decision. However, if it involves something that might be questionable to other Family members, the decision could go all the way to the Leadership Group. But the decision could be made by a single sub-Family member, too. A member of the Leadership Group stated,

> He'd just say that I want this guy in. It can be quite informal. After all, we're all equals. But, it must be remembered that everybody—from the dullest to the sharpest member—realizes that when this happens, don't make a mistake, because that's the individual's responsibility. We take

his word for it, but never have to say it—that's just assumed, or understood. It's like the con code—if you break it, all parties know—you don't have to talk about it.

There is no strict chain of command in Family. A member of the Leadership Group noted that a nonleadership member "would probably go to his Family father [sub-Family head], because that's his familiar territory, where he feels comfortable." However if he wishes, he is welcome to go to a member of the Leadership Group or a Money Man. But normally, if he wants the advice of someone who is in command of more information than he is, his sub-Family head is the man he will approach. Also, when a decision is made by the Leadership Group, it just filters on down to the members. All members who were in on the decision go to different places, and the decision is spread by word of mouth. A Leadership Group member noted that in a tight situation, such as when money has just been turned,

> We don't want the word to just filter down. I'd tell any member of my Family; and if I saw any Family member that I thought might not have come into contact with somebody who would have told him, I'd say, hey, have you heard that it's all money today. Even then, the word isn't spread through the sub-Family heads. It's still a very open kind of thing; but instead of casually telling, you make a point of telling. You don't care who you tell. In that respect, there's no real chain of command or fixed pattern of communication that must be followed.

Family members understand the absolute necessity to show strict loyalty to all four types of Family. When asked if there are varying degrees of loyalty accorded to the different types of Family, members answered with a definite no. However, when a hypothetical conflict situation between two types of Family posed (wherein an individual's brother—a member of Third Family—did something very serious against Second Family), it was admitted that there is a variance. Their loyalty would be in accord with the highest ethics of the group. The individual's brother would have to be taken care of, even executed if necessary. In such a situation, the man would not be expected to carry out the sanction against his brother; a member of Second Family would do it. However, the individual would not protest Second Family action. He would know that his brother had been judged by First Family and found guilty, and that sanctions against his brother would be necessary for the good of the group. Family does not prey on its members, and there have only been two "strays" in the history of Family. One, the punk noted earlier in this chapter, was allowed to be killed by a nonmember convict. The other was ordered executed. In both cases, there was no question about the validity of the decision. Among members, the general appreciation of the dangers of internal conflict seems to be an effective form of control; consequently, coercive force is not necessary to assure compliance with decisions of First Family.

The use of the kinship term, family, to name this group can be seen as an indication of the grave import that the members accord their group. Traditionally, Chicanos (both inside prison and on the streets) have always held their own kin (family) ties in high regard. Among Chicanos, the greatest loyalty and support is accorded one's own kin, with progressively diminishing degrees granted to friendship ties, *barrio* (neighborhood) ties, and Chicano ethnic identity. Therefore, one can see the choice of the term family (as a name for their group) as an extreme intensification of family loyalty, with Family being given the highest degree of allegiance by members.

Major Activities

The two major types of Family activities are economic and protective. Both are necessary for Family to attain its goals. Family economic activities have successfully provided the funds necessary to enable its members, most nonmember Chicano prisoners, and most convicts to live in a *macho* manner, with the pride and dignity of adult male human beings. Without these funds, Family could not exist and accomplish its goals. Consequently, economic activities must be tightly controlled at all times, and anything that interferes is a serious threat to Family's very existence. Such interference can be a matter of life and death for those involved.

. . . Family virtually controls the illegal economic activities. Through its control of all major amounts of prisoner illegal money and most major sources of contraband goods, Family is able to function much as banks and governments do. It has the means to regulate the flow of contraband money in all the larger California prisons. It can also control the value of this illegal money. It is the prisoners' bank throughout CDC, because all major loans are made either directly or indirectly through Family. It has an unquestioned stability because it has the power and means to collect and pay legitimate debts from one prison to another (or even on the streets), much as a bank can do from state to state. This makes dealing with Family a very positive, yet serious matter. For example, Family will collect or pay a legitimate debt, regardless of where the debtor or debtee might be transferred—even if he is released to the streets. In contrast, if a prisoner has financial dealings with an inmate, there is the constant threat that the inmate will be transferred to a different prison (or even be paroled or discharged to the streets)—which would present serious difficulties in tendering payment or collecting a debt.

Through its protective activities, Family is able to insure the secrecy necessary for its security, to prevent or eliminate threats to its economic enterprises, and to maintain its integrity as a group. These protective activities are absolutely necessary to preclude situations or conditions that ultimately could destroy Family. Although they may surface occasionally in the form of violence and death, such as an "ordered" execution, these activities usually are less extreme and quite subtle. Anyone who consciously deals with Family knows the seriousness with which members regard Family activities and the extent to which they will go to protect Family. Non-Family individuals who function on the lower levels of the prisoner culture understand the rules of the game, and even the extreme act of death to a snitch may seem justifiable to them. The mere possession of this knowledge usually is sufficient to keep prisoners from crossing Family in any way. For someone to snitch on Family, the stakes would have to be *very* high, and the informer would have to feel that he could get away with it. If he is discovered by Family, there would be no subtle reminders; there would be no discussion; there would only be deadly action. Members know very well that their group could never survive without such severe protective measures. . . .

With this background of the history, goals, ethics, membership, power structure, and major activities of Family, it is hoped that the reader will understand why this group has come into existence. As one Family member stated,

> The administration, by pushing on prisoners the way that it does and
> has been doing, is forcing new ideas and new ways into existence among

us. The Baby Mafia just happened to fall into a race thing and fits well into the Chicano background; but if it had not been that, it would have been something else.

Also, even though it may be difficult for outsiders to comprehend, Family could not work or survive without using extreme methods; they are of the utmost necessity. A strong degree of cultural relativity may be necessary for an outsider to understand the following Family view as it pertains to *all* prisoners, "The harm which may be caused by Family, or its activities, is *far* outweighed by the good it does."

DISCUSSION:
Pirates

Patterns for state-organized crime in the Americas were set in the late 1600s. At that time, entire fleets of privateers were commissioned to roam throughout the Caribbean and as far north as Rhode Island and were authorized to seize the ships of the enemy. Pirates roamed the waters, looting ships without proper authorization. Because their pay came from plunder and their attacks depended largely on opportunity and need, there was an extremely fine and variable line between privateering and piracy (Kenney & Finckenauer, 1995, p. 55). Piracy was an original and early form of OC. According to Carse (1965), piracy began the day after humans first learned to transport valuable goods over water.

The colonial spoils system benefited elites. The rich traded with pirates and promoted the smuggled traffic in plunder and stolen goods. The massive official corruption of the 1700s led many in the colonies to lose all respect for law and order. It was an economic free-for-all. Colonists were exploited and, because they had lost trust in British laws, there was no codified system of ethics that they agreed on (Browning & Gerassi, 1980). Piracy peaked in 1720 but quickly diminished thereafter, and over the next decade, pirates disappeared almost completely. Fundamental changes in the politics and economics of the colonies accounted for the collapse of piracy. Pirates could no longer buy protection from officials. As corruption diminished, piracy no longer thrived. Piracy grew with corrupt governments and also where government was absent (Kenney & Finckenauer, 1995). Most military and law enforcement efforts had little impact on piracy as a whole. Pirates and many colonial communities had become partners in a vast system of wholesale theft and fencing. Piracy flourished because the colonists wanted it to.

During the 1990s, a pattern of state-organized crime resembling piracy developed in the United States. Federal laws passed in 1970 and 1984 authorized forfeiture of OC assets and seizures by law enforcement officials. The laws were drafted to authorize the looting of enemies of the state, just as in the 1600s. After a decade, as the law was applied, it became opportunistic. Law enforcement agencies could not depend on regular, routine seizures of criminal assets. Opportunistic seizure of noncriminal assets have been documented. An extremely fine line developed between legitimate law enforcement activities and piracy on the highways. Forfeiture required that all property that was used in violation of the law be transferred to the government. Property in which the owner had no responsibility for its illegal use was still seized. Once probable cause was established, the burden of proof shifted to the defendant. It had to be demonstrated to the court by the preponderance of evidence that the property was not illegal gain. It was not necessary for prosecutors to trace assets to some specific act. The courts permitted the tracing of wealth to general narcotic trafficking, for example. Forfeiture was regularly upheld as legitimate in court. Federal forfeiture laws were expanded by state laws throughout the United States (Lombardo, 1990).

The right to seize assets gives law enforcement officers powers to plunder like those flaunted by privateers. In efforts against OC, lawmakers have been willing to impose sanctions against people who are beyond the reach of the criminal law. In justifying going beyond the law, the law itself provides a contradiction. Forfeiture laws open the doors to corruption and the repetition of age-old patterns.

10

Pirates and Profiteers

Frank Browning
John Gerassi

Chapter 4 (pp. 53-71) of *The American Way of Crime,*
by Frank Browning and John Gerassi (New York:
G. P. Putnam's Sons, 1980)

No sooner had crime become profitable in America than it became organized. And no sooner did it become organized than it became a regular part of the American way of life, thanks to the cooperation and collusion of government officials. Organized crime did not begin with twentieth-century Prohibition. It began with the colonial pirates.

Though they traded with almost total impunity all along the Atlantic coast, America's pirates, originally ocean-borne mercenaries hired by the English throne to harass Spain, actually lived in the various coves and inlets that honeycombed North Carolina, Virginia, Maryland, Long Island, and the Bahamas. One of their most notable way stations, Accomac, lay just across Chesapeake Bay from Jamestown, the seat of Virginia's colonial government, which was hardly eager to undercut the only commerce that kept its people alive. But Accomac was only one of many such towns. The letters and reports of the colonial governors abound with complaints about such trading posts in Pennsylvania, Delaware, North Carolina, New York, and Rhode Island.[1]

Pirate lore reached its highest pitch in Virginia and the Carolinas but especially in Charleston. Preeminent among the southern towns, Charleston had quickly captured the West Indian trade in rum, sugar, molasses—and eventually slaves. Ambitious Englishmen as well as restless, or landless, traders from the mid-Atlantic colonies gravitated there, bringing a cosmopolitan if lusty ambience to the town.[2]

Charleston was bound to the West Indies by more than punch and profits. Separated from the northern settlements by hundreds of miles of barren coastline, Carolina was the most precarious of all the English colonies. To the west were the Indian tribes. To the south were the Spanish, who retained their desire for a grand empire in North America and hence kept the people of Charleston under constant fear of attack. By the 1680s their most reliable defenders were the pirates and privateers of the West Indies—an anomaly that finds its explanation in the original French and English colonial conquests a hundred years earlier.[3]

Since the late 1500s, Jamaica and Barbados had been the special preserve of freebooters and buccaneers commissioned privately by the English kings and queens to attack, burn, loot or otherwise decimate Spain's military and commercial ships. As one war bubbled over into the next, usually to Spain's detriment, there appeared entire fleets of privateers ranging the Baltic, the Mediterranean, the Barbary Coast and the Caribbean. Though protected by commission from their own king and therefore technically innocent of committing piracy, the privateers fought for themselves, free of any normal military control. Too far away and rugged for any effective government by either the English or French, the smaller Caribbean islands provided a natural base for these seaworthy mercenaries. Gradually through the decades, a loose nomadic population of mariners began to cover the islands. These self-styled "Brethren of the Coast," as the English privateers were sometimes called, held an almost fanatical hatred of Spain. Moreover, it was profitable hatred, for unlike the English, Spain's colonial enterprise was dedicated to the simple extraction of native wealth. Her ships were nearly always loaded with gold, silver, and precious ornaments, items vital to any fighters who must live off their plunder.[4] In theory a privateer was commissioned only to seize enemy ships; seizure of neutral ships was piracy. That the privateer and his crew took their pay in plunder meant that the decision to seize a ship often depended upon opportunity, capability, and how desperate the crew was for supplies. Consequently the line between privateering and piracy was exceedingly fine and subject to change week by week. Among the hardiest of the lot were those called buccaneers, originally a mixture of English and French sailors who had settled on Tortuga and later Jamaica and who always seemed to be waging skirmishes with the Spanish authorities. Besides the bounty they could seize from Spanish ships, they added to their income by smuggling imports to the Spanish settlers in violation of restrictive colonial trade laws.

Contrary to the high-minded description of most colonial historians, the buccaneers were hardly groveling bands of vicious depraved men. Within their own ranks the standard of behavior tended to be both democratic and egalitarian. A direct account of the buccaneers' own rules come from the diary of a young French surgeon, Alexander Exquemeling, who in 1668 signed on to a buccaneer ship as surgeon-barber. Wild drinking bouts and pistol play fill many pages of Exquemeling's diary. But he also described the councils formed by the crew and the rules they established jointly for life at sea:

> Having got possession of flesh sufficient for their voyage, they return to their ship. Here their allowance, twice a day to everyone, is as much as he can eat, without either weight or measure. Neither does the steward of the vessel give any greater proportion of flesh or anything else to the captain than to the meanest mariner. . . . They mention how much the captain ought to have for his ship. Next the salary of the carpenter, or shipwright, who careened, mended or rigged the vessel. . . . They stipulate in writing what recompense or reward each one ought to have, this is either wounded or maimed in his body, suffering the loss of any limb, by that voyage. Thus they order for the loss of the right arm 600 pieces of eight or six slaves; for the loss of a left arm 500 pieces of eight, or five slaves; for an eye 100 pieces of eight, or one slave; for a finger of the hand the same reward as for an eye. . . . They observe among themselves very good order. For in the prizes they take it is severely prohibited to everyone to usurp anything in particular to themselves. Hence all they take is equally divided. . . . Yea, they make a common oath to each other not to abscond or conceal the least thing they find amongst the prey. If afterwards anyone is found unfaithful, who has contravened the said oath, immediately he is separated and turned out of the society.[5]

In all likelihood the buccaneers and other pirates of the Caribbean did not maintain their egalitarian relations perfectly. There is no record, from the young surgeon or elsewhere, of any kind of justice meted out to violators of the code. Indeed there were occasional accounts of pirate captains whose power was matched only by their caprice. The most notable example is that of the pirate Blackbeard, who in the middle of a card game blew out the candles, pulled his pistols and fired randomly beneath the table. Asked for an explanation by one crewman hit in the knee, he answered curtly that such displays were necessary occasionally to demonstrate who was in charge.[6]

Even flawed, the myth of brotherhood seems to have been a critical attraction for the men who became pirates. Cast against the social and political turmoil sweeping England in the late seventeenth century, the promise of such shipboard camaraderie doubtless offered a fine alternative to many a London laborer. For what inspired the strong young men to sail off to the pirate seas also led rebellious souls to fight for Oliver Cromwell's radical visions. The wild dreamers known as Diggers and Levellers, who sought to banish the king while twirling the English propertied establishment on its nose, were spiritual kinsmen to these adventurers. And of course these young men did not set out to be criminals; most pirates first went to sea as perfectly legitimate privateers.

In much of America, especially Charleston, there was no dire stigma attached to pirating and privateering. "For many years scarcely a month passed without seeing these licensed freebooters sail into Carolina, their vessels laden with the spoil of their latest expedition," one Carolina historian has written. "Not infrequently they would meet with rich prizes, ships of treasure and plate, and on coming into the colony would scatter their gold and silver about with so generous a hand that their appearance would soon come to be welcomed by the trading classes; and by means of their money they ingratiated themselves not only with the people, but with the highest officials of the government.[7]

Pirates were often simply regarded as gentlemanly outlaws. Their officers were regular guests in the city's finest homes, for it was the pirates who enabled the colonists to circumvent the English Trade and Navigation Acts. Enacted first under Cromwell's regime and later reaffirmed under the Restoration kings, the Navigation Acts forbade the colonists to buy or sell goods that had not been shipped through England and delivered on English boats. All the seaport town bristled under the restrictive laws, but the northern towns were too closely watched by the English governors to do much about them. Charleston, as the principal continental port for the Caribbean pirates and privateers, held a more advantageous position. The Charlestonians were able to buy their luxury items at prices far lower than the legal markets offered in Europe or the northern towns. Thus they graced their tables with the most elegant china and sterling, draped their windows in silk brocades, and otherwise created the veneer of sophistication—all through the services of the vast "underworld" fencing system.

For the captains, a privateer's commission could prove highly profitable. For the crew, the motive was twofold: brotherhood and profit. The adventurous English worker-turned-crewman would find his performance evaluated, for the most part, by a brotherhood of equals. And however improbable his dream of wealth, his chances were far better at sea than on the plantations of Virginia or in the slums of London.[8]

Officially, of course, Carolina authorities condemned piracy and its fruits. Strict laws were passed against trading with pirates, and as the pirates expanded their attacks against English ships, the king dispatched a regular stream of governors to crack down on them. None of the Royal emissaries achieved any real success, however, until the end of the century when the Carolinians themselves became prosperous enough, commercially and agriculturally, to produce their own exports, particularly rice. Then the tables began to turn, for the loss of sales to such a fragile community could soon have bankrupted the entire colony. Moreover, the development of exports increased the colonies' trade in general. More trade meant more ships, and more ships only heightened the pirates' appetite. Suddenly the shopkeepers, grain dealers, and bankers of colonial Charleston were no longer pleased with their former trading companions.

In the early 1700s, the West Indies—Barbados, the Bahamas, Jamaica, Tortuga, and Haiti—were teeming with freebooters, mercenaries, marooned sailors and countless unemployed fighters from the war England had just concluded with France. King William's War, the colonial name for Europe's War of the League of Ausburg, which lasted from 1688 to 1697, had mostly been fought along the colonies' northern frontiers. But it had greatly stimulated privateer and pirate activity along the Atlantic and Caribbean coasts, so much so that New York's governor, Lord Bellomont, solicited the support of Virginia in his attempt to impose the navigation laws. Virginia and Maryland were then at the edge of economic ruin, and the tight group of landholders who would eventually dominate Virginia's political and commercial life were determined to rid their busy bays and rivers of the pirate prey. "We are in a state of war with the pirates," Governor Nicholson of Virginia wrote to Lord Bellomont.[9]

In 1702, Queen Anne's War, known in Europe as the War of Spanish Succession, expanded into America. Spanish forces, usually aided by the French, repeatedly attacked Carolina settlers, while English troops tried to separate their opponents by raiding Spanish settlements in Florida. The war quickly eroded the Chesapeake colonies' tobacco and agricultural exports to England, and they were left teetering on the brink of bankruptcy. At the same time, Indians had begun to fight back against white expansion across the Blue Ridge and Great Smokey mountains, forcing Carolinians and Virginians to use much of their military energy to crush them, in what became known as the Tuscarora War (1711-12). This effectively stopped the Carolinians and Virginians from dealing with the pirates.[10]

The Treaty of Utrecht ended Queen Anne's War in 1713. But it did not curtail the pirates. On the contrary, so bold had they become during the colonies' preoccupation with the war that they had proved a serious menace, controlling many of the shipping lanes used by the colonies. By 1718, when the pirate Blackbeard died, between fifteen hundred and two thousand pirates navigated these waters, sometimes sailing openly into Long Island Sound and the ports of Rhode Island. Understandably, it had become time for the colonies, especially Virginia, which most depended on exports and which had long coveted Carolina's land, to put an end to piracy once and for all—and occupy the pirates' sanctuaries in the process.

Alexander Spotswood, who became Virginia's governor in 1710, did not even wait for the end of the war to launch an attack on the pirate outposts. But the pirates were formidable. Among them, four of their leaders were especially courageous and colorful: Stede Bonnet, Captain Kidd, Anne Bonney, and Blackbeard. Within ten years, from 1710 to 1720, they rose to the peak of their power and wealth—and then fell to death and oblivion, sacrificed to the burgeoning commercial movement that was sweeping America.[11]

Major Stede Bonnet apparently became a pirate out of boredom. Until about 1715 he had spent his life as a rich respectable farmer who kept a large manor in Barbados. Then he shocked his equally respectable neighbors and took off "a-pirating." Charles Johnson, who in 1724 published the first encyclopedia of pirate lives and lore, believed Bonnet suffered "a Disorder in his Mind, which has been but too visible in him some time before this wicked Undertaking and which is said to have been occasioned by some Discomfort he found in a married State." Bonnet joined Blackbeard for a while, but old and inexperienced, he was soon double-crossed. He and his crew continued to prey upon the South Carolina coast alone and with considerable success until they were captured in a bloody fight led by English customs collectors. Sympathy was so widespread for Bonnet among Charlestonians, however, that he was allowed to escape before his final trial. He was eventually recaptured and executed.[12]

The saga of female pirate Anne Bonney suggests she too had friends in South Carolina. In the pamphlets and journals of the early eighteenth century, Anne Bonney and her sometime companion Mary Read took on heroic grandeur. "Bonnie," known best for her "fierce and courageous temper," was said to be the bastard daughter of an Irish lawyer who had sailed to Carolina. Banished from the household by her father for having secretly married a sailor (who in the midst of the scandal chose to disappear), Anne Bonney soon found her match in a wild and handsome pirate called Captain John ("Calico Jack") Rackham. Together they plundered the seas, she as eager as her mate to leap aboard each newly captured prize ship.[13]

Anne Bonney was not the only woman aboard Rackam's ship when they were caught under attack by an armed sloop of the Jamaican governor one October morning in 1720. Mary Read was also a full member of the crew. Her zeal was said to be exceeded only by her skill. As the Jamaican warship drew up against Rackam's sloop, the king's men leapt aboard, gaining an early advantage. But while Calico Jack and his men fell back below deck, Anne Bonney and Mary Read stood their ground, bare-breasted, their swords and cutlasses flashing through the air.[14]

Cowardice has no place in the stories of these two women. Captured alive and brought to trial, Bonney begged mercy on the grounds of pregnancy—and was spared. But her lover, the dashing Calico Jack, won no such mercy. Shortly before his hanging, the two were permitted a final meeting, where, according to Johnson, she wasted no time weeping but declared "she was sorry to see him there, but if he had fought like a Man, he need not have been hang'd like a Dog."[15]

Apparently the same court would have granted clemency to Mary Read as well had her own iron will not been revealed in a statement regarded as too brazen for forgiveness. Once, the court was told, Rackam had asked her why such a fine attractive woman could want to risk death and danger among pirates. Her fateful response: "as to hanging, she thought it no great Hardship, for, were it not for that, every cowardly Fellow would turn Pyrate and so infest the Seas, that Men of Courage must starve." Read was convicted of piracy and would have hanged with the rest had she not contracted a "fatal fever" and died in prison.[16]

Had the burghers of Charleston retained their loyalties to their old pirate friends, Edward Teach might have retired to some manorial estate on the delta, planted rice and harvested indigo, and have contributed his name to one of the grand genealogies of the aristocratic South. Instead, his head, one November morning in 1718, was chopped off, and he is remembered as Blackbeard, the most notorious pirate in American history.

Blackbeard was a promoter in the grand style—mostly of himself. Improbable tales of his brutality, his wiliness, his charm, even of his birth and his dozen or more wives were repeated up and down the entire coast. He cultivated mystery and fostered a reputation for volcanic unpredictability. For he knew his ability to survive depended mostly upon his capacity to entertain, to draw out the venal interests of an ambitious and insecure population, huddled along the shores of England's least successful colony. In 1699, in order to crush piracy, the king had allowed the colonies to establish their own admiralty courts for the prosecution of pirates and other violators of the Navigation Acts. Blackbeard then decided that as long as his wild and romantic reputation preceded him, he would always find colonial allies susceptible to his charms, people whose greed so exceeded their social position that they were willing to gamble on the quick profits of the pirate's traffic.

Taller than most men of his time, he wore a great, curly, black beard which, according to one account, "like a frightful meteor, covering his whole face, frightened America more than any comet that has appeared there a long time." Under his broad leather hat, his beard, festooned with bright colored ribbons, tumbled to his waist. He kept pistols strapped to his shoulders. On occasion he achieved novel nighttime effects by attaching small lighted wicks to his hat just above his ears so that his eyes flickered in the shadow of his beard.[17]

Teach's first definitive appearance was in the Bahamas beneath a hill just east of the site that is now downtown Nassau. If the fragmentary accounts are to be believed, he maintained an invincible position aided by a great watchtower at the top of the hill from which he could survey the entire expanse of the Bahamian waters. Just as well could he maintain careful watch of the pirate denizens who swarmed about the island. "Occasionally Blackbeard would descend the tower steps and the steep, narrow trail to the pathway below, where he and some of his favorites from the crew had set up a few tents. There under a huge tree, he held court—trading loot, interviewing volunteers for his next cruise, planning its itinerary, and drinking more rum," according to one historian of colonial piracy.[18]

He appeared off Charleston in June 1718 with a French merchant ship he had named *Queen Anne's Revenge,* loaded with four hundred men and forty cannons, and a fleet of three lesser sloops. Within a week he had stopped at least eight outbound ships, seized what cargo he wanted, and taken several prominent Charlestonians hostage. One of them was province council member Samuel Wragg.

Blackbeard then dispatched one of his deputies to town to bring back needed medicines. Upon delivery, all hostages would be released, he said. After two days passed, Blackbeard threatened to slaughter the hostages. He relented when he learned his deputy's sloop had capsized in a squall. When the deputy did finally land in Charleston, panic swept the town. Angry citizens were itching to attack Blackbeard's fleet with sailboats and lynch the pirate's deputy. But the council and the governor, backed against the wall, quickly acceded and sent Blackbeard a cache of medicines worth between three and four hundred English pounds. Before releasing his hostages, Blackbeard stripped them to the waist, relieving council member Wragg personally of the equivalent of $6,000 in cash.[19]

The pirates had a short voyage as they sailed out of Charleston harbor. For Blackbeard's new base had become Ocracoke Inlet, near the mouth of the Pamlico River in North Carolina. He had come to North Carolina a few years earlier in the wake of the new British campaign against West Indian pirates. Devoid of much commerce or many people, the North Carolinians responded as had the people of Charleston in the 1680s. The pirates were friendly, and they brought in as much trade and fun as could be found in most of the colony. They had established thoroughly cordial relations with Charles Eden, North Carolina's governor. Six months before their Charleston raid, Blackbeard and his crew had surrendered to Eden under terms of a pirate amnesty proclamation offered by George I. Having settled along the coast in apparent legitimacy, the crew had waited until spring before getting local merchants to outfit the ships for their new exploits.[20]

After the Charleston raid, Blackbeard disbanded his company, keeping one sloop, which he called the *Revenge,* and only his most trusted men. He promised Governor Eden he would carry out only honest trading missions. But the summer had hardly ended when he returned from one such mission, a French merchant sloop in tow. He had "found the French ship at sea without a soul on board her," he reported to Governor Eden on September 24, adding that since it was such a leaky vessel it should be towed back to sea and burned to avoid any hazard to the harbor. Eden, egged on by his customs chief, Tobias Knight, agreed. Knight, who happened to be the judge of the vice-admiralty court responsible for certifying the ship abandoned, quickly convened the court and issued judgment in favor of the reformed pirate.[21]

Blackbeard of course kept the bulk of the "abandoned" ship's cargo. Sixty hogsheads of sugar, however, were delivered to Governor Eden, while twenty more, ostensibly a customs tax, were taken to Secretary Knight's personal barn. This led some North Carolinians to doubt Blackbeard's claim that he had found the ship abandoned. Before long the tale of the extraordinary episode reached Governor Spotswood's chambers in Virginia and went on to Philadelphia where that colony's angry governor issued a warrant against Teach for past depredations. Some have argued that Teach then entered his long-deferred dream of respectable "semiretirement" hobnobbing with the gentry of Ocracoke.[22]

Regardless of Blackbeard's own intentions, Alexander Spotswood was hardly ready to rest quietly on the James and miss a fine opportunity. Instead, he launched his mission against Blackbeard with care. First he had Blackbeard's former quartermaster, William Howard, arrested on the harbor docks on trumped-up charges. The governor's agents confiscated £150 from Howard, then indicted him for vagrancy. Spotswood prevailed against adamant protests from Howard's lawyer, who was a former Speaker in the House of Burgesses and mayor of Williamsburg. Howard was then compelled at his trial to testify against Blackbeard and assist the Virginians in identifying his Ocracoke hideout.

Autumn 1718 was half over by the end of Howard's trial, and Spotswood moved fast. He appealed to the British naval commander for help in mounting an expedition, but was rebuffed. Under a blanket of total secrecy, Spotswood then solicited Captains George Gordon and Ellis Brand to lead the mission, financed privately from the governor's personal account. Only certain selected members of the governor's council were informed.

On November 13 Spotswood asked the House of Burgesses to offer a special reward for Blackbeard's capture, charging that information taken at William Howard's trial indicated the pirate was planning new revenge against the Virginians. Providing no explanation, Spotswood insisted the legislation be approved immediately. On November 24, after the bill had been rushed past the Burgesses with almost no debate, Spotswood signed into law a proclamation offering £100 reward for the capture of Blackbeard and his crew.[23]

But Blackbeard had been killed by Captain Brand's men two days earlier. Brand himself was not in command of the final assault. Instead he had led an expedition overland to Governor Eden's home at Plum Point, across Bath Creek from Blackbeard's home. Brand left his ship, the *Pearl*, under command of his lieutenant, Robert Maynard. A second sloop, commanded by Captain George Gordon, accompanied Maynard. Maynard slipped into Ocracoke Inlet at sunset on Thursday, November 21, waiting for the high tides of morning to ease him over the unmarked shoals. Just before dawn Friday he hoisted anchor. Several men were dispatched in rowboats to trace a route through the shoals. As soon as the scouts were spotted, Blackbeard fired warning shots and they retreated to the *Pearl*. Blackbeard's final battle was under way, and he chose to stand rather than retreat through the scores of obscure channels upstream.

Blackbeard grabbed a flask of liquor, so the story was told, and announced to all of Maynard's men: "Damnation seize my soul if I give you quarter or take any from you!" He cut cable and maneuvered his ship beyond a submerged sandbar upon which Maynard quickly ran aground.[24]

As Maynard's ship slid free from the sandbar and he began to close in, Blackbeard unleashed a barrage of crude grenades made of bottles filled with powder and small pieces of jagged lead and iron. But Maynard moved the *Pearl* alongside the *Revenge*, keeping his men below deck, safe from the grenades.

The pirates stormed aboard Maynard's ship, its decks slippery with the blood of twenty sailors killed by Blackbeard's earlier broadside. Blackbeard led the assault, flailing his cutlass about his head like a great razored windmill until he came face to face with Maynard.

Each man fired his pistol. Though he was hit, Blackbeard was not stopped, and the two drew their swords, Blackbeard still swinging his cutlass. It snapped Maynard's sword just below the hilt and would have cut him down when one of Maynard's men struck Blackbeard "a terrific wound in the neck and throat." Blackbeard flung his cutlass a final time, then stumbled, before several of Maynard's men closed in on him with their swords. Within minutes the other pirates surrendered, and Blackbeard's head was chopped from his body and mounted on a spike on the bow of the *Pearl*.

By battle's end, Blackbeard and nine of his men lay dead. Twenty-nine of Spotswood's expeditionary force were killed or wounded. The surviving pirates were transported back to Virginia and tried on March 12, 1719. Fourteen of the fifteen prisoners were convicted and hanged, one having persuaded the court he had only come aboard ship for a party the previous night. The seized booty sold at auction for £2,238.[25]

Evidence produced at the trial so implicated Customs Chief Tobias Knight that he too was later indicted by the North Carolina provincial council. The most damning evidence against Knight was a letter found on the *Revenge* dated November 19, addressed to Teach:

> My friend,
>   If this finds you yet in harbor I would have you make the best of your way up as soon as possible your affairs will let you. I have something more to say to you than at present I can write; the bearer will tell you the end of our Indian war, and Ganet can tell you in part what I have to say to you, so referr you in some measure to him.
>   I really think these three men are heartily sorry at their difference with you and will be very willing to ask your pardon; if I may advise, be friends again, it's better than falling out among your selves.
>   I expect the Governor this night or tomorrow, who I believe would be likewise glad to see you before you go. I have not time to add save my hearty respects to you, and am your real friend.
>   And servant
>   T. Knight

Knight was acquitted by the council of all charges, in part because the key witnesses against him were four black slaves, and testimony by blacks was never admitted into court in any of the southern colonies. Knight also argued that he had written the letter to Blackbeard on explicit instructions from Governor Eden. A member of the famed aristocratic English family from which British prime minister Sir Anthony Eden descended, Eden was already ill and died within a few months.[26]

Outside North Carolina Alexander Spotswood was lionized for having eliminated the colonies' most fearsome brigand. The North Carolinians, however, harbored more than passing resentment for his invasion
of their territory, for the embarrassment he caused them, and for refusal
to recognize their legal jurisdiction after the pirates had been captured.
There were also other, more profound, reasons for their antagonism
toward the Virginia governor.

Before Spotswood was appointed governor (technically he was lieutenant governor as a stand-in for the English earl of Orkney), he had been
a colonel in the army and acquired vast land holdings. North Carolinians
complained that he had been continuously prejudiced against their
province since its formal separation from South Carolina in 1712. He had
discouraged adventurers and new arrivals from settling there, they said,
largely because he sought to profit from the sale or lease of his own large
wilderness tracts on the Virginia frontier.

Some historians partial to the Carolina viewpoint have explained
Spotswood's eagerness to embarrass Governor Eden as part of a grand
design to annex the colony of Virginia. If so, he obviously failed. Nonetheless by the end of his term as governor, Spotswood had accumulated
more than eighty-five thousand acres in Spotsylvania County alone,
much of it covered by seven-year tax exemptions from the date of
transfer. He had secretly granted himself much of this land by putting it
in the name of friends with whom he had special transfer agreements.[27]

If Spotswood gloated over Blackbeard's death, other powerful men
wept—among them several New York and Long Island import brokers
whose involvement with the pirates stretched back over an entire generation to the 1690s. Taking advantage of a corrupt colonial administration,
these importers had become virtual partners with the pirates in massive
smuggling schemes aimed at subverting the trade and customs laws.

The one who did most to create this corrupt administration was
Benjamin Fletcher, governor of New York between 1692 and 1698. Fletcher
was a man caught in a hopeless web of contradiction. Today, few standard historians ever mention him by name, or if they do, it is to note only
parenthetically that he was the most corrupt governor in colonial history.
Yet Fletcher did little that might not have fallen under the mantle of
patriotism half a century later.

Governor Fletcher was quite simply the leading commercial courte-
san for the pirate trade of the North Atlantic coast. He liked most of the
pirates who visited New York. He found them clever, amusing, and

worldly. They were expert sailors whose skills, and confidence in their own skills, easily distinguished them from the plodding preachers and bureaucrats of the colonial council. They were also well liked by the rising class of merchants and import brokers who were the governor's most loyal backers.[28]

Fletcher had been named governor in 1692 in the wake of a failed rebellion led by a New York shopkeeper named Jacob Leisler. A German immigrant who bitterly resented his static position in a social structure that blocked the rising middle class from political power, Leisler was not a democrat. But, as a captain in the citizen militia, he successfully led his troops into deposing the royal deputy, and afterwards he did call for a constituent assembly. Defeated by Loyalist forces, Leisler was hanged on March 30, 1691, before Fletcher became governor. Fletcher decided to wipe out whatever remained of Leisler's movement by rigging three consecutive elections for the New York Assembly. In the election of 1695, he even forced voters to cast their ballots orally in front of soldiers and sheriffs, who pistol whipped anyone who dared vote against his candidates.[29]

Once securely backed by a rubber-stamp assembly, Fletcher proceeded to develop New York as the colony's foremost trading center, for the benefit of its dominant class and, of course, himself. He realized New York would have to create an independent world of commerce, unhampered by such obstacles as the king's Navigation Acts. Fletcher encouraged the pirates and the colonial merchants to sidestep these laws, and built up his own power with the latter's support. His principal mistake was to expect that these upstart capitalists would continue to back him in his hour of need.

The charges that eventually drove Fletcher from office in 1698 were devastating: He had given protection to notorious pirates in exchange for payoffs; he had jailed his political opponents; he had armed various rogues and nonuniformed soldiers with clubs and sent them to the voting polls to intimidate dissident voters; he had offended friendly Indians; he had made huge land grants, totaling over two thousand square miles, to his friends and political cronies.[30]

While Leisler and his men had reacted spontaneously out of growing frustration with the old brazen colonial regime, Fletcher's rule fomented real polarization. He frequently alluded to his close connections at Whitehall, London, implying that he could easily open doors to new trade for those who would support him. He went out of his way to characterize the Leislerians as anarchic rogues and radicals who had no respect for the law or commerce and who could not be trusted with political power. In that way he eagerly sought to ingratiate himself with the tiny elite of manorial gentry, while simultaneously cementing his alliance with the fast-rising businessmen of the coast. Thus, as historian Herbert Osgood put it, "the official merchant and landed aristocracy of New York was again in the saddle."[31]

Fletcher made a point of displaying his taste for spectacle from the very beginning of his rule, employing a coach and six horses for his inauguration—"a pomp this place had never seen in any Governor." Fanfare and splendor were frequently his response to local crises. When Iroquois tribal leaders asked for supplies and men in their loyal battles against the French, Fletcher pleaded poverty. Responding later to charges that he had treated the Indians poorly, Fletcher answered without a trace of embarrassment:

> I have been at great pains to gain the hearts of the Heathen. . . . I have taken their chief Sachims to my table; some of the principal leading men of the Five nations came down the River to pay me a visit, whom I treated with all manner of kindness and Courtesy. I ordered them on board the greatest ships we have and guns to be fired, the King's birthday happening in that time. . . . I ordered six horses to be put into my coach and coachmen to drive them around the City and into the country to take the air, by which they were extremely obliged, and dismissed them with considerable presents, at which they did express satisfaction.[32]

In his acceptance of gifts and favors, Fletcher was equally nonchalant. It had been custom in the colony for the assembly to assess a onetime tax of a penny per pound against estate owners for the newly arrived governors. Such pennies were niggardly sums, Fletcher informed the assembly, adding as one of his first statements that he would throw the estate owners in jail if they would not pay him more. "He takes a particular delight," wrote one of his opponents, "in having presents made to him, declaring he looks upon them as marks of their esteem of him, and he keeps a catalogue of persons who show their good manners as men most worthy of his favor. This knack has found employment for our silversmiths and furnished his Excellency with more plate (besides variety of other things) than all our former Governors ever received."[33]

Gift-taking was minor compared to the charge, later corroborated in court, that Governor Fletcher encouraged trafficking by pirates:

His Excellency gives all due encouragement to these men, because they make all due acknowledgements to him; one Coats a captain of this honorable order presented his Excellency with his ship, which his Excellency sold for £800 and every one of the crew made him a suitable present of Arabian Gold for his protection; one Capt. Twoo who is gone to the Red Sea upon the same errand was before his departure highly caressed by his Excellency in his coach and six horses and presented with a gold watch to engage him to make New York his port at his return. Twoo retaliated the kindness with a present of jewells.[34]

The evidence against Fletcher was damning. Pirate Coates, for example, testified directly that he had been forced to pay Fletcher £1,300 protection money. But Fletcher seemed nonplussed and eagerly explained his behavior with imaginative tales, especially when talking about Captain Tew (Twoo), who was as notorious a pirate as Blackbeard.

"This Tew appeared to me," Fletcher said, "not only a man of courage and activity, but of the greatest sense and remembrance of what he had seen, of any seaman I had met. He was also what they call a very pleasant man; so that at some times when the labours of the day were over it was some divertisment as well as information to me to hear him talke. I wished in my mind to make him a sober man, and in particular to reclaime from him a vile habit of swearing."[35]

Meanwhile, frontier forts had fallen into disrepair. Soldiers constantly deserted from the militia because of the low pay, yet Fletcher had never failed to deduct a half penny per day from each soldier's pay. He had even inflated the payroll figures to show four hundred men on the muster rolls when at times there were hardly half that many. When these collections were added to the pirate payoffs, Fletcher's total profit became impressively large; Coates, Tew, and a certain Hoare alone paid him £6,000 for his "commissions." The assembly of 1694 had asked Fletcher for an account of the three previous years' appropriations, revenues amounting to about £40,000. The governor refused, admonishing them that theirs was to appropriate, his was to spend.[36]

The hearings against Fletcher continued at Whitehall until late 1697. Richard Coote, the earl of Bellomont, who eventually replaced Fletcher in 1698, had been given free rein two years earlier to suppress pirate traffic in the northern colonies. Bellomont's reports, combined with local testimony drawn mostly from the old Leislerian faction, finally became overwhelming and Fletcher was replaced.

Not six months after his arrival, Lord Bellomont found himself surrounded by corruption and inequity. In September 1698, the New York Board of Trade reported, "we can not but with his Lordship conclude the great corruption of the whole body of that people, both officers and traders." They and Bellomont determined that from 1687 to 1697 the Royal revenues from customs and duties had actually decreased despite immense expansion of trade.[37]

In June 1698, Bellomont failed to secure approval from his council on an order requiring four suspected pirate ships to post security before departing for Madagascar, an infamous pirate hangout. As it turned out, at least one council member, Frederick Phillips, had warned the pirates not to sail into the harbor but to drop anchor off Delaware where he would sail out to bring in the booty on his own craft. When Bellomont did carry off successful seizures of booty and imports, he found few witnesses willing to testify in court. At one trial some twenty-two merchants conspired to block incriminating testimony, and shortly afterward, the customs agent resigned rather than effect the seizure ordered by Bellomont.[38]

Frustrated at every turn, Bellomont wrote his London superiors in July 1699 of his despair:

> Arabian Gold is in great supply [in New York], and indeed till there be a good judge or two and an honest active Attorney General to prosecute for the King, all my labor to suppress piracy will signify even just nothing. The people there are so impudent in abetting and sheltering pirates and their goods, that without such assistance as I have now proposed, I can never expect to check that vile practice of theirs.[39]

Lord Bellomont never succeeded in crushing the violators of the Navigation Acts. Eventually the same commercial instincts that lay at the root of the illegal trade became a battle cry of the American Revolution. At best Bellomont helped stop northern piracy. Some of his gambits, however, failed miserably—notably his employment of Captain William Kidd in 1695 on a privateer's commission to suppress the pirates. Two years later, having spent some £6,000 paid him by Bellomont, the famed Captain Kidd was convicted and hanged for having himself become a "notorious" pirate.[40]

Severe pressure was applied to colonial administrations in Delaware, New Jersey, and Rhode Island, where piracy had been a major problem to the English. Even in godly, pacifist Pennsylvania, certain colonial governors developed rather comfortable relations with the pirates. William Penn, by that time rather antiquated but ever mindful of his own interests, wrote to the English authorities in 1700 that he should not be forgotten in disposal of booty seized from the scurrilous pirates: "I confess I think my interest in these cases ought not wholly to be overlooked, who as Lord of the Soil, erected into a Seigneury, must needs have a royalty, and share in such seizures, else I am in much meaner circumstances than many Lords of Manors upon the seacoasts of England, Ireland and Scotland." Penn merely wanted his cut, now that the dreaded pirates had been liquidated.[41]

Piracy drew slowly to an end as the new century began. English determination to stop it had simply made the price too high; only a few colorful figures in the weaker southern colonies hung on. Within another generation they too would disappear. Naval power, however, could never have crushed the pirate fleets had the colonies themselves not entered a new era. By the eighteenth century, the coasts were no longer harsh frontiers.

Colonial America had become commercial America. Some of her industries, especially shipbuilding, rivaled England's. And crewmen on American ships were better paid than they were in England. Simple piracy—the outright seizure of commercial vessels—had become a blight against the colonists as well as the king. Smuggling was another matter, however. One might even presume the furious industry in small shipcraft construction bore a special relation to the proliferation of coastal smugglers.[42]

The deeper Lord Bellomont probed into the commercial corruption of New York, the more he began to discover that piracy was not his toughest problem:

> There is a great trade between Boston and Newfoundland and I have been told there is a constant trade between St. Sebastian and Newfoundland and that there is great store of French and Spanish wines and Spanish iron in Newfoundland. If the merchants of Boston be minded to run their goods, there's nothing to hinder them. . . . 'Tis a common thing as I have heard to unload their ships at Cape Ann and bring their goods to Boston in wooden boats.[43]

The new century was transforming pirates into patriots—and smuggling into free trade.

To say that piracy brought prosperity to North America would be facile and untrue. Nothing could have kept the lid on the whistling engine of colonial commerce once the throttle began to be opened in the late 1600s. But prosperity could not have come so rapidly or so fully without the pirate heritage. . . .

Notes

1. Shirley H. Hughson, "The Carolina Pirates and Colonial Commerce, 1670-1740," *Johns Hopkins University Studies in History and Political Science*, vol. XII, 9-34. Alexander O. Exquemelin, *The Buccaneers of America*, New York: 1924, part I, 9-79. Lloyd H. Williams, *Pirates of Colonial Virginia*, Richmond, Va.: 1937, 24-26. Herbert L. Osgood, *The American Colonies in the Seventeenth Century*, vol. II, New York: 1904, 221-22. William B. Weeden, *Economic and Social History of New England*, vol. I, New York: 1963, chapter 9, 337-78.

2. Carl Bridenbaugh, *Cities in the Wilderness*, New York: 1938, 177-78, 203-4.

3. Hughson, 12-18.

4. Philip Gosse, *A History of Piracy*, New York: 1932, 141-75. Hughson, 12-18.

5. Exquemelin, 59-60.

6. Gosse, *A Pirate's Who's Who*, Boston: 1924, 293.

7. Hughson, 13-14.

8. For a general discussion of the effect of the Navigation Acts on the colonial economy, see Weeden, vol. I, 232-67. See also Hughson, 17-23; Bridenbaugh, 177; and Charles A. and Mary R. Beard, *The Rise of American Civilization*, New York, 1930.

9. Hughson, 44-49.

10. Ibid., 57-60, 71-72. Osgood, vol. II, 428-31. Craven, 303.

11. Hughson, 59. Osgood, vol. I, chapter XVI, esp. 546-47. Alexander Spotswood, *The Official Letters of Alexander Spotswood, Lieutenant Governor of the Colony of Virginia, 1710-1722*, R. A. Brock, ed., vol. II, Richmond, Va.: 1882, 45.

12. Gosse, *A History of Piracy*, 193. Osgood, vol. I, 549-50.

13. Captain Charles Johnson, *A General History of the Robberies and Murders of the Most Notorious Pirates*, New York: 1926, 130-41.

14. Ibid., 205.

15. Ibid., 203. Johnson, 141.

16. Gosse, *A Pirate's Who's Who*, 256, and *A History of Piracy*, 203-5. Johnson, 135.

17. Robert E. Lee, *Blackbeard the Pirate: A Reappraisal of His Life and Times*, Winston-Salem, N.C.: 1976, 20-21. Gosse, *A Pirate's Who's Who*, 255-56. Williams, 83-85. Johnson, 5.

18. Gosse, *A History of Piracy*, 193. Lee, 11-13. See also Cyrus H. Karraker, *Piracy Was a Business*, Rindge, N.H.: 1953, 134-64. Addison B. C. Whipple, *Private Rascals of the Spanish Main*, New York: 1957, 182-83.

19. Hughson, 70-72. Osgood, *The American Colonies in the Eighteenth Century*, vol. II, New York: 1924, 561-64.

20. Hughson, 74-75. Williams, 100-1. Osgood, *Eighteenth Century*, 548. Lee, 28-30.

21. Hughson, Ibid. Williams, 101-4.

22. Hughson, 76-78. Spotswood, 273. Lee, 56-57.

23. Spotswood, 274, 305, 318. Williams, 107-8. Hughson, 76-78. Leonidas Dodson, *Alexander Spotswood*, Philadelphia: 1932, 217-19. Lee, 99-105, 108-12.

24. Williams, 109-12. Lee, 113-26.

25. Lee, 123-25. Osgood, *Eighteenth Century*, 548-49. Hughson, 82-83.

26. Lee, 143-56. "Council Journals," *North Carolina Colonial Records*, vol. II, 343-44, 349, 359. Hughson, 82-83.

27. Osgood, *Eighteenth Century*, 225, 252. Dodson, 282. Lee, 94-97.

28. Weeden, 344-45. Osgood, *Eighteenth Century*, vol. I, 531-32. Edward B. O'Callaghan, ed., *Documents Relative to the Colonial History of the State of New York*, Albany: 1853-57, vol. IV, 307, 459, 480. (Hereafter, *N.Y. Docs.*).

29. N.Y. Docs., 447. See also Thomas J. Archdeacon, "The Age of Leisler—New York City, 1689-1710," in Jacob Judd and Irwin H. Polishook, eds., *Aspects of Early New York Society and Politics*, Tarrytown, N.Y.: 1974.

30. *N.Y. Docs.*, 433-34. Craven, 280-81. For a discussion of class instability and the quest for legitimacy in America during the Glorious Revolution, see Michael Kammen, *People of Paradox*, chapter 2. Osgood, *Eighteenth Century*, vol. I, chapter 7, especially 253-57.

31. *N.Y. Docs.*, 221. Osgood, *Eighteenth Century*, 228.

32. *N.Y. Docs.*, 275.

33. *Ibid.*, 221-24.

34. *Ibid.*

35. *Ibid.*, 304, 447.

36. *Ibid.*, 323, 381, 397. For a general summary see Weeden, 346-48.

37. *N.Y. Docs.*, 389-403.

38. *Ibid.*, 390-91, 323-24.

39. *Ibid.*, 531-37.

40. Weeden, 349-52.

41. *Calendar of State Papers, Colonial Series, American and West Indies, 1700*, London: 1862-1939, 83.

42. Weeden, 366-78.

43. *N.Y. Docs.*, 532, 781-97.

EPILOGUE:
Beyond the Mafia

A gang is what a gang does.
Knox (1994, p. 40)

OC generates profit for gangsters by corrupting the authority structure. From corporate criminals to pirates, the patterns are similar. Their goal is entrepreneurial. They are bonded by necessity for secrecy. They use violence as a tool and as an expression of power. They are constrained by the opportunity structures that exist, but they take advantage of them as well. Their crimes come from corruption of authorities, but also their crimes are organized in response to crime control efforts. OC's long history since the early 1600s has been marked by successes and failures in efforts at control. Yet in almost 400 years, some things remain constant. In the Americas, OC grows out of connections between politicians, law enforcement people, businesspeople, labor leaders, and finally gangsters.

Another lesson from history is that economic changes and monetary controls have had the most success as policies to thwart OC groups. Because the goal is profit, control means removing profits. Law enforcement efforts have had short-run successes, but in the long run, police control is often ineffective. It may have unintended negative consequences and is likely to become corrupted.

History also shows the essential role of consumers of the illicit goods and services provided by OC. That means taking a look at contradictions in policies to control, prohibit, and limit goods and services that become the basis for a black market. It also means examining the basic values and morals that are corrupted by OC and the willingness of citizens to deal with an illegal market.

Other, more explicit factors of OC were revealed by the studies included in this book:

- As an illicit enterprise, OC takes on the transglobal characteristics of legitimate enterprise.
- OC grows in climates of prohibition.
- OC groups develop a lifestyle characteristic of secret societies.
- OC groups grow increasingly indistinguishable from legitimate organizations.
- The most violent OC members are the younger ones; early socialization prepares the way for violent careers.
- There are neighborhoods in the margins of society where gangs became substitute families. In some ways, these places resemble frontiers.
- Sexuality as a commodity—the sex trade—means OC groups are gender segregated.
- Exaggerated masculinity roles place females at a disadvantage in the OC marketplace.
- In some cases, legitimate authorities and the OC groups reach a level of complex interaction by which enforcement efforts maintain and perpetuate the group.
- Strong efforts to curb OC that depend on law enforcement and authorize going "outside the law" are likely to reap more corruption and greater disillusionment and disrespect for authorities.

Moving away from history, scholars have lost sight of larger connections and bigger patterns of which OC is a part. This book attempts to look toward the future of OC without losing the vision of history. It is meant to point the way for more useful studies of OC that will inform more effective policies to deal with OC. The issues that were addressed in this book are certainly not new. Historians and journalists as well as social scientists have provided a wealth of information about OC. There is no shortage of studies. What is needed is a perspective on the future that considers the historical moment. In the global market being created, there is a fertile field for transnational OC. It will challenge our combined efforts as nations and citizens to control this superprofit-oriented illicit enterprise. It calls for rethinking many of the taken-for-granted notions about gangs and gangsters. It calls for self-examination of the ways in which each of us personally contributes to OC, as observer, customer, investor, or business agent, or even as contributors or supporters of efforts that are supposed to combat it. Without the willing participation of ordinary people, OC is no threat. Yet because of acceptance by common citizens, OC groups have become major menaces threatening the international financial system. Wherever politicians are for sale, OC can corrupt the political and the economic systems.

For the future, studies of OC must take size and potential size into account. OC is no longer confined within the borders of nations. Studies must also consider the acceptance that OC receives from huge numbers of people who grow accustomed to dealing with an illegal market. Finally, studies must also be informed about the single, driving focus of profit and its potential for corruption and control. Without these elements, studies of OC remain descriptions of gangs and gangsters that are not much more than paper cutouts without any background.

The processes by which OC was created went far beyond the experiences of one gang and one place and time, but they inevitably involved corruption. The consequences of OC have been vast and beyond measuring, but they have also inevitably involved corruption. It is the beginning and the end. Corruption causes contradictions, leading to conflicts that may be addressed but not solved. Efforts at control lead to more contradictions and different conflicts. The corruption of the system is not separate from the corruption of individuals; they are connected in predictable ways. Everyone is involved, even though not everyone participates. Lack of attachment to the legal system, lack of commitment to the future, lack of involvement in constructive activities, and lack of confidence in the system of authority are common personal ways in which the corruption of the system is felt by almost everyone at one time or another.

The potential for corruption is minimized by providing for a legitimate authority and fair treatment. Corruption is less where a positive outlook for the future and legitimate career opportunities exist. The motivation for corruption is also reduced in a society where citizens are inspired by a legal system in which they are treated with respect. There will be no meaningful change in the processes and consequences of OC without eliminating the corruption on which it is based.

References

Abadinsky, H. (1994). *Organized crime* (4th ed.). Chicago: Nelson Hall.

Albanese, J. (1996). *Organized crime in America* (3rd ed.). Cincinnati: Anderson.

Allsop, K. (1961). *The bootleggers and their era.* Garden City, NY: Doubleday.

Barleycorn, M. (1975). *Moonshiners manual.* Willits, CA: Oliver.

Block, A. (1980). Searching for women in organized crime. In S. Datesman & F. Scarpitti (Eds.), *Women, crime, and justice* (pp. 192-213). New York: Oxford University Press.

Block, A. (1981). Aw! Your mother's in the Mafia: Women criminals in progressive New York. In L. H. Bowker (Ed.), *Women and crime in America.* New York: Macmillan.

Block, A. A., & Chambliss, W. J. (1981). *Organizing crime.* New York: Elsevier North Holland.

Browning, F., & Gerassi, J. (1980). *The American way of crime.* New York: G. P. Putnam's Sons.

Camp, G., & Camp, C. (1985). *Prison gangs: Their extent, nature and impact.* Washington, DC: Government Printing Office.

Campbell, A. (1984). *The girls in the gang: A report from New York City.* New York: Basil Blackwell.

Carse, R. (1965).*The age of piracy.* New York: Grosset & Dunlap.

Chambliss, W. J. (1978). *On the take: From petty crooks to presidents.* Bloomington: Indiana University Press.

Chambliss, W. J. (1995). State organized crime: The American society of criminology. In N. Passas (Ed.), *Organized crime* (pp. 183-280). Brookfield, VT: Dartmouth.

Chang, D. H. (1995). A new form of international crime: The human organ trade. *International Journal of Comparative and Applied Criminal Justice, 19*(1), 1-18.

Chesney-Lind, M., & Shelden, R. G. (1998). *Girls, delinquency, and juvenile justice* (2nd ed.). Belmont, CA: Wadsworth.

Chin, K. (1990). *Chinese subculture and criminality: Non-traditional crime groups in America.* Westport, CT: Greenwood.

Chin, K. (1995). Triad societies in Hong Kong. *Transnational Organized Crime, 1*(1), 47-64.

Chin, K. (1996). *Chinatown gangs: Extortion, enterprise, and ethnicity.* New York: Oxford University Press.

Clinard, M. B., & Yaeger, P. C. (1980). *Corporate crime.* New York: Free Press.

Courtwright, D. T. (1986). *Violent land: Single men and social disorder from the frontier to the inner city.* Cambridge, MA: Harvard University Press.

Cressey, D. R. (1995). Methodological problems in the study of organized crime as a social problem. In N. Passas (Ed.), *Organized crime* (pp. 3-14). Brookfield, VT: Dartmouth.

Criminal Intelligence Service Canada. (1996). *Annual report on organized crime in Canada.* Ottawa: Author.

Dawley, D. (1972). *A nation of lords: The autobiography of the Vice Lords.* Prospect Heights, IL: Waveland.

Dawley, D. (1992). *A nation of lords: The autobiography of the Vice Lords* (2nd ed.). Prospect Heights, IL: Waveland.

Fennell, T. (1994). Risky business: Tax weary Canadians help support a boom in smuggled alcohol. *Maclean's, 107*(28), 14.

Freemantle, B. (1995). *The octopus: Europe in the grip of organized crime.* London: Orion.

Gambetta, D. (1995). Fragments of an economic theory of the Mafia. In N. Passas (Ed.), *Organized crime* (pp. 171-190). Brookfield, VT: Dartmouth.

Goodson, R., & Olson, W. (1995, January/February). International organized crime. *Society,* pp. 18-29.

Grassi, A. (1990). The role of the courts in combating international crime. In J. R. Buckwalter (Ed.), *International perspectives on organized crime* (pp. 37-47). Chicago: University of Illinois at Chicago, Office of International Criminal Justice.

Handelman, S. (1994). The Russian mafya. *Foreign Affairs, 73*(2), 83-96.

Hoffman, D. E. (1987). Tilting at windmills. In T. Bynum (Ed.), *Organized crime in America: Concepts and controversies* (pp. 83-102). Monsey, NY: Willow Tree.

Huey Long Song, J., & Huripz, L. (1995). Victimization patterns of Asian gangs in the United States. *Journal of Gang Research, 3*(1), 41-49.

Jackson, C., & Wilson, G. D. (1993). Mad, bad or sad? The personality of bikers. *Personality and Individual Differences, 14*(1), 241-242.

Jankowski, M. S. (1991). *Islands in the street: Gangs and American urban society.* Berkeley: University of California Press.

Kaplan, D. E., & Dubro, A. (1986). *Yakuza: The explosive account of Japan's criminal underworld.* Menlo Park, CA: Addison-Wesley.

Keiser, R. L. (1969). *The Vice Lords: Warriors of the streets.* New York: Holt, Rinehart & Winston.

Keiser, R. L. (1979). *The Vice Lords: Warriors of the streets* (fieldwork ed.). New York: Holt, Rinehart & Winston.

Kenney, D. J., & Finckenauer, J. O. (1995). *Organized crime in America.* Belmont, CA: Wadsworth.

Kerry, J. (1997). *The new war.* New York: Simon & Schuster.

Knox, G. W. (1994). *An introduction to gangs* (rev. ed.). Chicago: Wyndham Hall.

Lavey, D. (1990). Interpol's role in combating organized crime. In J. R. Buckwalter (Ed.), *International perspectives on organized crime* (pp. 87-93). Chicago: Office of International Criminal Justice.

Lee, R. W., III. (1995). Colombia's cocaine syndicate. In N. Passas (Ed.), *Organized crime* (pp. 281-317). Brookfield, VT: Dartmouth.

Licensed Beverage Industries. (1966, October). *Moonshine merchants: A study and report.* New York: Author.

Licensed Beverage Industries. (1974, January). *Moonshine: Formula for fraud and slow death.* New York: Author.

Lombardo, R. M. (1990). Asset forfeiture: Civil remedies against organized crime. In J. R. Buckwalter (Ed.), *International perspectives on organized crime* (pp. 49-62). Chicago: University of Illinois at Chicago, Office of International Criminal Justice.

Lupsha, P. A. (1995). Individual choice, material culture and organized crime. In N. Passas (Ed.), *Organized crime* (pp. 105-125). Brookfield, VT: Dartmouth.

Ma, Y. (1995). Crime in China: Characteristics, causes and control strategies. *International Journal of Comparative and Applied Criminal Justice, 19,* 247-256.

MacDonald, S. B. (1988). *Dancing on a volcano: The Latin American drug trade.* New York: Praeger.

Mackenzie, N. (Ed.). (1967). *Secret societies.* New York: Holt, Rinehart & Winston.

Martens, F. T. (1990). African-American organized crime. In J. R. Buckwalter (Ed.), *International perspectives on organized crime.* Chicago: University of Illinois at Chicago, Office of International Criminal Justice.

Martin, J. M., & Romano, A. T. (1992). *Multinational crime: Terrorism, espionage, drugs and arms trafficking.* Newbury Park, CA: Sage.

Martinez, R., Jr. (1996). Latinos and lethal violence: The impact of poverty and inequality. *Social Problems, 43,* 131-146.

McDonald, W. F. (1995). The globalization of criminology: The new frontier is the frontier. *Transnational Organized Crime, 1*(1), 1-12.

McDonald, W. F. (1997). Crime and illegal immigration: Emerging local, state, and federal partnerships. *National Institute of Justice Journal, 232,* 2-10.

Moore, J. W. (1978). *Homeboys: Gangs, drugs, and prisons in the barrios of Los Angeles.* Philadelphia: Temple University Press.

Moore, J. W. (1991). *Going down to the barrio.* Philadelphia: Temple University Press.

Moore, J. (1994). The chola life course: Chicana heroin users and the barrio gang. *International Journal of the Addictions, 29,* 1115-1126.

Myers, W. H., III. (1996). ORB weavers: The global webs, the structure and activities of transnational ethnic Chinese criminal groups. *Transnational Organized Crime, 1*(4), 1-36.

Naylor, R. T. (1996). From underworld to underground enterprise crime: Informal sector business and public policy response. *Crime, Law and Social Change, 24,* 79-150.

Neapolitan, J. (1996). Cross national crime data: Some unaddressed problems. *Journal of Crime and Justice, 19*(1), 95-112.

Pace, D. F. (1991). *Concepts of vice, narcotics, and organized crime* (3rd ed.). Englewood Cliffs, NJ: Prentice Hall.

Paris-Steffens, S. (1990). The role of the United Nations in combating organized crime. In J. R. Buckwalter (Ed.), *International perspectives on organized crime* (pp. 13-17). Chicago: University of Illinois at Chicago, Office of International Criminal Justice.

Parsels, E. (1996). Capitalism fosters gang behavior. In C. P. Cozic (Ed.), *Gangs: Opposing viewpoints.* San Diego, CA: Greenhaven.

Patrick, J. (1973). *A Glasgow gang observed.* London: Eyre Methuen.

Potter, G. W. (1994). *Criminal organizations: Vice, racketeering, and politics in an American city.* Prospect Heights, IL: Waveland.

Quinn, J. F. (1987). Sex roles and hedonism among members of outlaw motorcycle clubs. *Deviant Behavior, 8*(1), 47-63.

Rhodes, R. P. (1984). *Organized crime: Crime control vs. civil liberties.* New York: Random House.

Romo, R. (1983). *East Los Angeles: History of a barrio.* Austin: University of Texas Press.

Ruggiero, V. (1996). War markets: Corporate and organized criminals in Europe. *Social and Legal Studies, 5*(1), 5-20.

Ruth, D. E. (1996). *Inventing the public enemy: The gangster in American culture.* Chicago: University of Chicago Press.

Scarpitti, F. R., & Block, A. A. (1987). America's toxic waste racket: Dimensions of the environmental crisis. In T. S. Bynum (Ed.), *Organized crime in America: Concepts and controversies.* Monsey, NY: Willow Tree.

Schlegel, K. (1987). Violence in organized crime. In T. Bynum (Ed.), *Organized crime in America: Concepts and controversies* (pp. 55-70). Monsey, NY: Willow Tree.

Seymour, C. (1996). *Yakuza diary: Doing time in the Japanese underworld*. New York: Atlantic Monthly.

Shelley, L. I., Saberschinski, H., & Sinuraja, T. (1995). East meets West in crime. *European Journal on Criminal Policy and Research, 3*(4), 7-107.

Slaughter, T. P. (1986). *The Whiskey Rebellion: Frontier epilogue to the American Revolution*. New York: Oxford University Press.

Smith, D. (1995). Paragons, pariahs and pirates. In N. Passas (Ed.), *Organized crime* (pp. 127-158). Brookfield, VT: Dartmouth.

Stamler, R. (1990). Controlling organized crime in Canada. In J. Buckwalter (Ed.), *International perspectives on organized crime* (pp. 1-12). Chicago: University of Illinois at Chicago, Office of International Criminal Justice.

Steffensmeier, D. J. (1983). Organizational properties and sex segregation in the underworld: Building a sociological theory of sex differences in crime. *Social Forces, 61*, 1010-1032.

Sutherland, E. H. (1949). *White collar crime*. New York: Holt, Rinehart & Winston.

Taylor, C. S. (1993). *Girls, gangs, women and drugs*. East Lansing: Michigan State University Press.

Thompson, H. S. (1966). *Hell's Angels: A strange and terrible saga*. New York: Ballantine.

U.S. Department of Health and Human Services. (1992). Elevated blood lead levels associated with illicitly distilled alcohol: Alabama, 1990-1991. *Morbidity and Mortality Weekly Report, 41*(17), 294.

U.S. Department of Justice. (1985). *Prison gangs: Their extent, nature and impact on prisons* (Grant No. 84-NI-AX-0001). Washington, DC: Government Printing Office.

U.S. General Accounting Office. (1996). *Drug control: U.S. heroin program encounters many obstacles in Southeast Asia*. Washington, DC: Author.

U.S. Senate, Committee on Governmental Affairs, Permanent Subcommittee on Investigations. (1992). *The new international criminal and Asian organized crime: Report* (Report Item No. 1037-CMF). Washington, DC: Government Printing Office.

Vaksberg, A. (1991). *The Soviet mafia* (J. Roberts & E. Roberts, Trans.). New York: St. Martin's.

Van Duyne, P. C. (1996). The phantom and threat of organized crime. *Crime, Law and Social Change, 24*, 341-377.

Varese, F. (1994). Is Sicily the future of Russia? Private protection and the rise of the Russian Mafia. *Archives of European Sociology, 35*, 224-258.

Vigil, J. D. (1988). *Barrio gangs: Street life and identity in southern California*. Austin: University of Texas Press.

Vigil, J. D. (1997). *Learning from gangs: The Mexican American experience* (Rep. No. RC 020 943). Los Angeles: University of California at Los Angeles. (ERIC

Clearinghouse on Rural Education and Small Schools Temporary Accession No. RC 020 943)

Volobuev, A. (1990). Combating organized crime in the U.S.S.R.: Problems and perspectives. In J. R. Buckwalter (Ed.), *International perspectives on organized crime* (pp. 75-82). Chicago: University of Illinois at Chicago, Office of International Criminal Justice.

Wessell, N. H. (Ed.). (1995). Special issues on crime in Russia. *Russian Politics and Law, 33*(4), 3-72.

Woodiwiss, M. (1988). *Crime, crusades and corruption: Prohibition in the United States, 1900-1987.* Totowa, NJ: Barnes & Noble.

Zhang, S. X., & Gaylord, M. S. (1996). Bound for the golden mountain: The social organization of Chinese alien smuggling. *Crime, Law and Social Change, 25,* 1-16.

Zimbardo, P. (1985). *Psychology and life* (12th ed.). New York: HarperCollins.

Additional
Selected Readings

Albanese, J. (1989). *Organized crime in America* (2nd ed.). Cincinnati: Anderson.

Baker, M. (1996). *Badguys.* New York: Simon & Schuster.

Block, A. (1994). *Space, time, and organized crime* (2nd ed.). New Brunswick, NJ: Transaction.

Booth, M. (1990). *The triads: The growing global threat from the Chinese criminal societies.* New York: St. Martin's.

Bowker, L. H. (Ed.). (1981). *Women and crime in America.* New York: Macmillan.

Brookhiser, R. (1995, June 16). Patriots, rebels and founding fathers: Analysis of the Shays' Rebellion and the Whiskey Rebellion. *New York Times,* pp. A15, A27.

Buckwalter, J. R. (Ed.). (1990). *International perspectives on organized crime.* Chicago: University of Illinois at Chicago, Office of International Criminal Justice.

Burney, J. (1912). *History of the buccaneers of America.* London: Allen & Unwin.

Butterfield, F. (1997, August 17). Study: Cohesion in community lowers violence. *Daytona Beach Sunday News Journal,* p. 3A.

California Department of Justice, Bureau of Investigation. (1996). *Russian organized crime: California's newest threat.* Sacramento: Author.

Chambliss, W. (1988). *On the take: From petty crooks to presidents* (2nd ed.). Bloomington: Indiana University Press.

Chu, Y. (1996). Triad societies and the business community in Hong Kong. *International Journal of Risk, Security and Crime Prevention,* 1(1), 33-40.

Clinard, M. B. (1990). *Corporate corruption: The abuse of power.* New York: Praeger.

Crowgey, H. G. (1971). *Kentucky bourbon: The early years of whiskeymaking.* Lexington: University Press of Kentucky.

Cummins, E. (1995). *California prison gang project (final report)* (EDRS No. 387 616, CE No. 069 978). Chicago: Spencer Foundation.

Datesman, S. K., & Scarpitti, F. R. (Eds.). (1980). *Women, crime, and justice.* New York: Oxford University Press.

Davidson, R. T. (1974). *Chicano prisoners: The key to San Quentin.* Prospect Heights, IL: Waveland.

Debnam, B. (1997, August 19). The most famous pirate of all: Blackbeard the feared. *Daytona Beach News Journal,* p. 2C.

Demont, J. (1996). Moonshine revival: History and hard times mean more illegal booze. *Maclean's, 109*(37), 18.

Dobnik, V. (1997, January 25). Report: Chinese being paid slave wage. *Daytona Beach News Journal,* p. 12A.

Duzán, M. J. (1994). *Death beat: A Colombian journalist's life inside the cocaine wars* (P. Eisner, Trans.). New York: HarperCollins. (Original work published 1992)

Exquemelin, J. (n.d.). *The buccaneers of America* (W. S. Stallybrass, Ed. & Trans.). New York: E. P. Dutton. (Original work published 1684-1685)

Fong, R. S., & Buentello, S. (1991). The detection of prison gang development: An empirical assessment. *Federal Probation, 55*(1), 66-69.

Gibbs, N. R. (1995, September 19). Yummy. *Time Magazine,* pp. 55-59.

Gilbert, J. N. (1996). Organized crime on the western frontier. *Journal of Criminal Organizations, 10*(2), 7-13.

Handelman, S. (1995). *Comrade criminal: Russia's new mafya.* New Haven, CT: Yale University Press.

Hopper, C., & Moore, J. (1990). Women in outlaw motorcycle gangs. *Journal of Contemporary Ethnography, 18,* 359-369.

Huff, C. R. (Ed.). (1996). *Gangs in America* (2nd ed.). Thousand Oaks, CA: Sage.

Jacobs, J. B. (1974). Street gangs behind bars. *Social Problems, 21,* 395-409.

Jamieson, A. (1995). Transnational dimensions of Italian organized crime. *Transnational Organized Crime, 1,* 151-172.

Jones, L., & Newman, L. (1997). *Our America: Life and death on the south side of Chicago.* New York: Scribner.

Kellner, E. (1971). *Moonshine, its history and folklore.* Indianapolis: Bobbs-Merrill.

Kinnear, K. L. (1996). *Gangs: A reference handbook.* Santa Barbara, CA: ABC-CLIO.

Kleinknecht, W. (1996). *The new ethnic mobs: The changing face of organized crime in America.* New York: Free Press.

Knox, G. W. (1994). *National gangs resource handbook: An encyclopedic reference.* Chicago: Wyndham Hall.

Kotlowitz, A. (1991). *There are no children here.* Garden City, NY: Doubleday.

Lamott, K. (1963). *Chronicles of San Quentin: The biography of a prison.* London: John Long.

Lang, A. (n.d.). Adventures of buccaneers [Introduction]. In J. Exquemelin, *The buccaneers of America* (pp. xiii-xix). New York: E. P. Dutton.

Maltz, M. D. (1990). *Measuring the effectiveness of organized crime control efforts* (Monograph No. 9). Chicago: University of Illinois at Chicago, Office of International Criminal Justice.

Marx, G., & Parsons, C. (1996, November 11). Guard feels caught in the middle. *Chicago Tribune*, pp. 1-8.

McCormack, R. J. (1996). *Organized crime: A North American perspective.* Trenton: College of New Jersey, Department of Law and Justice.

Monti, D. J. (1994). *Wannabe gangs in suburbs and schools.* Cambridge, MA: Blackwell.

Moore, J. (1985). Isolation and stigmatization in the development of the underclass: The case of Chicano gangs in east Los Angeles. *Social Problems, 33,* 1-10.

New York State Organized Crime Task Force: New York State Commission of Investigations, & New Jersey Commission. (1996). *An analysis of Russian emigre crime in the tri-state region.* Albany, NY: Tri-State Joint Soviet-Emigre Organized Crime Project.

Passas, N. (Ed.). (1995). *Organized crime.* Philadelphia: Temple University Press.

Posner, G. L. (1988). *Warlords of crime: Chinese secret societies: The new Mafia.* New York: McGraw-Hill.

Rankin, H. (1969). *The golden age of piracy.* New York: Holt, Rinehart & Wilson.

Renard, R. D. (1996). *The Burmese connection: Illegal drugs and the making of the golden triangle.* Boulder, CO: Lynne Rienner.

Royal Canadian Mounted Police Training and Development Branch. (1994). Outlaw motorcycle gangs. *Royal Canadian Mounted Police Gazette, 56*(3 & 4), 1-39.

Ryan, P. J. (1995). *Organized crime: A reference handbook.* Santa Barbara, CA: ABC-CLIO.

Saga, J. (1991). *Confessions of a Yakuza: A life in Japan's underworld.* Tokyo: Kodansha.

Sale, R. T. (1971). *The Blackstone Rangers: A reporter's account of time spent with the street gang on Chicago's south side.* New York: Random House.

Salzano, J. (1994). It's a dirty business: Organized crime in deep sludge. *Criminal Organizations, 8*(3 & 4), 17-20.

Sanders, W. B. (1994). *Gangbangs and drive-bys: Grounded culture and juvenile gang violence.* Hawthorne, NY: Aldine de Gruyter.

Sanz, K., & Silverman, I. (1996). The evolution and future direction of Southeast Asian criminal organizations. *Journal of Contemporary Criminal Justice, 12,* 285-294.

Sato, I. (1991). *Kamikaze biker: Parody and anomy in affluent Japan.* Chicago: University of Chicago Press.

Schatzberg, R., & Kelly, R. J. (1996). *African-American organized crime: A social history.* New York: Garland.

Seibel, G., & Pincomb, R. A. (1994). From the Black P Stone Nation to the El Rukns. *Criminal Organizations, 8*(3 & 4), 3-9.

Silberman, M. (1995). *A world of violence.* Belmont, CA: Wadsworth.

Small, G. (1995). *Ruthless: The global rise of the Yardies.* London: Warner.

Walther, S. (1994). Forfeiture and money laundering laws in the United States. *Crime, Law and Social Change, 21,* 1-13.

Wilkinson, A. (1985). *Moonshine: A life in pursuit of white liquor.* New York: Knopf.

Williams, P., & Savona, E. (1995). The United Nations and transnational organized crime. *Transnational Organized Crime, 1*(3), 1-194.

Wolf, D. R. (1991). *The Rebels: A brotherhood of outlaw bikers.* Toronto: University of Toronto Press.

Index

About the Editors

Sue Mahan is the coordinator of the Criminal Justice Program at the University of Central Florida-Daytona Beach. She has written three books: *Unfit Mothers; Women, Crime & Criminal Justice* (with Ralph Weisheit); and *Crack Cocaine, Crime and Women.* She is also the author of numerous book chapters, articles, and papers about women and crime, corrections, prison violence, and related topics. From 1991 to 1993, she was a Kellogg International Fellow, and in 1996, she was a Fulbright Distinguished Lecturer in Peru.

Katherine O'Neil works as a court liaison for Stewart Marchman Treatment Center in Daytona Beach, Florida. She is a Certified Criminal Justice Addiction professional with experience as a substance abuse evaluator, counselor, and criminal justice therapist. She first worked as a criminal justice research assistant in 1989 while earning her BA degree at the University of Central Florida. As a graduate student, she has a research interest in prison industries.

About the Contributors

Frank Browning has contributed articles to *Ramparts*, the *Washington Post*, the *Village Voice*, and *New Times*. In addition to *The American Way of Crime*, he has written and edited numerous books and articles and was an associate editor of Pacific News Service.

Ko-lin Chin has been studying *Chinatown Gangs* since the 1980s. His participant observation studies followed the inspiration of Marvin Wolfgang and the tradition of sociological studies of the subculture of violence.

Marshall B. Clinard examined corporate behavior for more than 10 years with grants from the U.S. Department of Justice. In addition to *Corporate Corruption*, he has published three other books on corporate misbehavior and has testified before congressional committees dealing with corporate ethics and law violation.

R. Theodore Davidson is an anthropologist who conducted formal fieldwork in San Quentin Prison for 20 months from 1966 to 1968. *Chicano Prisoners—The Key to San Quentin* was begun as the research for his doctoral dissertation from the University of California at Davis.

Alec Dubro is a journalist who wrote *Yazuka* and articles about such subjects as drug enforcement and surveillance technology. He has been a private investigator, editor, television news writer, and consultant to the President's Commission on Organized Crime.

María Jimena Duzán became a journalist at the age of 16 in her native Colombia. She inherited her father's column in *El Espectador,* a major newspaper in her country and owned by her uncle. She became a strong critic of human rights abuses despite death threats and bombing attacks, and wrote *Death Beat* to expose the corruption that threatens Columbia.

John Gerassi is a journalist who has worked for the *New York Times* and *Newsweek* and was the Latin American editor for *Ramparts.* In addition to the *American Way of Crime,* he is known for his biography of Che Guevera, titled *Veneremos!*

David E. Kaplan is staff writer at the Center for Investigative Reporting in San Francisco. In addition to *Yazuka,* he is also the editor of the book *Nuclear California* and the author of numerous articles. He won the Thomas M. Storke International Journalism award in 1984.

William Kleinknecht wrote *The New Ethnic Mobs* from more than 100 interviews with law enforcement officials, community leaders, social workers, and street sources. He is a journalist who covered organized crime for the *New York Daily News,* the *Detroit Free Press,* and others.

Alex Kotlowitz is a celebrated journalist. He won the Sandburg award for *There Are No Children Here.* He has written on urban affairs, social policy, poverty, and race in the *New York Times* and the *Wall Street Journal* and on NPR and the MacNeil-Lehrer News Hour.

Wilbur R. Miller became interested *Revenuers and Moonshiners* while studying federal civil rights law enforcement. He is a historian and has written extensively on late 19th-century institutional history.

Daniel R. Wolf wrote *The Rebels* to explain the world of outlaw bikerdom from an insider's perspective. He established himself as a friend of the club in order to carry out a participant observational study of the outlaw-biker subculture.